AVENGERS: ENDLESS WARTIME

WARREN ELLIS

MIKE MCKONE • JASON KEITH

AVENGERS: ENDLESS WARTIME
First printing 2013.
ISBN# 978-0-7851-8467-6.
Published by MARVEL WORLDWIDE, INC.,
a subsidiary of MARVEL ENTERTAINMENT, LLC.
OFFICE OF PUBLICATION:
135 West 50th Street, New York, NY 10020.
Copyright © 2013 Marvel Characters, Inc.
ALAN FINE, EVP: Office of the President, Marvel
Worldwide, Inc. and EVP & CMO Marvel Characters B.V.
DAN BUCKLEY: Publisher & President: Print, Animation &
Digital Divisions
JOE QUESADA: Chief Creative Officer
TOM BREVOORT: SVP of Publishing
DAVID BOGART: SVP of Operations & Procurement,
Publishing
C.B. CEBULSKI: SVP of Creator & Content Development
DAVID GABRIEL: SVP of Print & Digital Publishing Sales
JIM O'KEEFE: VP of Operations & Logistics
DAN CARR: Executive Director of Publishing Technology
SUSAN CRESPI: Editorial Operations Manager
ALEX MORALES: Publishing Operations Manager
STAN LEE: Chairman Emeritus
For information regarding advertising in Marvel Comics
or on Marvel.com, please contact Niza Disla, Director of
Marvel Partnerships, at ndisla@marvel.com.
For Marvel subscription inquiries, please call
800-217-9158. Manufactured between 7/5/2013 and
8/19/2013 by R.R. DONNELLEY, INC., SALEM, VA, USA.

10 9 8 7 6 5 4 3 2 1

Warren Ellis
Author

Mike McKone
Illustrator

Jason Keith with Rain Beredo
Color Artist

VC's Chris Eliopoulos
Lettering

Rian Hughes
Book Design

Jake Thomas
Assistant Editor

Tom Brevoort With Lauren Sankovitch
Editors

Axel Alonso
Editor In Chief

Joe Quesada
Chief Creative Officer

Dan Buckley
Publisher

Alan Fine
Executive Producer

Photo by Blake Gardner

It was my brother, Andrew, who first got me into comics. It was the '70s and I was buried in sci-fi novels - Bradbury, Asimov, Philip K. Dick - until the day Andrew walked through the door with an issue of *Iron Man* drawn by Jim Starlin. I peeled through the pages in awed silence. The stories were dark and powerful, but what took my breath away was the artwork - the detail, the worlds, the emotion etched onto faces. I bought more *Iron Man*, whose lack of super-powers and human frailty I found endlessly compelling. Soon I added *Luke Cage,* then *The Avengers*, and since Bruce Lee was our hero we both got heavily into *Iron Fist.* But my deepest passion was Starlin. I searched comic shops and garage sales for his 'books.' I found his *Daredevil* and *Captain Marvel* and became obsessed with *Warlock.* So obsessed, in fact, that when I recently dug up an old middle school notebook, the pages were so dominated by sketches of Adam Warlock that the school work was crammed into a few rumpled sheets in the back. Which is, of course, how one ends up with a career in the arts.

Many years later, I read that my neighbor, Jon Favreau, was directing an origin movie of Iron Man, produced by Marvel with an amazing cast headed by Robert Downey Jr. as Tony Stark. I felt a rush of boyish excitement at the thought of even seeing the film. So when Jon offered me a minor role as a mysterious government agent named Coulson, the chance to interact with Tony Stark outside the pages of a spiral notebook was more than I could resist.

My first day on the film was like taking my 12-year-old self to work. I gaped at Robert's brilliant, razor-witted Tony Stark, but somehow managed to keep my geek-outs internal and even said most of my lines. When I got a call a few days later saying that they wanted to add more scenes for Agent Coulson, I quickly volunteered to clear my schedule. I soon found myself, as Agent Coulson, explaining to Tony Stark that I worked for "the Strategic Homeland Intervention Enforcement and Logistics Division." Between takes I asked young Marvel exec, Jeremy Latcham, if that acronym meant what I thought it meant. When Jeremy quietly confirmed my suspicion, I confessed to the twenty-five year gap in my Marvel timeline. The very next day a thing of beauty arrived at my door - a thick, illustrated Iron Man 'bible' filled with chapters on Nick Fury, S.H.I.E.L.D. and the evolution of Tony Stark, including riveting panels from Warren Ellis' influential graphic novel, *Iron Man: Extremis.* As I curled up on a couch to pore through the encyclopedic tome, I half expected to hear my mother call me down to dinner.

Six years and one epic movie demise later, I'm still playing Agent Phil Coulson. My time with Marvel has given me an unusual opportunity to reconnect with boyhood heroes (often quite thrillingly in the flesh) and with the rich pop mythology that fills their stories. In addition, I've had the pleasure of watching Marvel and brilliant filmmakers like Jon Favreau, Kenneth Branagh and Joss Whedon

bring those characters to cinematic life with a wit and sophistication that makes them as resonant and entertaining for me now as they were when I was a boy. So I was honored when Marvel asked me to write a forward to *Avengers: Endless Wartime,* a brilliant new graphic novel by Warren Ellis himself.

Avengers: Endless Wartime is a movie length epic that launches a new graphic novel line for Marvel with characters from the cinematic *Avengers,* like Captain America, Thor, Hawkeye, Black Widow and the Hulk, as well as beloved comic book Avengers like Wolverine and my personal favorite, the new female/alien incarnation of Captain Marvel. These Avengers are forced into combat with demons (quite literally) from Cap and Thor's shared past who turn out to be an unholy blend of cybernetic drone technology and a lost breed of Asgardian monsters.

Ellis is in prime form here and his crisp, edgy banter is brought to thrilling life by the incomparable panels of Mike McKone and the ensuing battle royal is even more badass than one might think possible. So, to Kevin Feige, Joe Quesada, Jeph Loeb and all the rest of my visionary friends at Marvel who, like me, never entirely grew up, thank you for once again pushing the envelope of your bold, imaginative world, and for giving me the opportunity to return to it.

Clark Gregg began his acting career as a founding member of the Atlantic Theater Company in NY, then moved to Los Angeles in the mid '90s where he landed roles in films including *Lovely and Amazing, In Good Company, Mr. Popper's Penguins, Thor, Iron Man* and *Iron Man 2, 500 Days of Summer, Marvel's The Avengers, The To Do List* and Joss Whedon's *Much Ado About Nothing.* On television he did recurring roles on *The West Wing, Sex and the City, Will and Grace* and co-starred with Julia Louis-Dreyfus on *The New Adventures of Old Christine.* Also a screenwriter and director, Gregg's screenwriting debut was *What Lies Beneath,* starring Harrison Ford and Michelle Pfeiffer. His directing debut, *Choke,* which he adapted from the novel by Chuck Palahniuk, won a special jury prize at the 2008 Sundance Film Festival. His second film, *Trust Me,* premiered at the 2013 Tribeca Film Festival. Gregg is poised to reprise his role of Agent Phil Coulson on *ABC's Marvel's Agents of S.H.I.E.L.D.*

Clark Gregg
June 16, 2013

INVENTORY

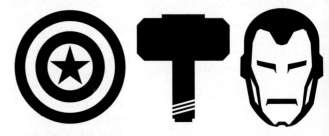

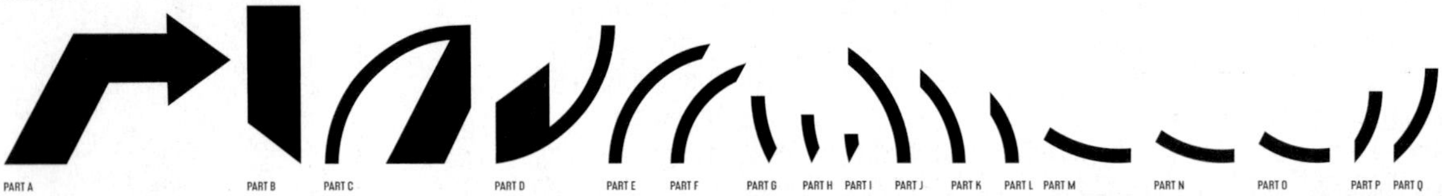

PART A   PART B   PART C   PART D   PART E   PART F   PART G   PART H   PART I   PART J   PART K   PART L   PART M   PART N   PART O   PART P   PART Q

TEAM MEMBER IDENTIFICATION   CAPTAIN AMERICA   THOR   IRON MAN

EMBLEM CONSTRUCTION   **TYPEFACE: KOROLEV MILITARY STENCIL** (includes international character set)

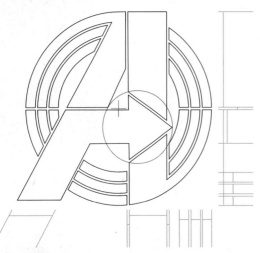

ABCDEFGHIJKLM
NOPQRSTUVWXYZ
aabcdefghijklmno
pqrstuvwxyz éëě
1234567890 ©®@
!@£$%^&*()-_+:;'''<>?

IO/I3-A REV.2

These guidelines are here excerpted for informational purposes only.
Their use on any product or event implies no endorsement by The Avengers or their affiliates,
other than by prior arrangement via authorized agents. EAOE.
Please refer to the full Corporate Guidelines for detailed usage instructions.
Subject to change.

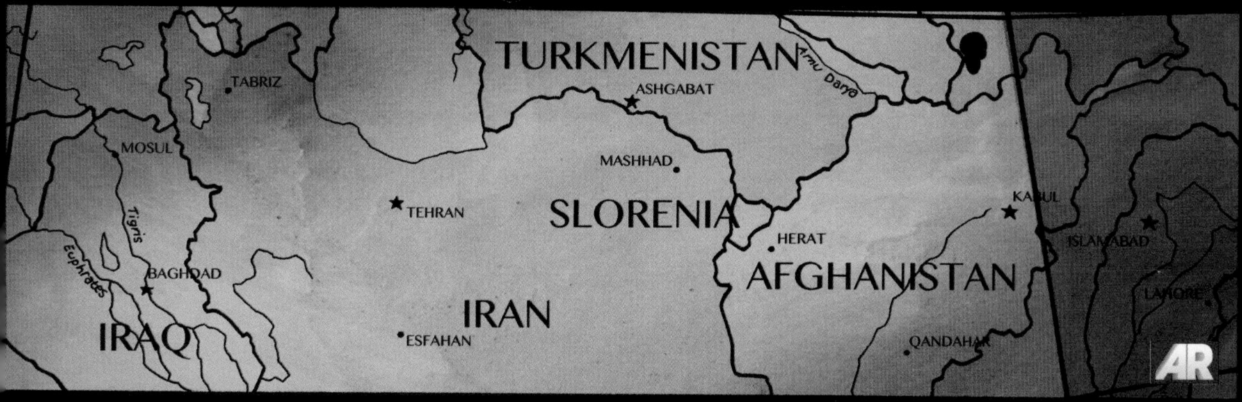
TURKMENISTAN
TABRIZ
ASHGABAT
Amu Darya
MOSUL
MASHHAD
Tigris
TEHRAN
SLORENIA
KABUL
HERAT
ISLAMABAD
Euphrates
BAGHDAD
AFGHANISTAN
LAHORE
IRAN
IRAQ
ESFAHAN
QANDAHAR
AR

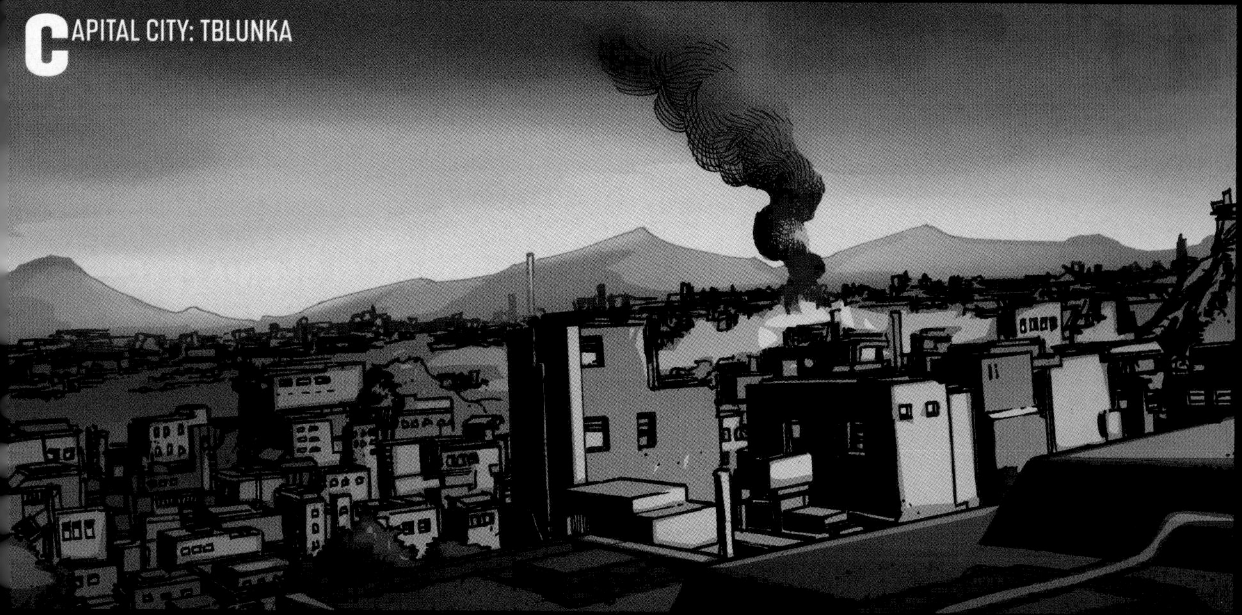
CAPITAL CITY: TBLUNKA

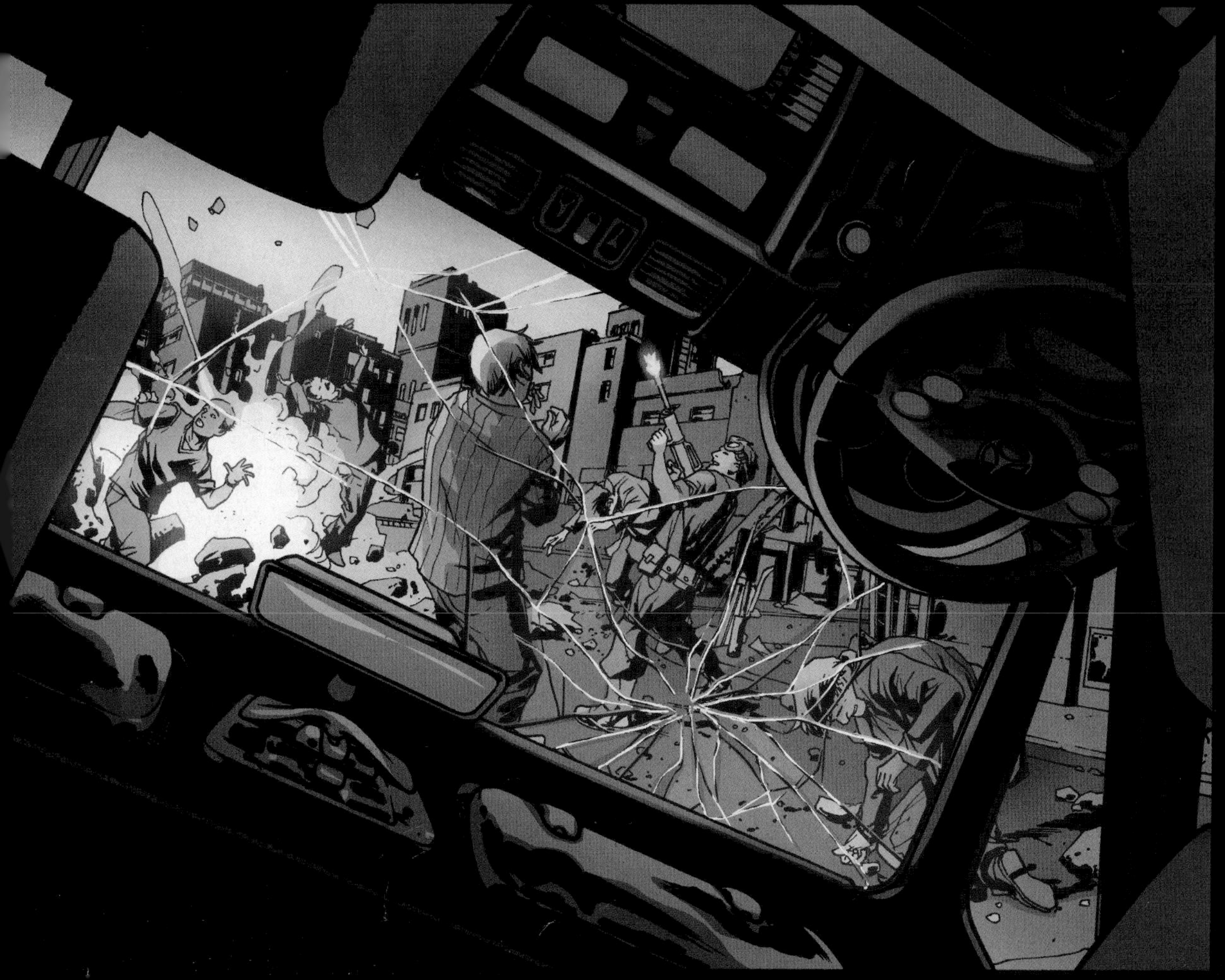

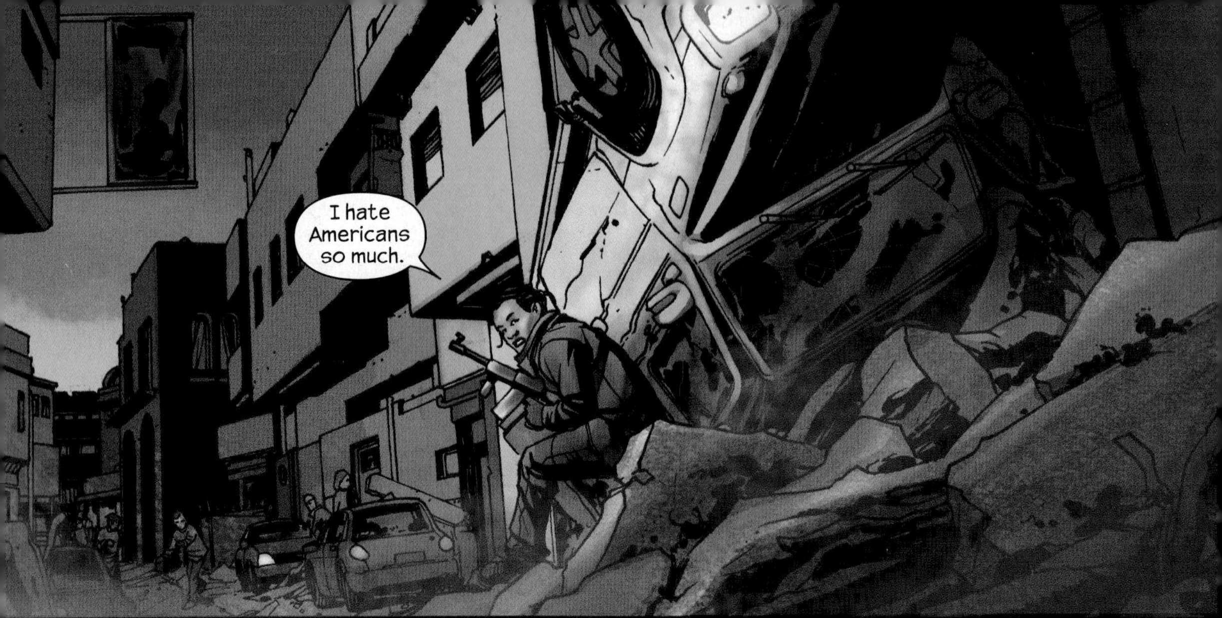
I hate Americans so much.

S.H.I.E.L.D. HANDBOOK: SLORENIA [EXCERPT]

The unseated regime council, the Tabissara, formed a mercenary force (now also generically referred to as the Tabissara) to attempt to take Slorenia back from the democratically elected government. Given Slorenia's strategic position, military aid from America was swiftly forthcoming.

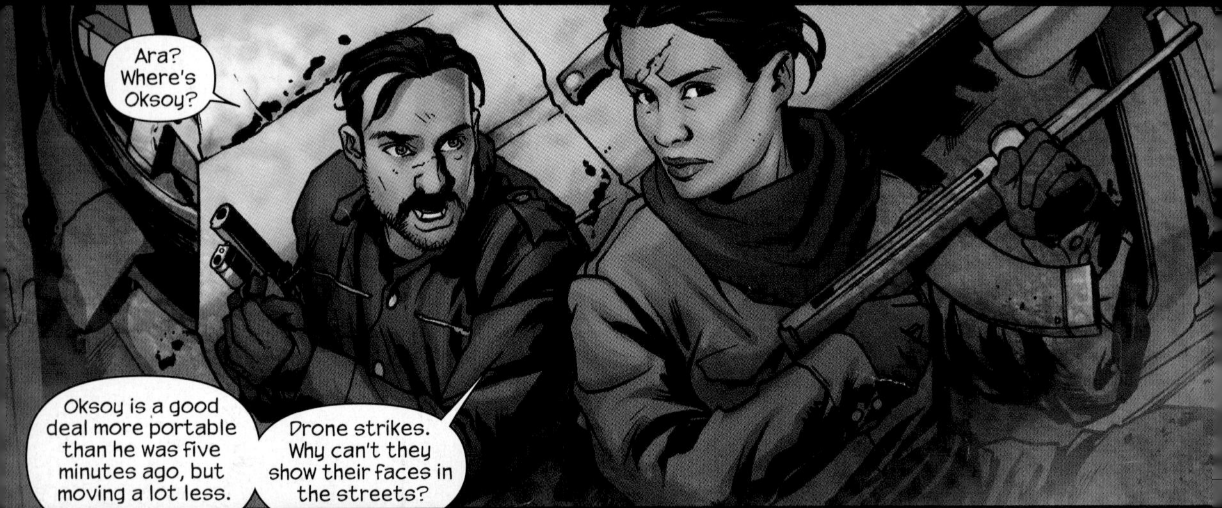
Ara? Where's Oksoy?
Oksoy is a good deal more portable than he was five minutes ago, but moving a lot less.
Drone strikes. Why can't they show their faces in the streets?

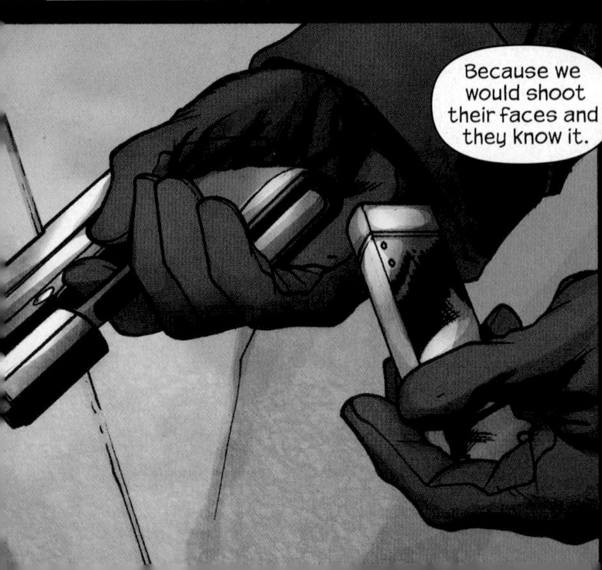
Because we would shoot their faces and they know it.

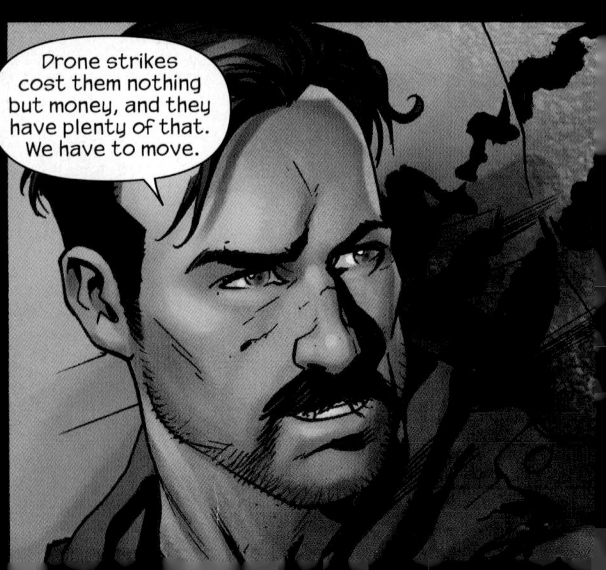
Drone strikes cost them nothing but money, and they have plenty of that. We have to move.

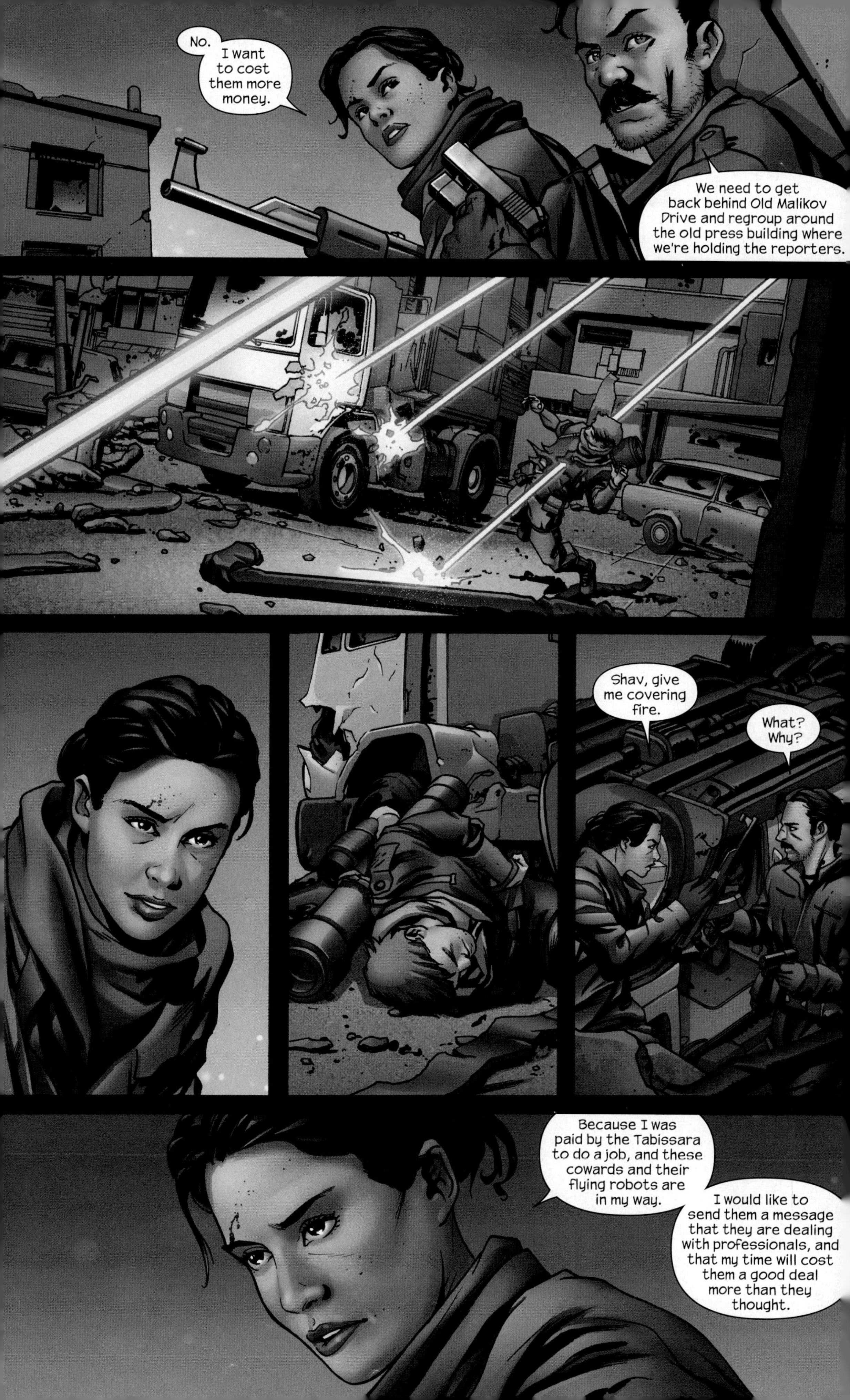
No.
I want to cost them more money.
We need to get back behind Old Malikov Drive and regroup around the old press building where we're holding the reporters.
Shav, give me covering fire.
What? Why?
Because I was paid by the Tabissara to do a job, and these cowards and their flying robots are in my way.
I would like to send them a message that they are dealing with professionals, and that my time will cost them a good deal more than they thought.

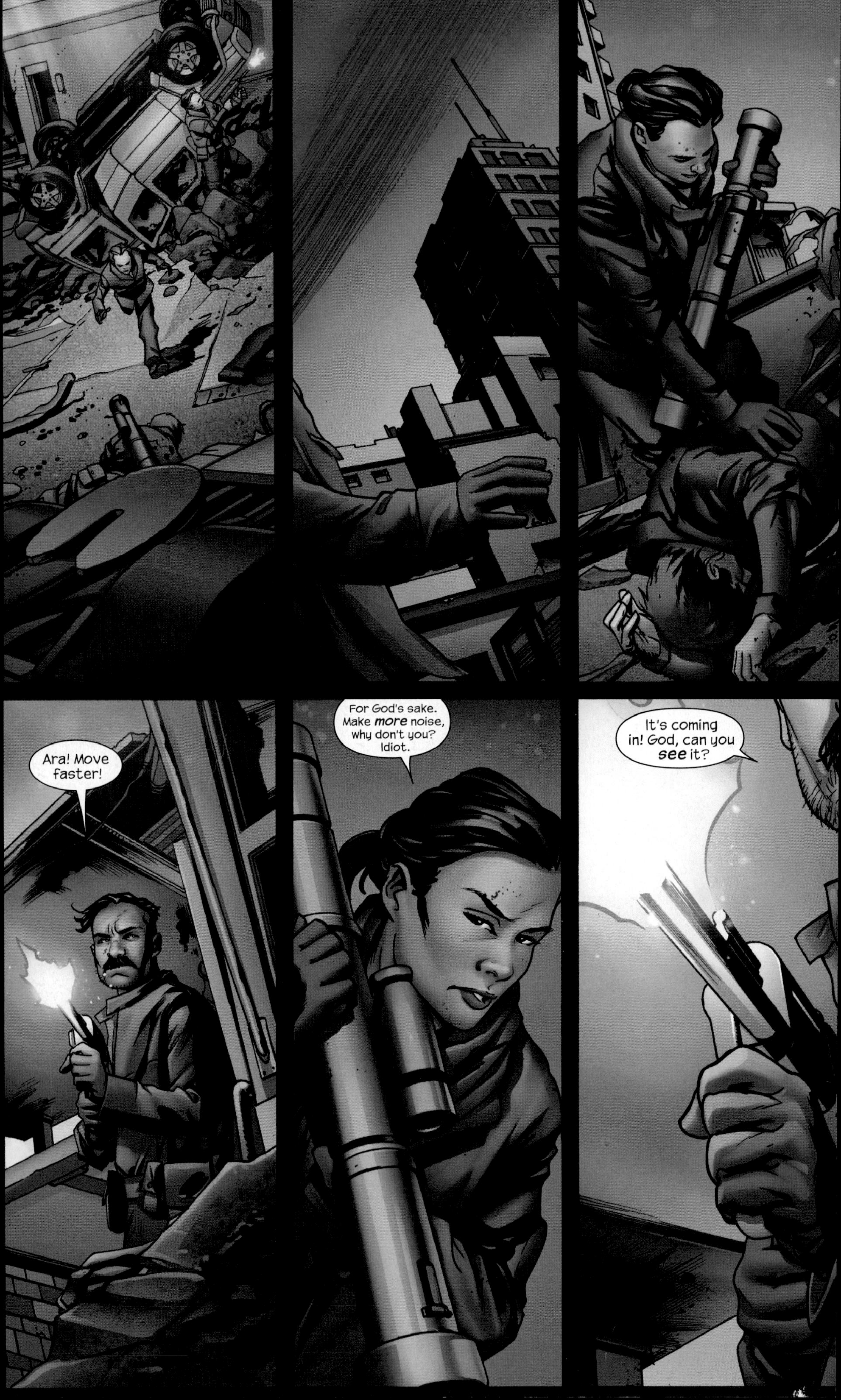
Ara! Move faster!
For God's sake. Make *more* noise, why don't you? Idiot.
It's coming in! God, can you *see* it?

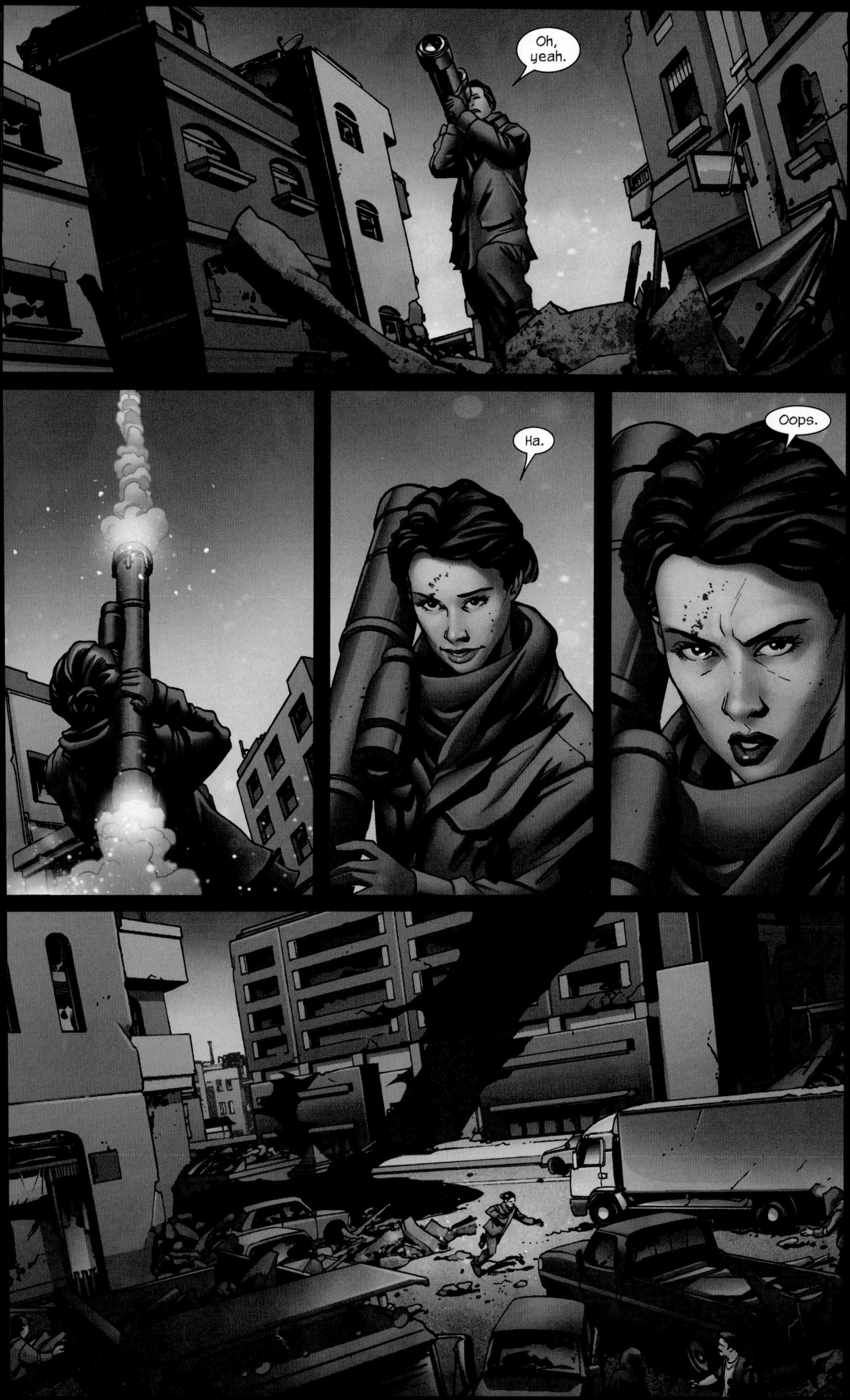
Oh, yeah.
Ha.
Oops.

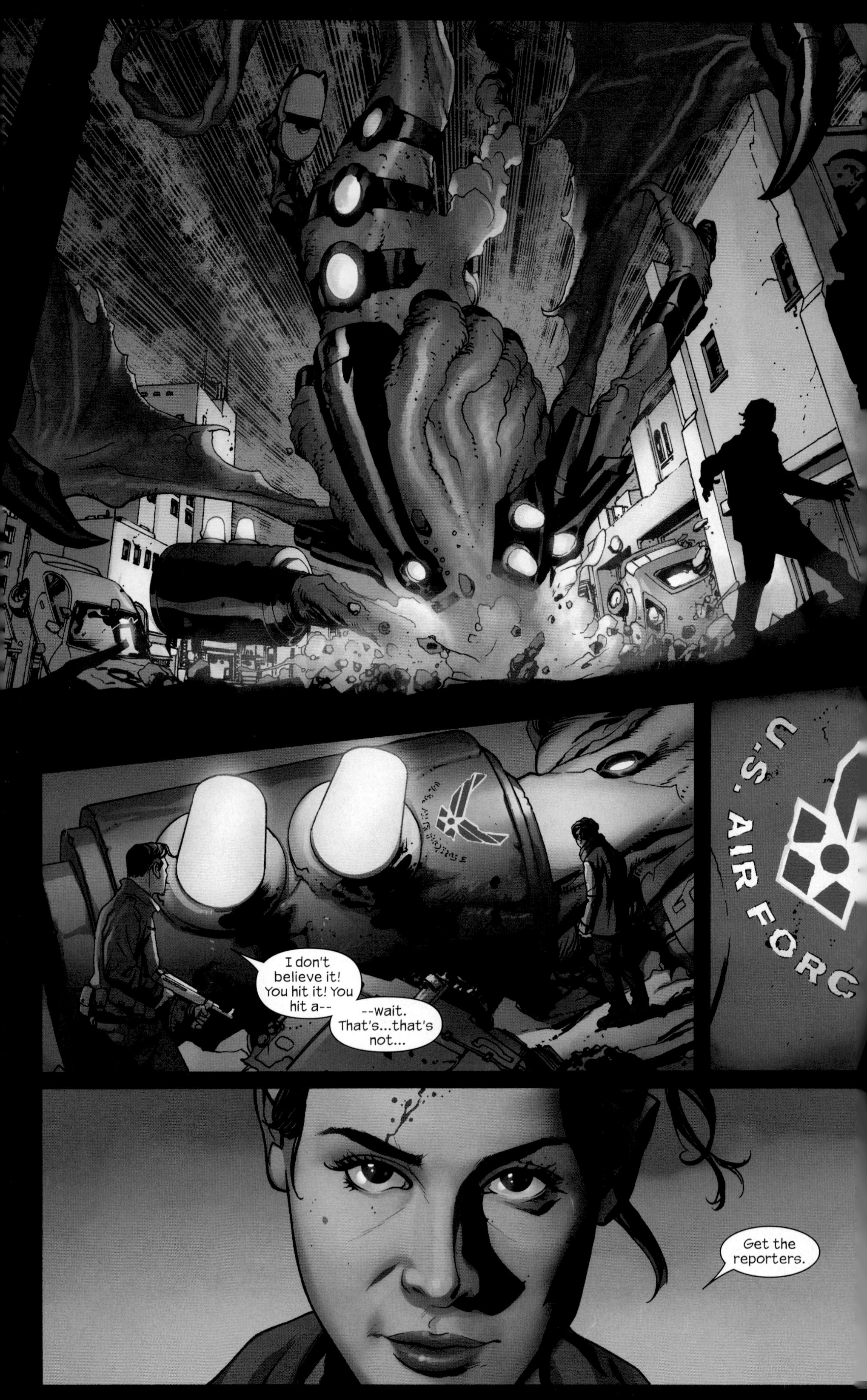

I don't believe it! You hit it! You hit a--
--wait. That's...that's not...
U.S. AIR FORC
Get the reporters.

It says "Stark" on the front, but everyone in New York City knows it as Avengers Tower.

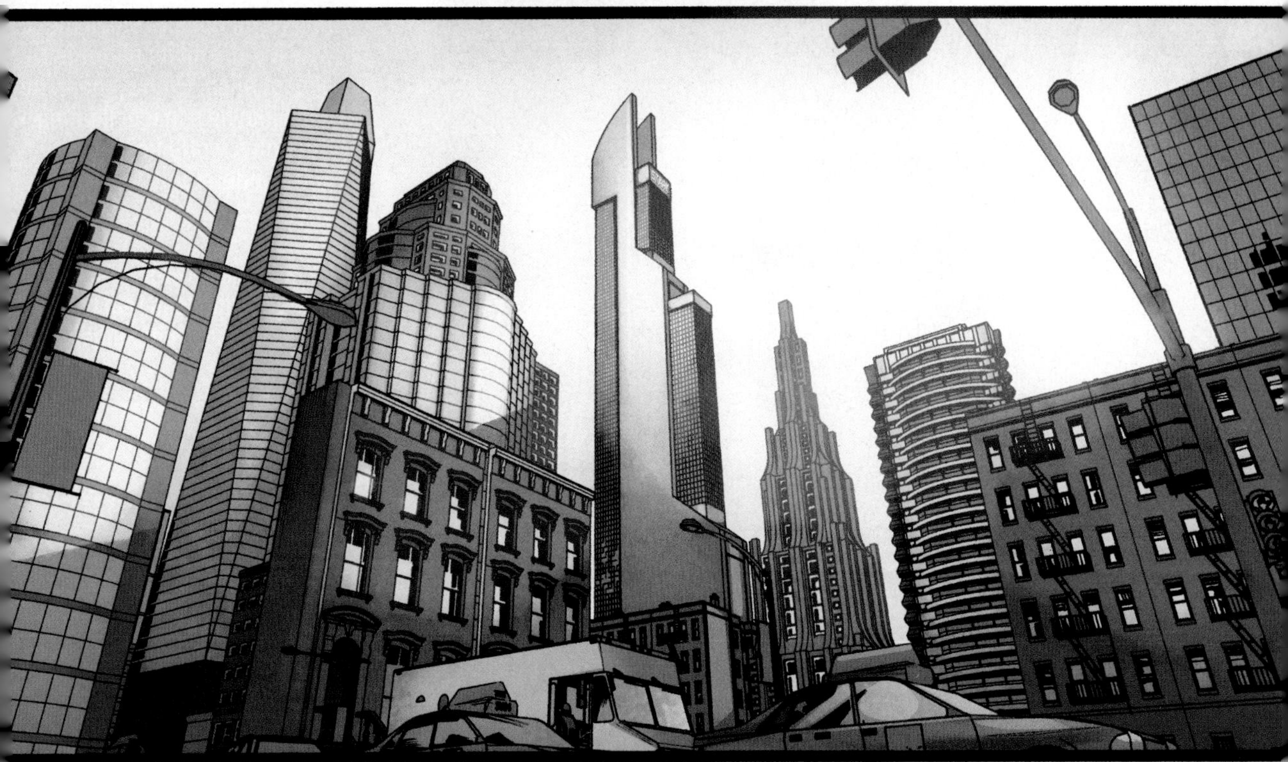

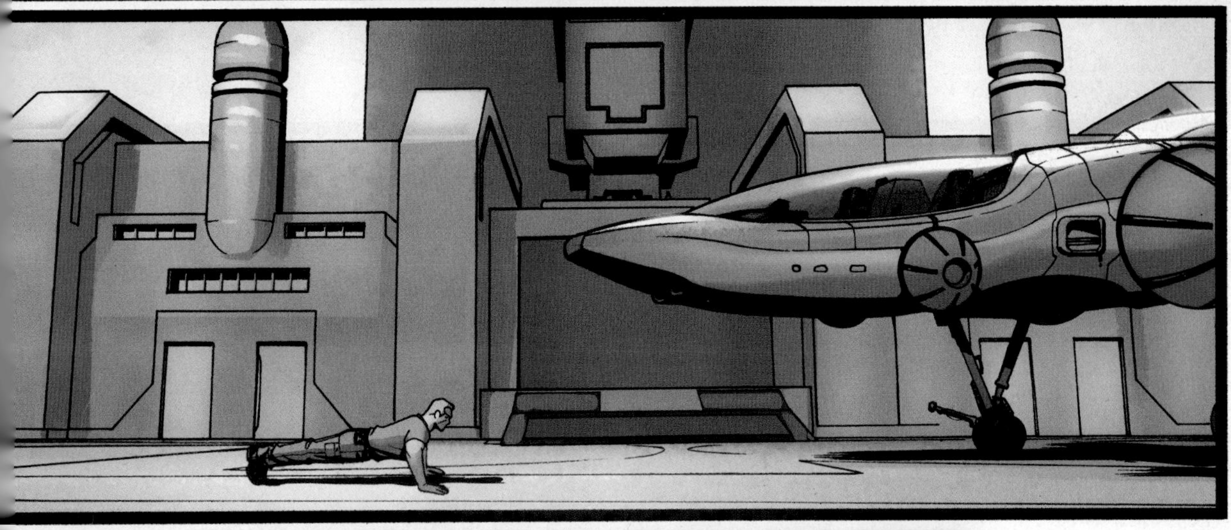

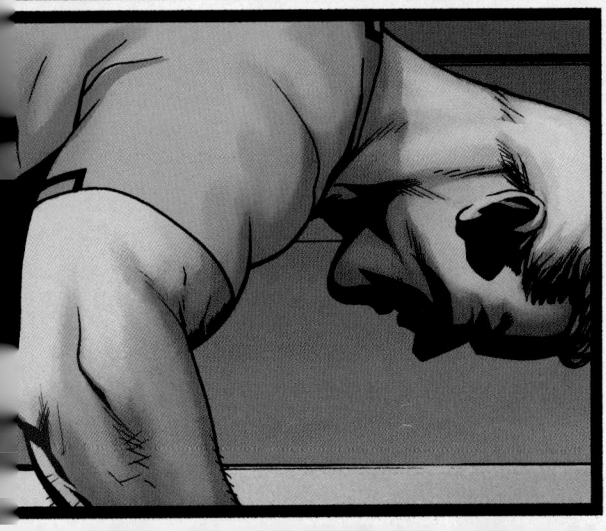

His name's Steve Rogers, but everyone knows him as Captain America, and the tower is home to him for part of each year.

As much as anything is home to him, even in part.

Even up here, he feels like he lives in a foreign country called The Future.

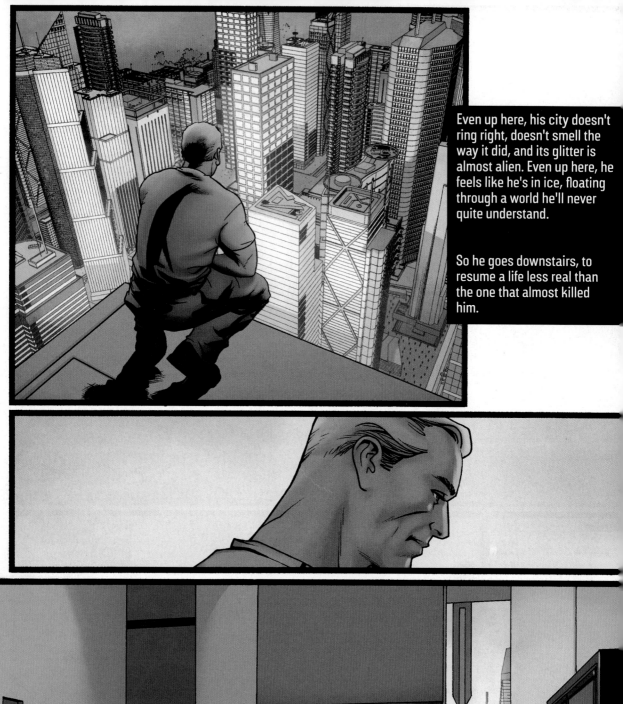

Even up here, his city doesn't ring right, doesn't smell the way it did, and its glitter is almost alien. Even up here, he feels like he's in ice, floating through a world he'll never quite understand.

So he goes downstairs, to resume a life less real than the one that almost killed him.

20 car pile-up reported near River Vale, NE

$50 million in diamonds stolen from world's largest deposit of ra

Coffee, sir?

I can do it myself, Jarvis. Really.

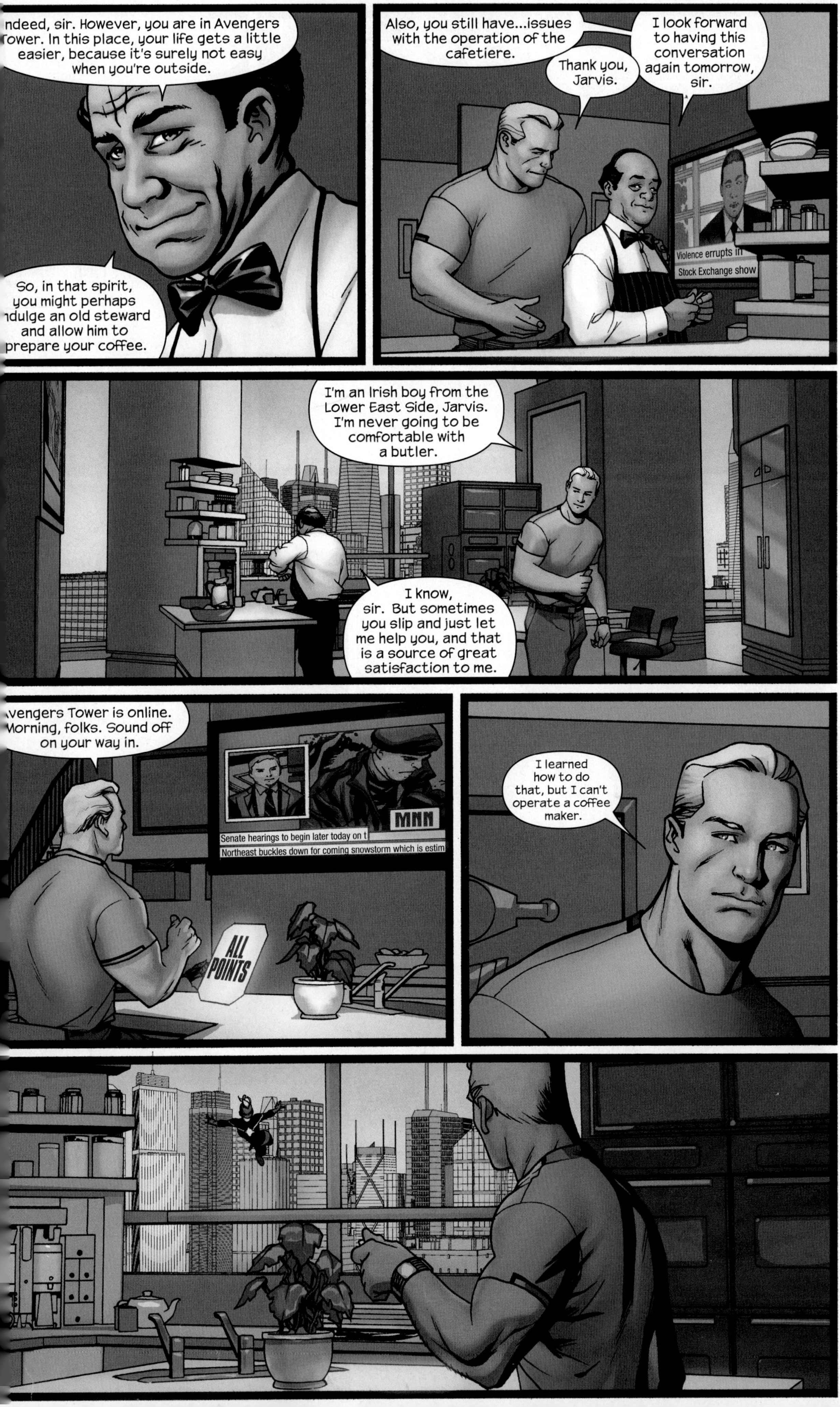
ndeed, sir. However, you are in Avengers Tower. In this place, your life gets a little easier, because it's surely not easy when you're outside.
So, in that spirit, you might perhaps ndulge an old steward and allow him to prepare your coffee.
Also, you still have...issues with the operation of the cafetiere.
Thank you, Jarvis.
I look forward to having this conversation again tomorrow, sir.
Violence errupts in
Stock Exchange show
I'm an Irish boy from the Lower East Side, Jarvis. I'm never going to be comfortable with a butler.
I know, sir. But sometimes you slip and just let me help you, and that is a source of great satisfaction to me.
vengers Tower is online. Morning, folks. Sound off on your way in.
MNN
Senate hearings to begin later today on t
Northeast buckles down for coming snowstorm which is estim
ALL POINTS
I learned how to do that, but I can't operate a coffee maker.

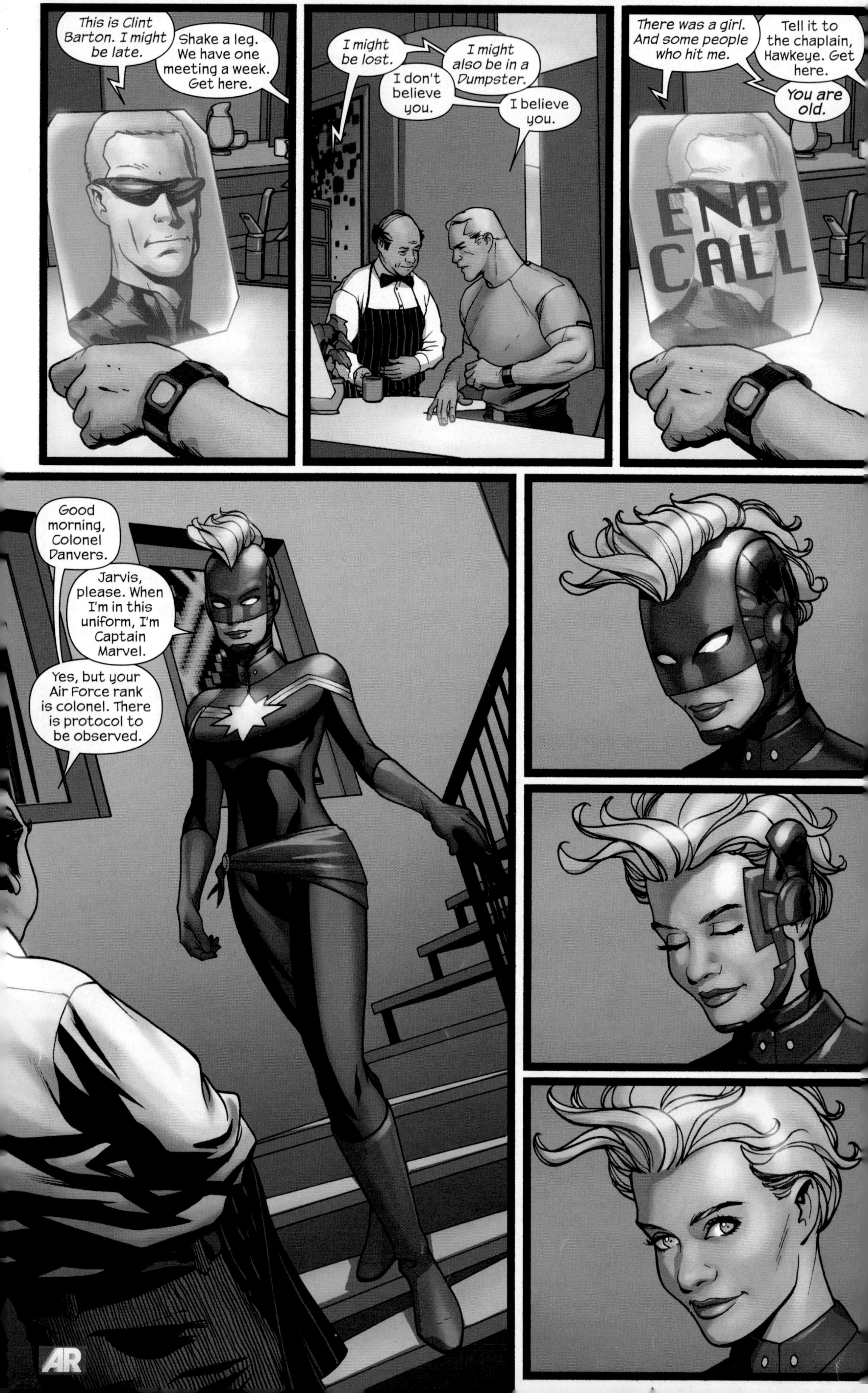
This is Clint Barton. I might be late.
Shake a leg. We have one meeting a week. Get here.
I might be lost.
I might also be in a Dumpster.
I don't believe you.
I believe you.
There was a girl. And some people who hit me.
Tell it to the chaplain, Hawkeye. Get here.
You are old.
END CALL
Good morning, Colonel Danvers.
Jarvis, please. When I'm in this uniform, I'm Captain Marvel.
Yes, but your Air Force rank is colonel. There is protocol to be observed.

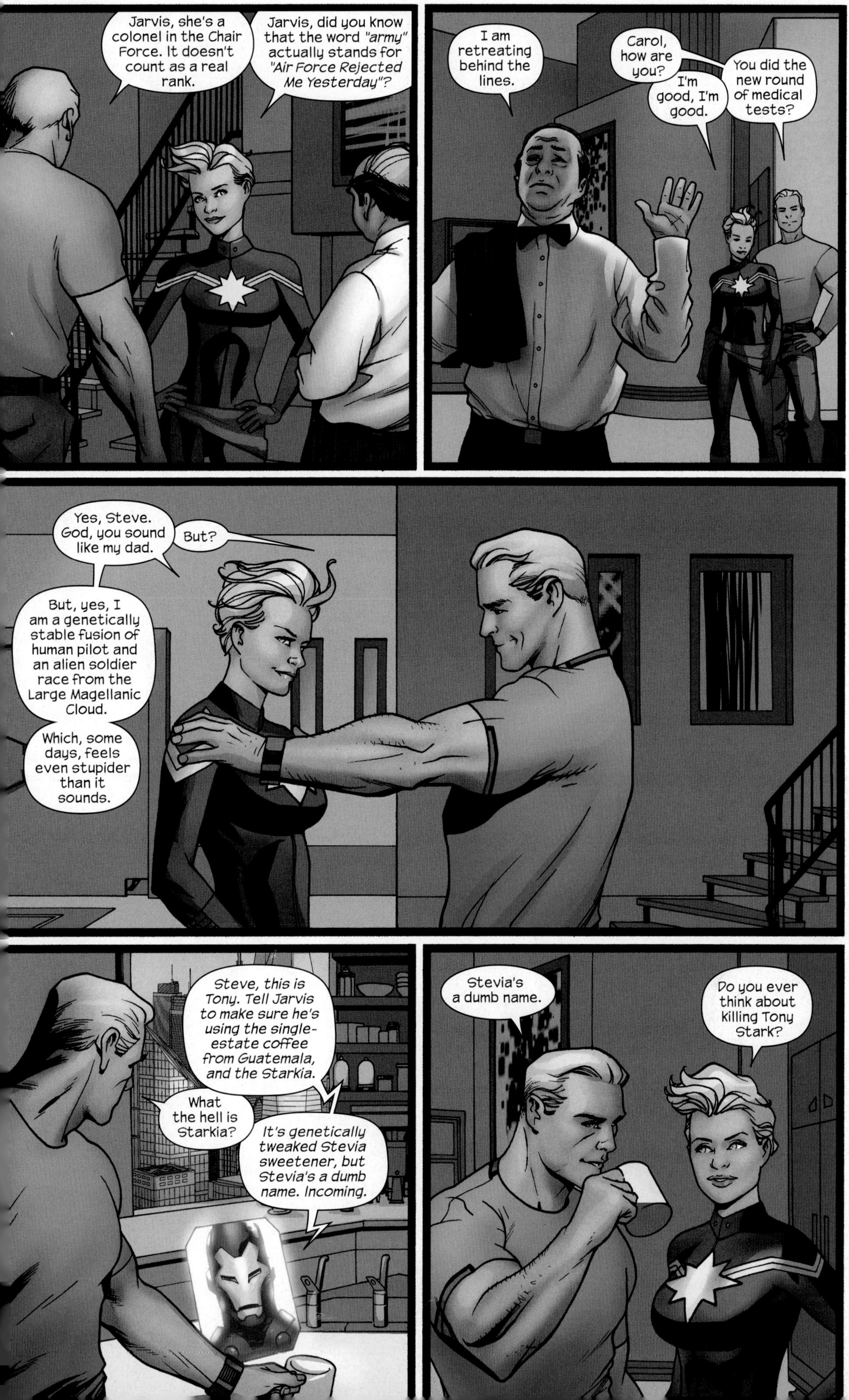

Jarvis, she's a colonel in the Chair Force. It doesn't count as a real rank.
Jarvis, did you know that the word *"army"* actually stands for *"Air Force Rejected Me Yesterday"*?
I am retreating behind the lines.
Carol, how are you?
I'm good, I'm good.
You did the new round of medical tests?
Yes, Steve. God, you sound like my dad.
But?
But, yes, I am a genetically stable fusion of human pilot and an alien soldier race from the Large Magellanic Cloud.
Which, some days, feels even stupider than it sounds.
Steve, this is Tony. Tell Jarvis to make sure he's using the single-estate coffee from Guatemala, and the Starkia.
What the hell is Starkia?
It's genetically tweaked Stevia sweetener, but Stevia's a dumb name. Incoming.
Stevia's a dumb name.
Do you ever think about killing Tony Stark?

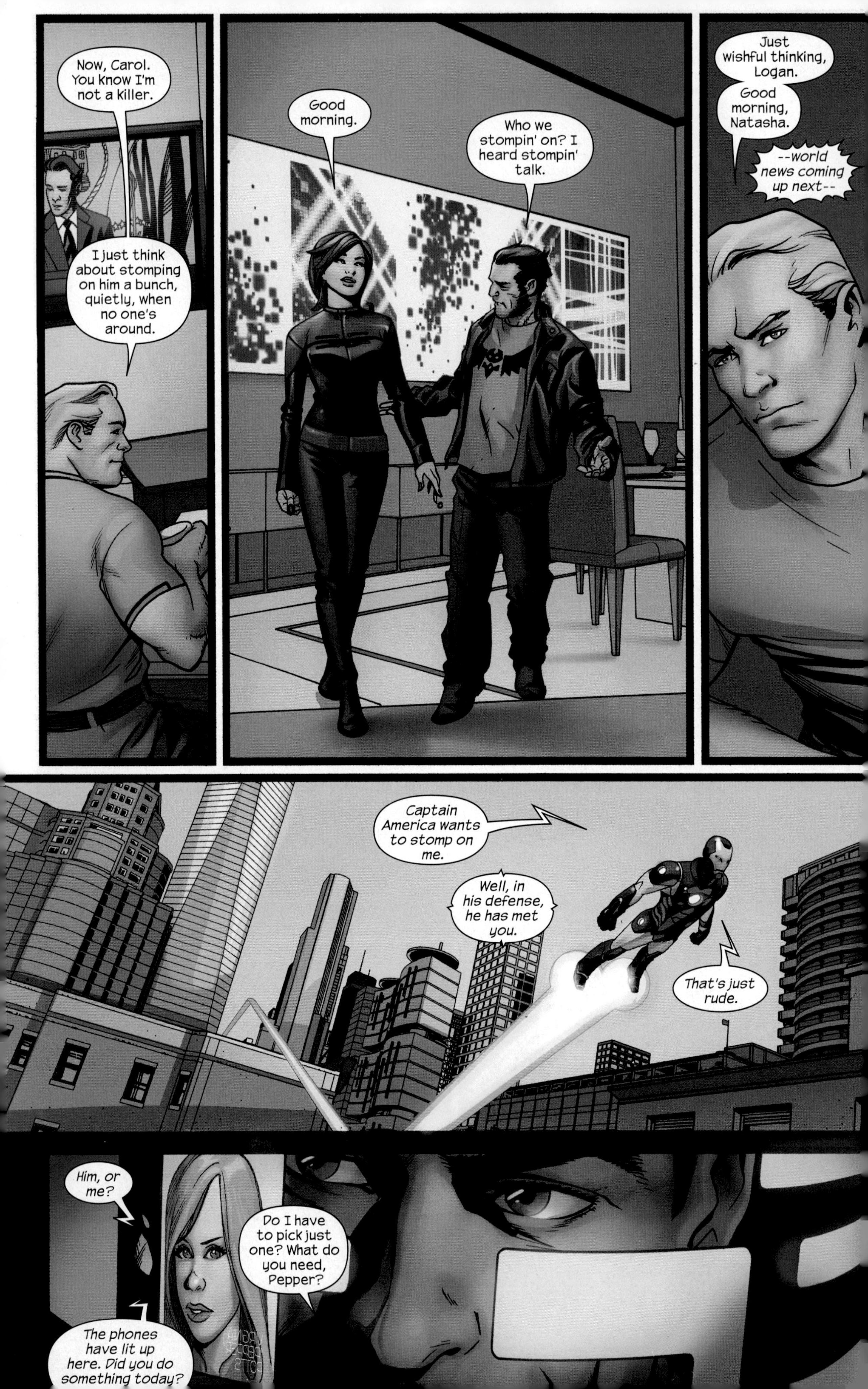
Now, Carol. You know I'm not a killer.
I just think about stomping on him a bunch, quietly, when no one's around.
Good morning.
Who we stompin' on? I heard stompin' talk.
Just wishful thinking, Logan.
Good morning, Natasha.
--world news coming up next--
Captain America wants to stomp on me.
Well, in his defense, he has met you.
That's just rude.
Him, or me?
Do I have to pick just one? What do you need, Pepper?
The phones have lit up here. Did you do something today?

What do you mean? Why do you say it like that? You treat me like I'm some brain-damaged criminal.

Oh, please. It's like you're just handing me the ammunition to use on you.

...I've been good.

Well, I'm getting a lot of journalists wanting to talk to you today. Defense correspondents, mostly. Can I feed you to a couple?

Do I know any of them?

No.

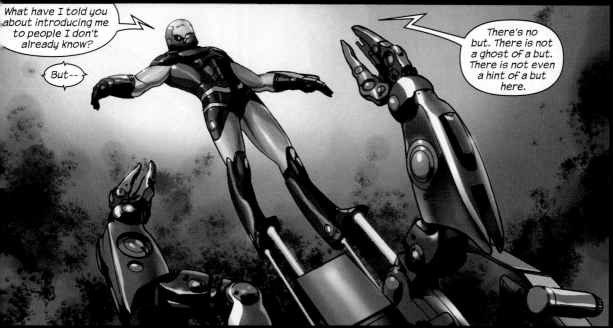

What have I told you about introducing me to people I don't already know?

But--

There's no but. There is not a ghost of a but. There is not even a hint of a but here.

Now, I have to go and sit with my awesome and awesomely boring quote friends unquote for a while.

Why are you just saying "butt" at me?

And you should sit in a dark room and think about what you've done. Okay? Love you.

End call. Launch teardown systems.

Good morning, beloved. Did anyone check the Dumpsters for Clint yet?

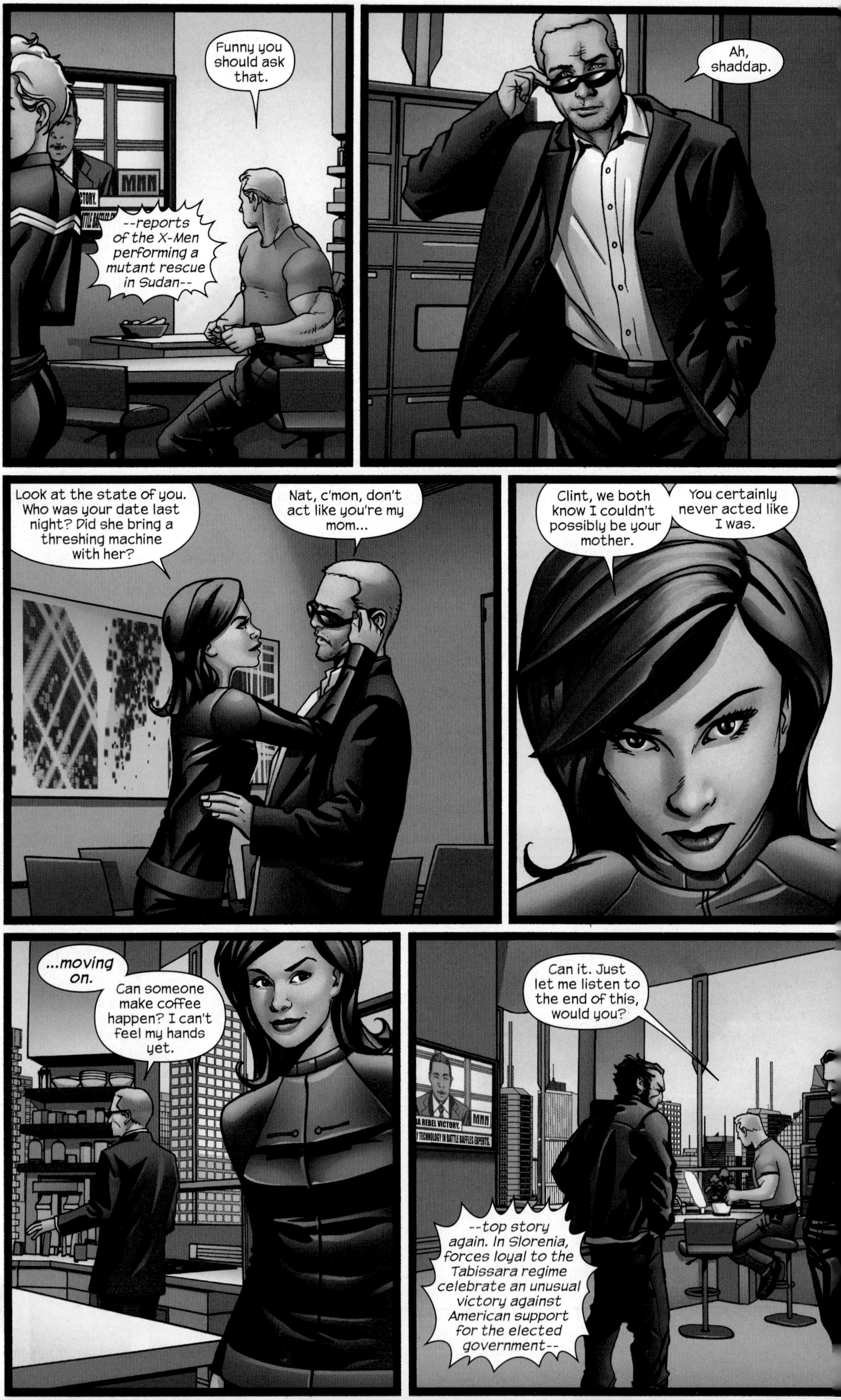
MNN
Funny you should ask that.
--reports of the X-Men performing a mutant rescue in Sudan--
Ah, shaddap.
Look at the state of you. Who was your date last night? Did she bring a threshing machine with her?
Nat, c'mon, don't act like you're my mom...
Clint, we both know I couldn't possibly be your mother.
You certainly never acted like I was.
...moving on.
Can someone make coffee happen? I can't feel my hands yet.
Can it. Just let me listen to the end of this, would you?
MNN
--top story again. In Slorenia, forces loyal to the Tabissara regime celebrate an unusual victory against American support for the elected government--

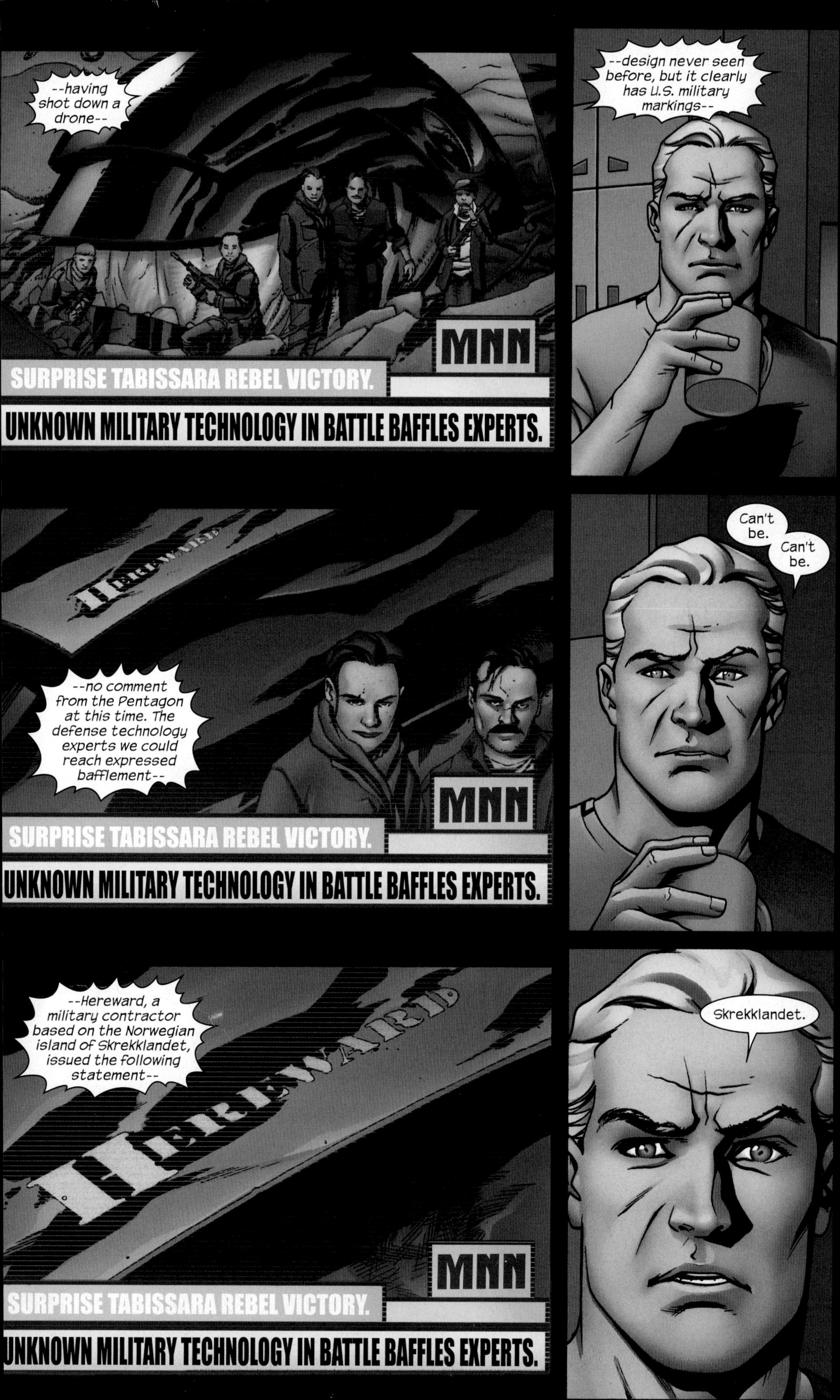
--having shot down a drone--
MNN
SURPRISE TABISSARA REBEL VICTORY.
UNKNOWN MILITARY TECHNOLOGY IN BATTLE BAFFLES EXPERTS.
--design never seen before, but it clearly has U.S. military markings--
HEREWARD
--no comment from the Pentagon at this time. The defense technology experts we could reach expressed bafflement--
MNN
SURPRISE TABISSARA REBEL VICTORY.
UNKNOWN MILITARY TECHNOLOGY IN BATTLE BAFFLES EXPERTS.
Can't be.
Can't be.
--Hereward, a military contractor based on the Norwegian island of Skrekklandet, issued the following statement--
HEREWARD
MNN
SURPRISE TABISSARA REBEL VICTORY.
UNKNOWN MILITARY TECHNOLOGY IN BATTLE BAFFLES EXPERTS.
Skrekklandet.

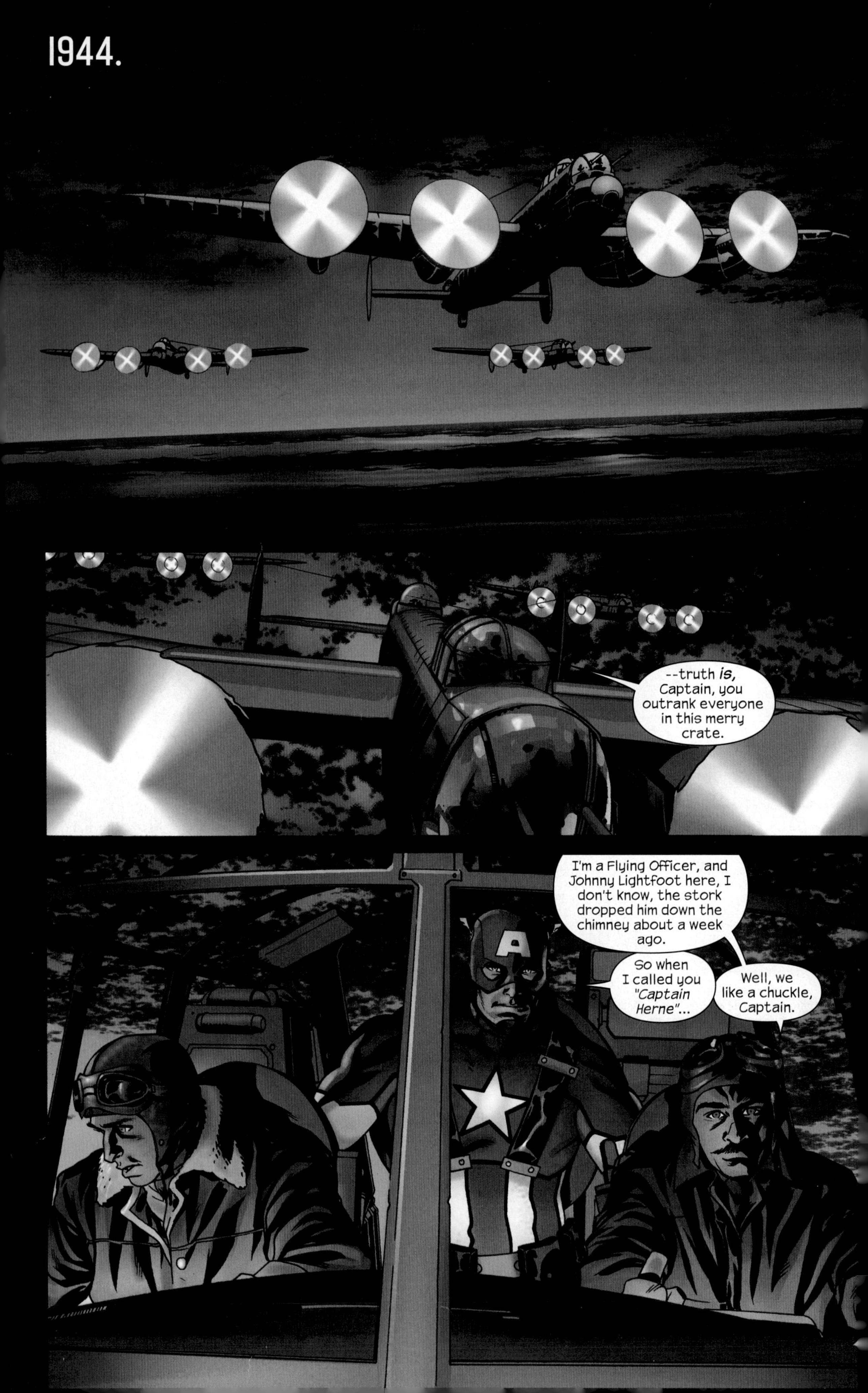
1944.
--truth *is,* Captain, you outrank everyone in this merry crate.
I'm a Flying Officer, and Johnny Lightfoot here, I don't know, the stork dropped him down the chimney about a week ago.
So when I called you *"Captain Herne"*...
Well, we like a chuckle, Captain.

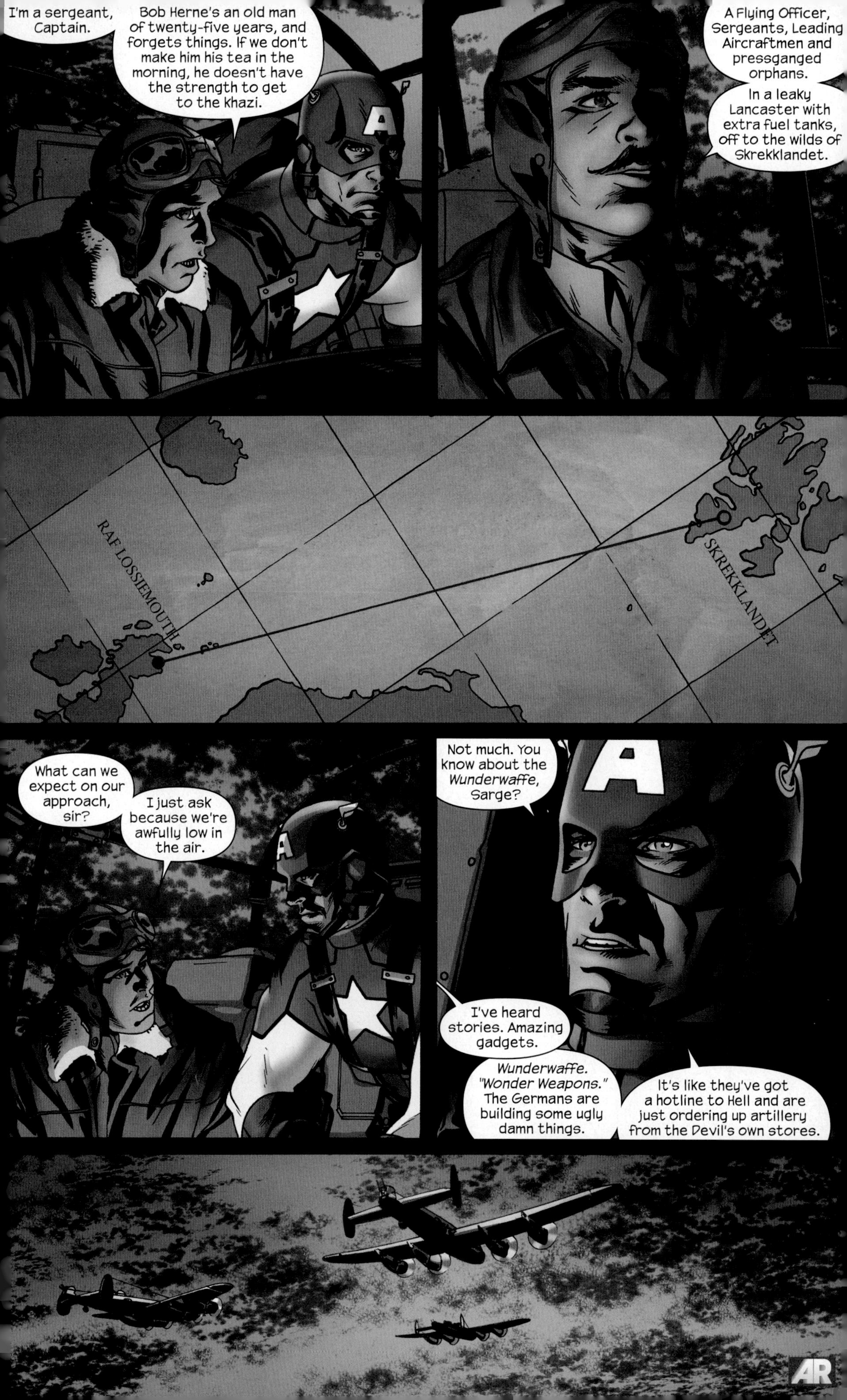
I'm a sergeant, Captain.
Bob Herne's an old man of twenty-five years, and forgets things. If we don't make him his tea in the morning, he doesn't have the strength to get to the khazi.
A Flying Officer, Sergeants, Leading Aircraftmen and pressganged orphans.
In a leaky Lancaster with extra fuel tanks, off to the wilds of Skrekklandet.
RAF LOSSIEMOUTH
SKREKKLANDET
What can we expect on our approach, sir?
I just ask because we're awfully low in the air.
Not much. You know about the *Wunderwaffe*, Sarge?
I've heard stories. Amazing gadgets.
Wunderwaffe. "*Wonder Weapons.*" The Germans are building some ugly damn things.
It's like they've got a hotline to Hell and are just ordering up artillery from the Devil's own stores.

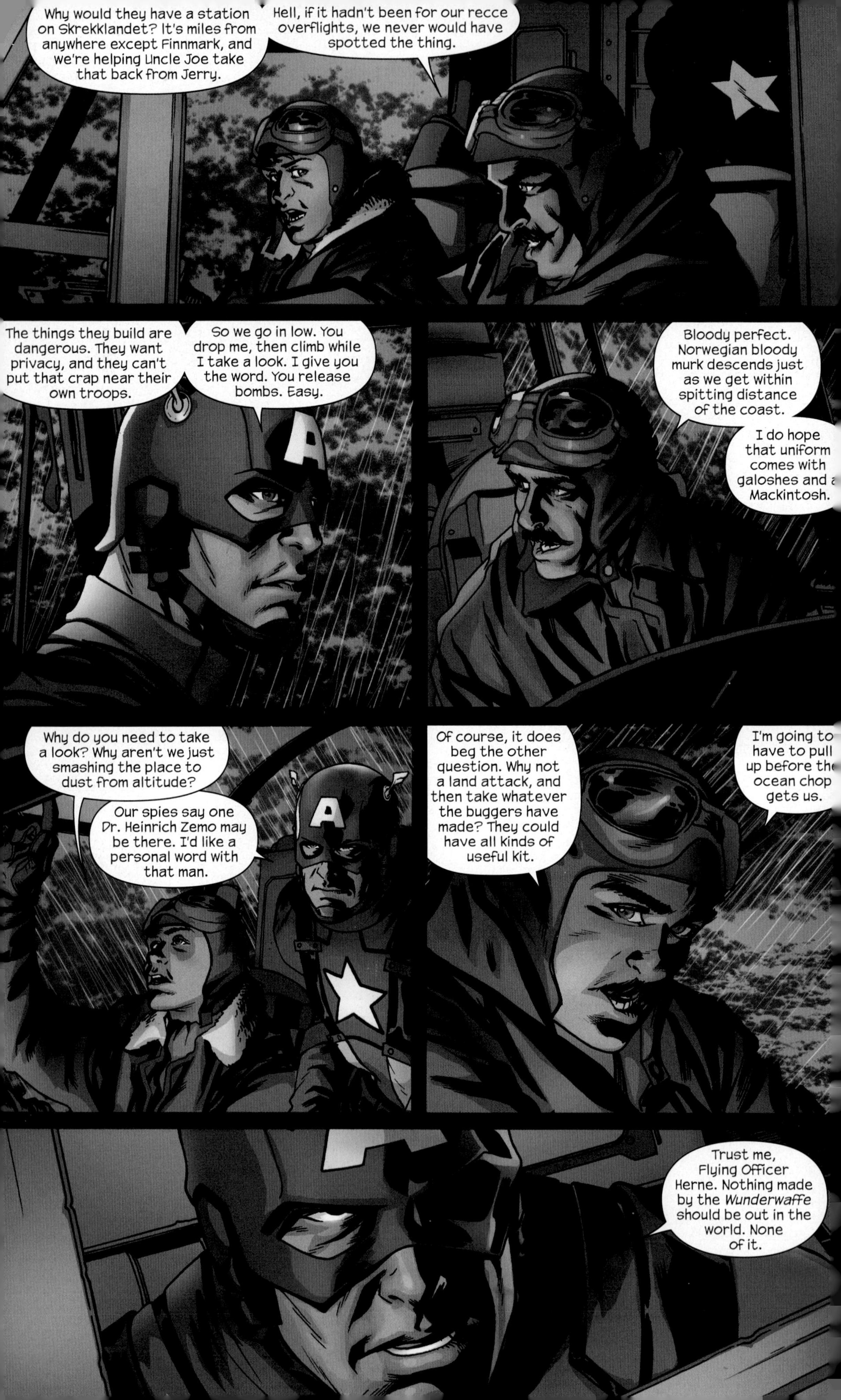

Why would they have a station on Skrekklandet? It's miles from anywhere except Finnmark, and we're helping Uncle Joe take that back from Jerry.
Hell, if it hadn't been for our recce overflights, we never would have spotted the thing.
The things they build are dangerous. They want privacy, and they can't put that crap near their own troops.
So we go in low. You drop me, then climb while I take a look. I give you the word. You release bombs. Easy.
Bloody perfect. Norwegian bloody murk descends just as we get within spitting distance of the coast.
I do hope that uniform comes with galoshes and a Mackintosh.
Why do you need to take a look? Why aren't we just smashing the place to dust from altitude?
Our spies say one Dr. Heinrich Zemo may be there. I'd like a personal word with that man.
Of course, it does beg the other question. Why not a land attack, and then take whatever the buggers have made? They could have all kinds of useful kit.
I'm going to have to pull up before the ocean chop gets us.
Trust me, Flying Officer Herne. Nothing made by the *Wunderwaffe* should be out in the world. None of it.

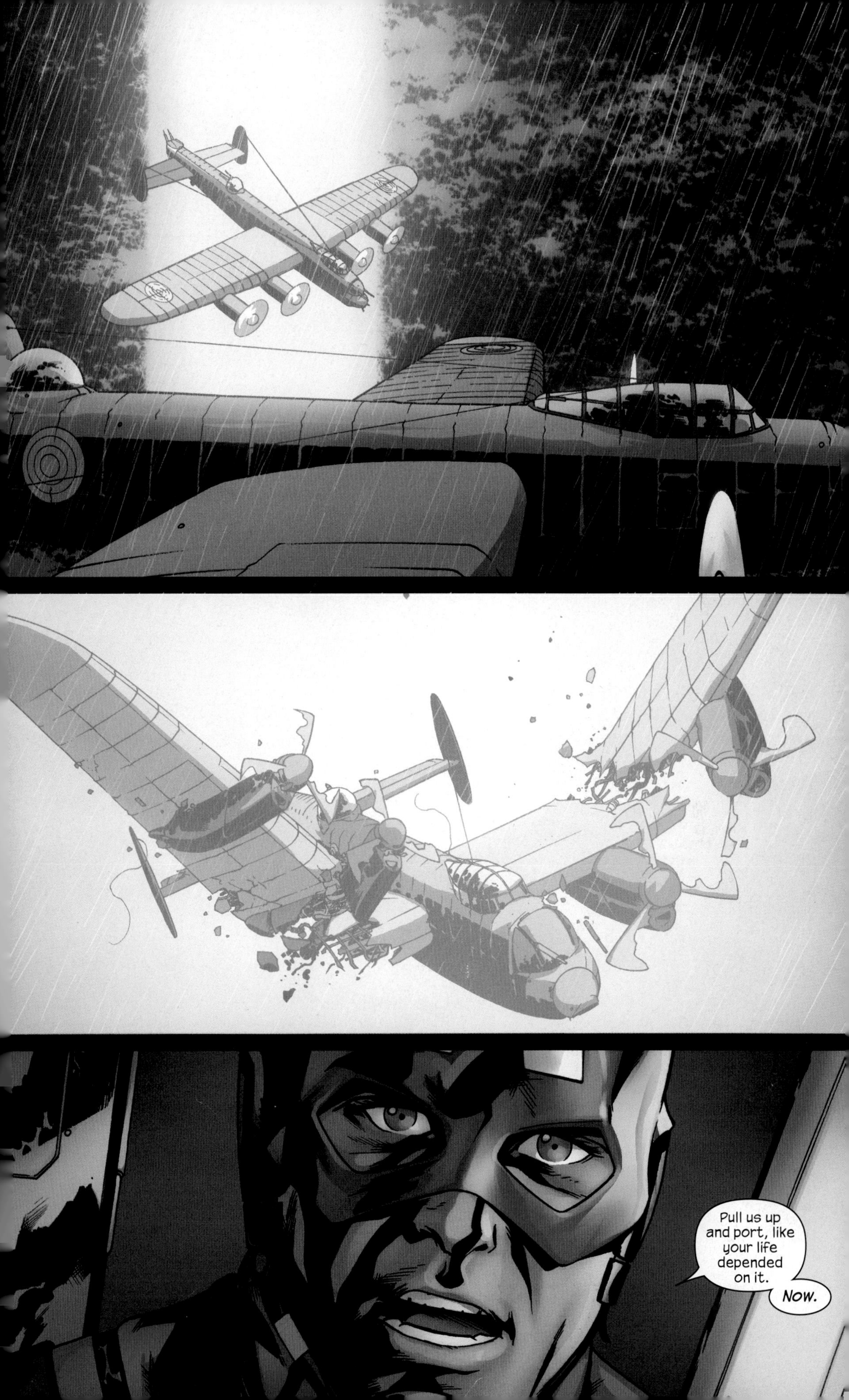
Pull us up and port, like your life depended on it.
NOW.

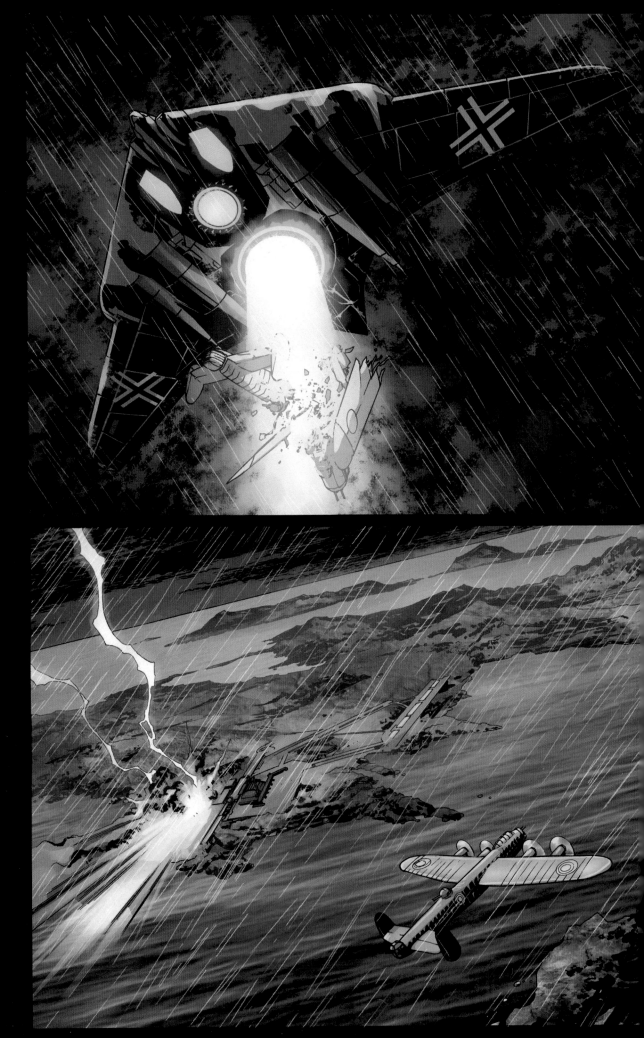

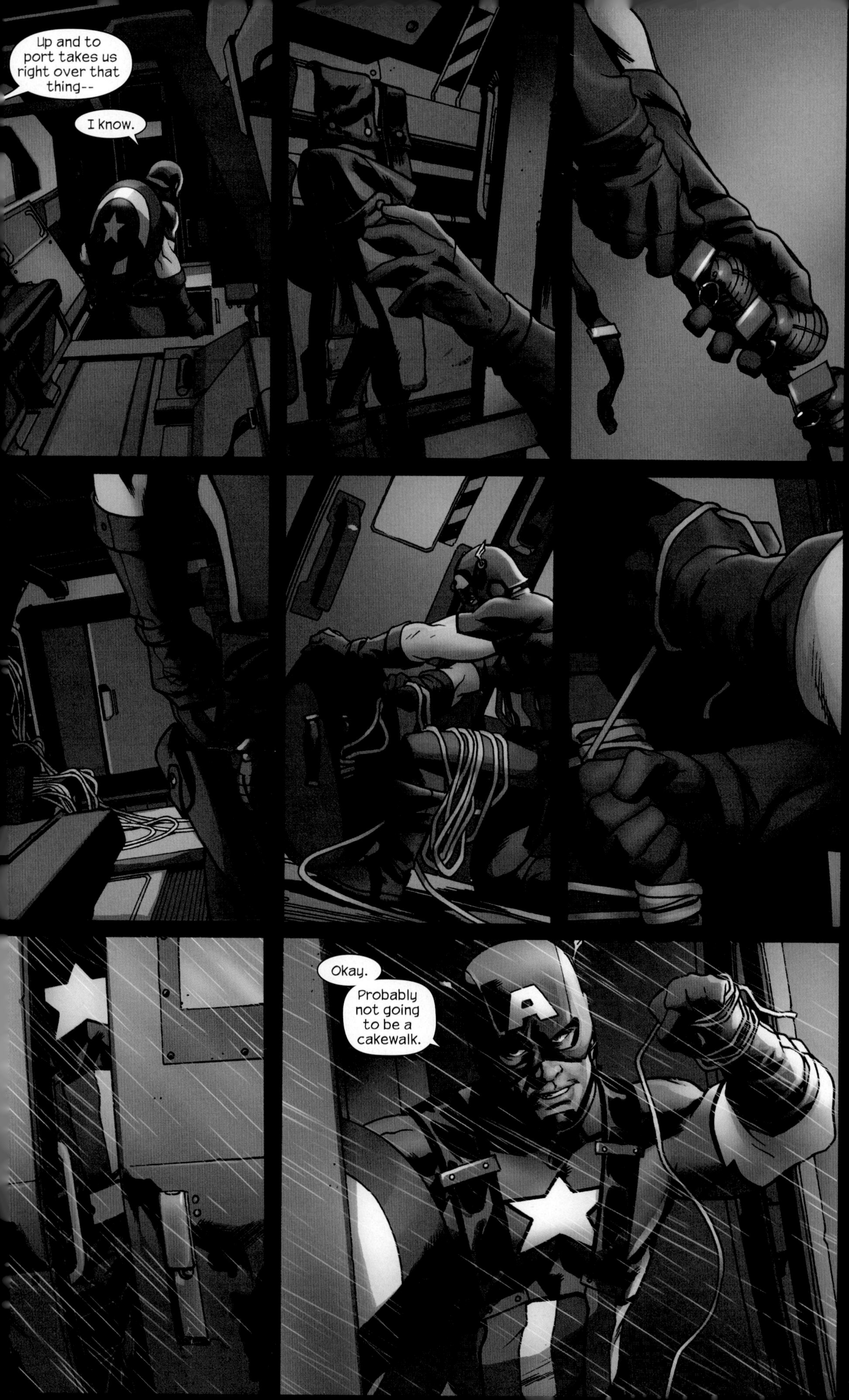
Up and to port takes us right over that thing--
I know.
Okay.
Probably not going to be a cakewalk.

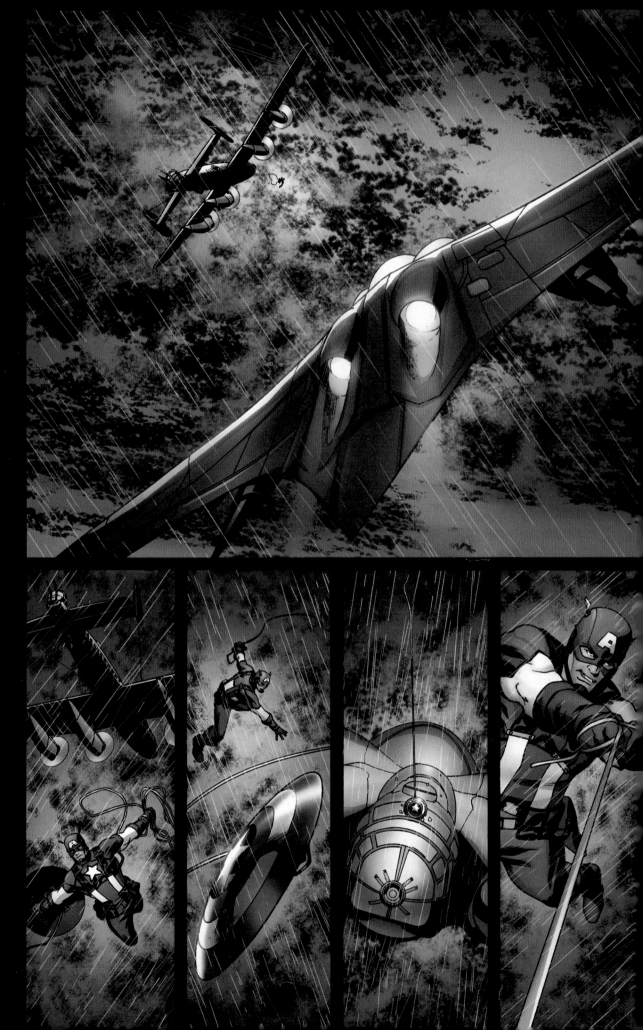

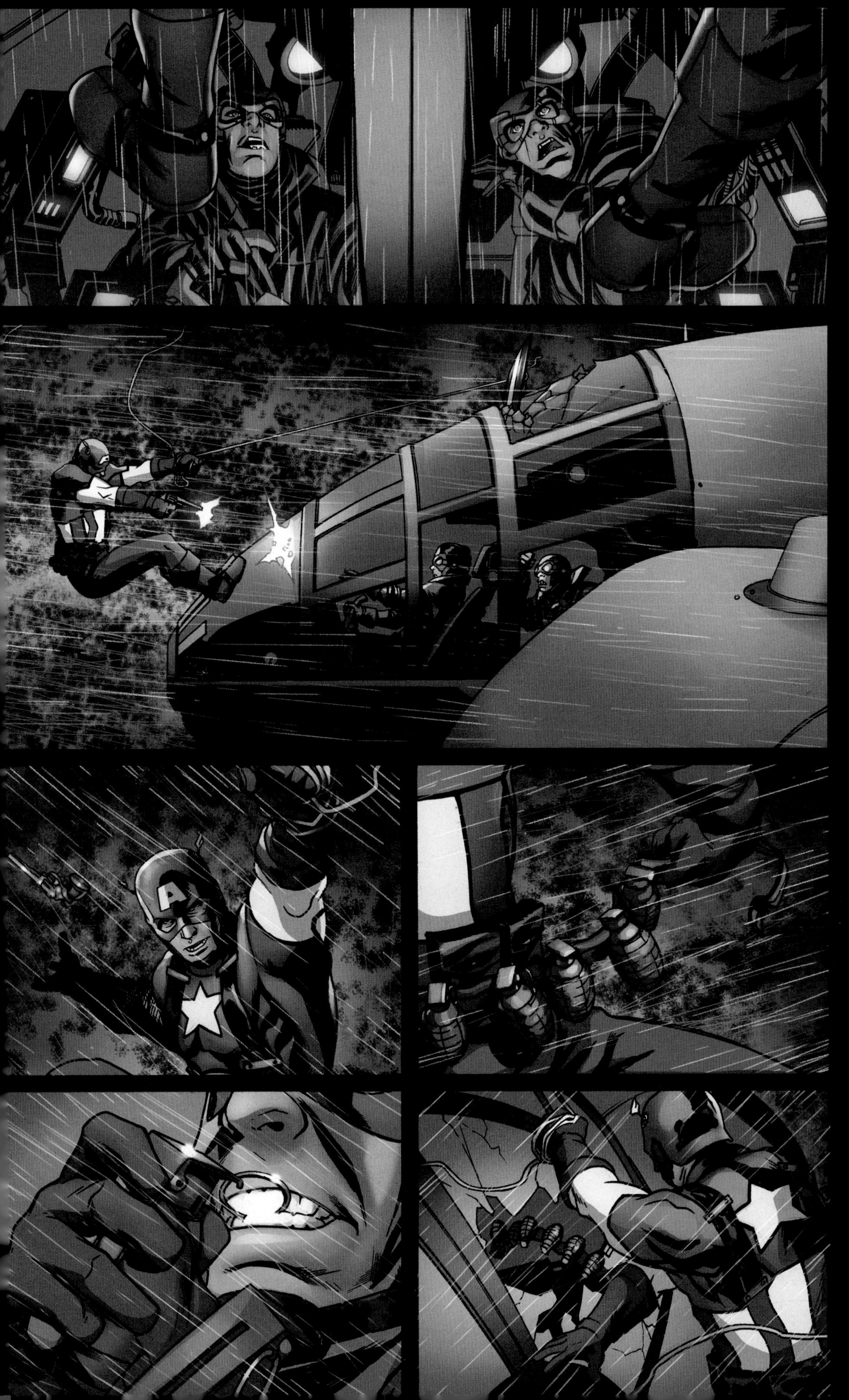

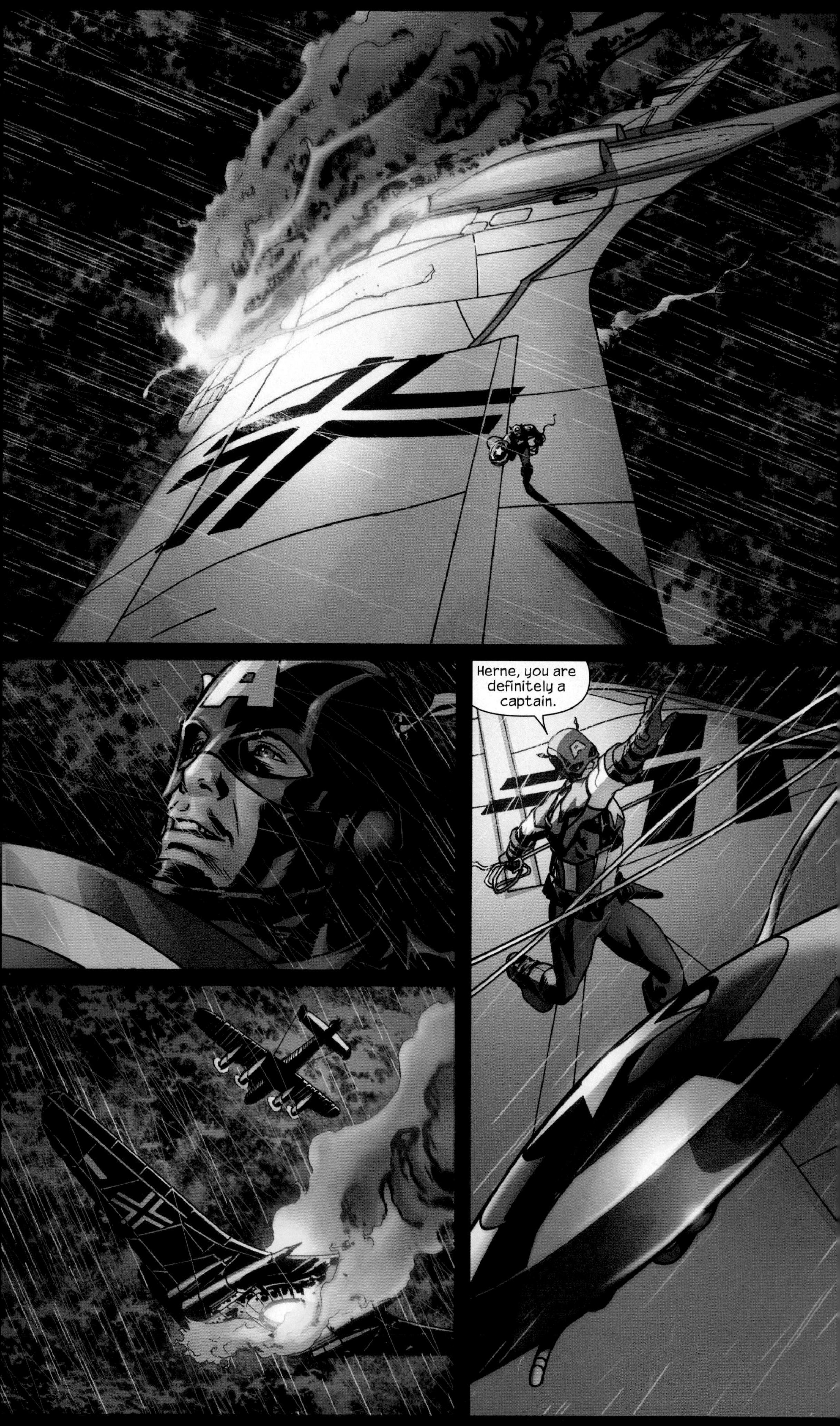
Herne, you are definitely a captain.

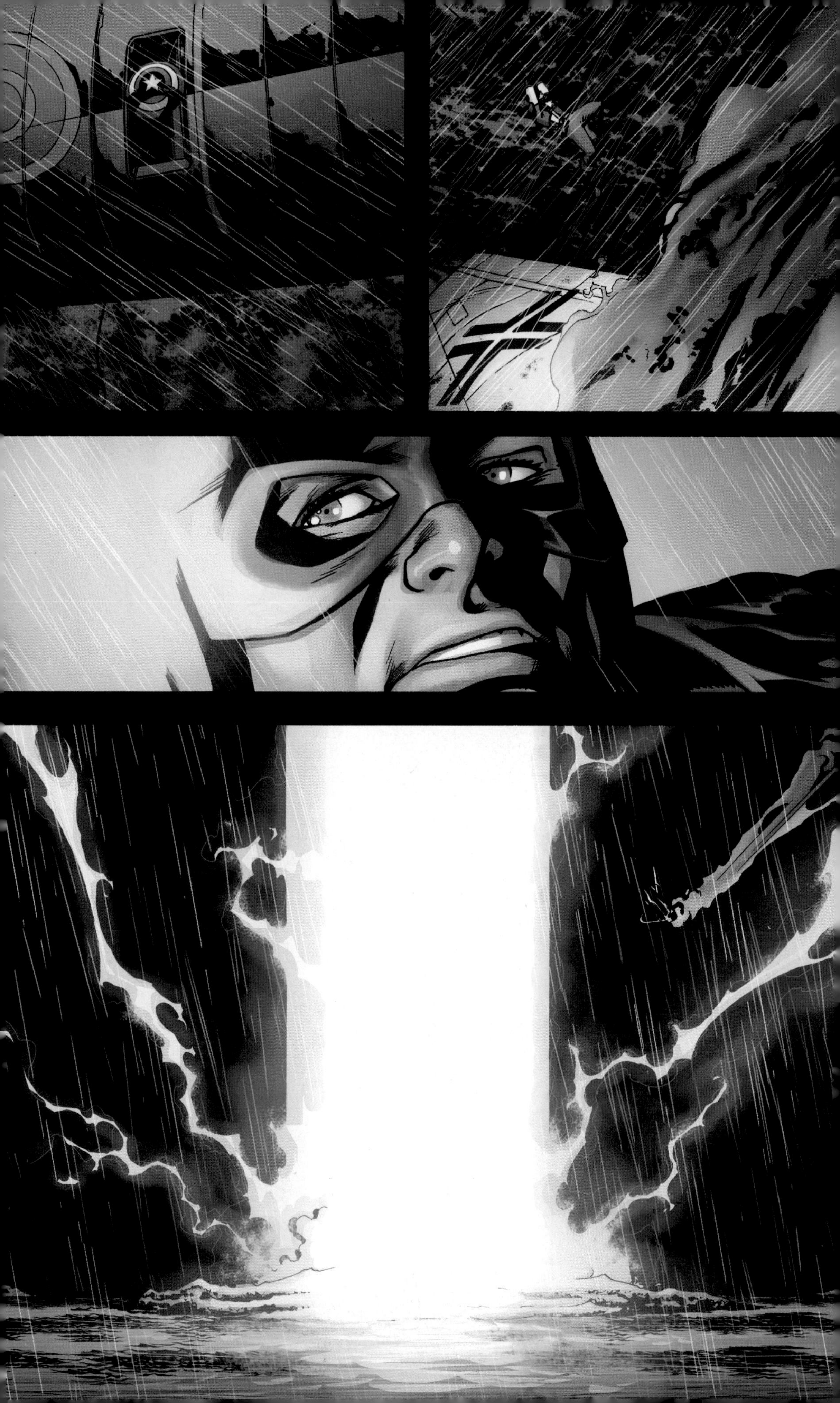

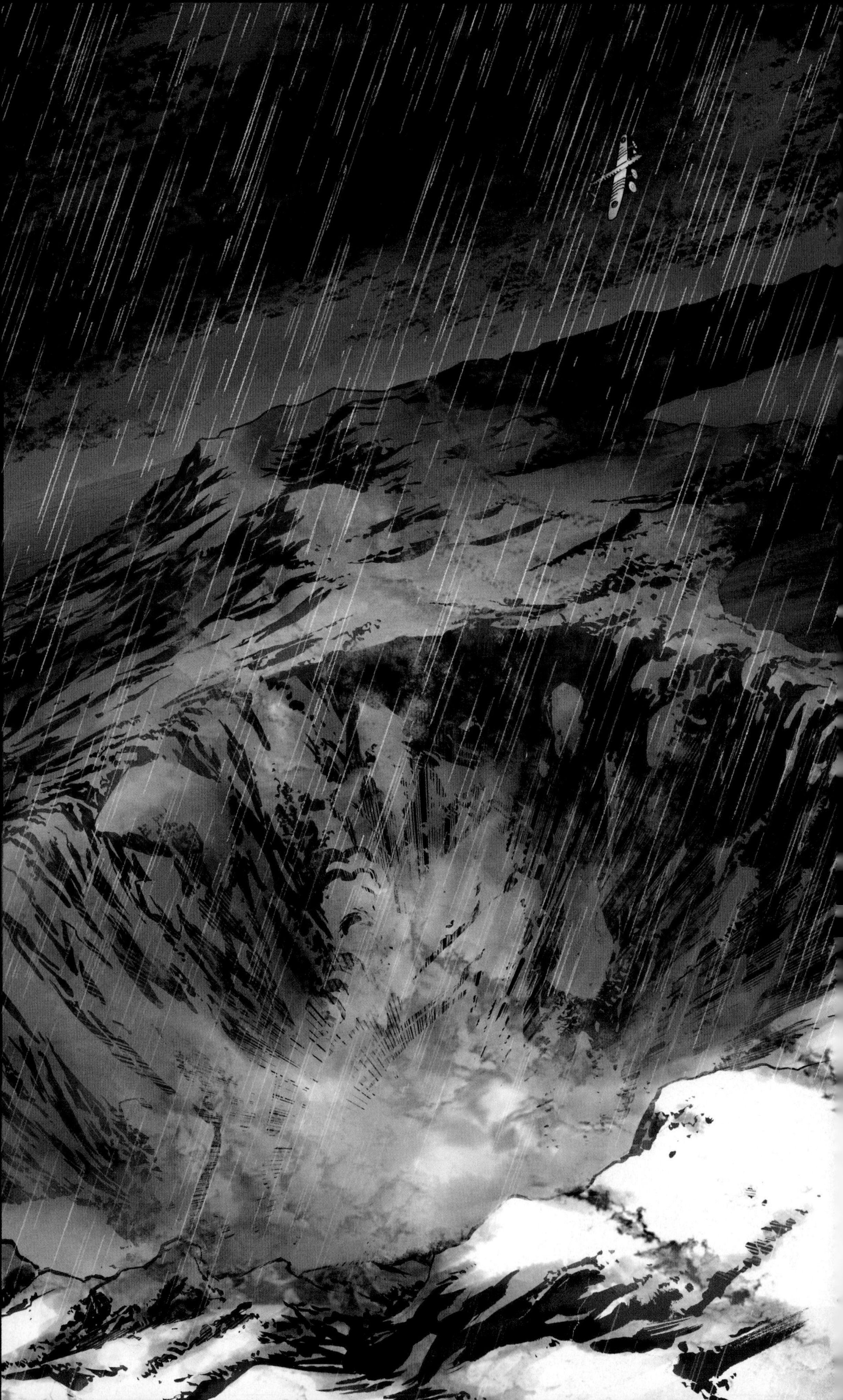

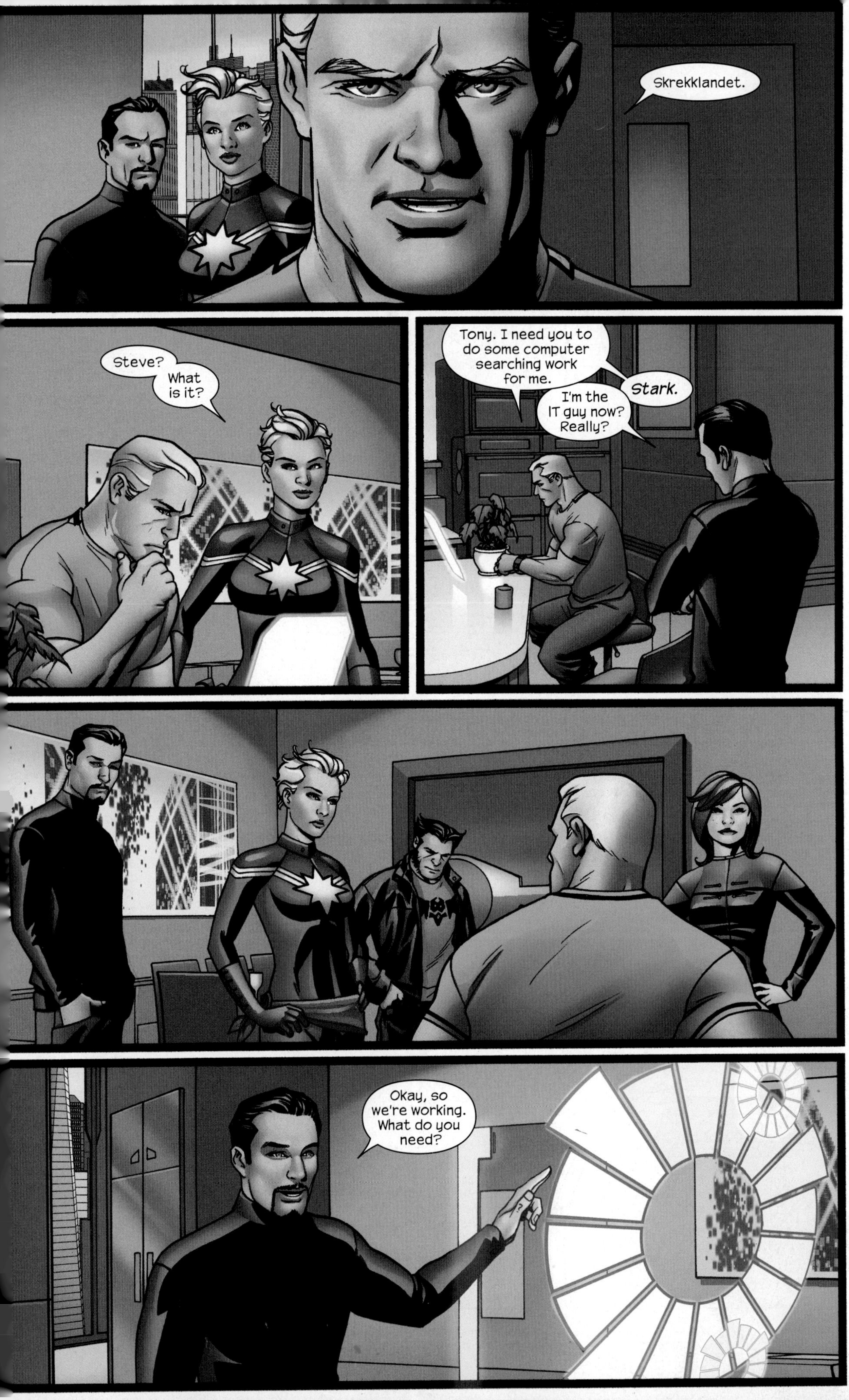
Skrekklandet.
Steve?
What is it?
Stark.
Tony. I need you to do some computer searching work for me.
I'm the IT guy now? Really?
Okay, so we're working. What do you need?

Panel 1:
Pull up the last five minutes of this news channel. You can do that, right?

Chapterized for your pleasure. What are we looking for?

Right about there.

Panel 2 (news caption):
Hold the still. Run the audio, twenty seconds on either side of it.

What is that thing?

In Slorenia, forces loyal to the Tabissara regime celebrate an unusual victory against American support for the elected government in the capital city, Tblunka, having shot down a drone--

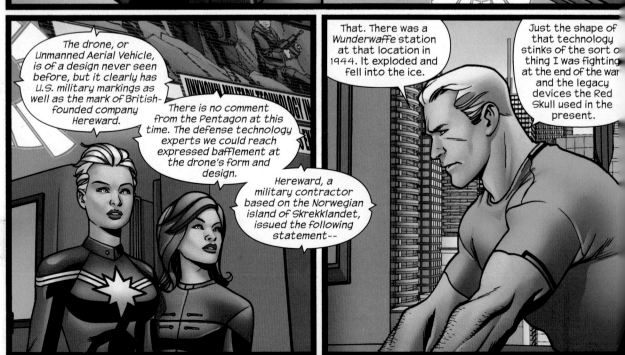

Panel 3:
The drone, or Unmanned Aerial Vehicle, is of a design never seen before, but it clearly has U.S. military markings as well as the mark of British-founded company Hereward.

There is no comment from the Pentagon at this time. The defense technology experts we could reach expressed bafflement at the drone's form and design.

Hereward, a military contractor based on the Norwegian island of Skrekklandet, issued the following statement--

Panel 4:
That. There was a Wunderwaffe station at that location in 1944. It exploded and fell into the ice.

Just the shape of that technology stinks of the sort of thing I was fighting at the end of the war and the legacy devices the Red Skull used in the present.

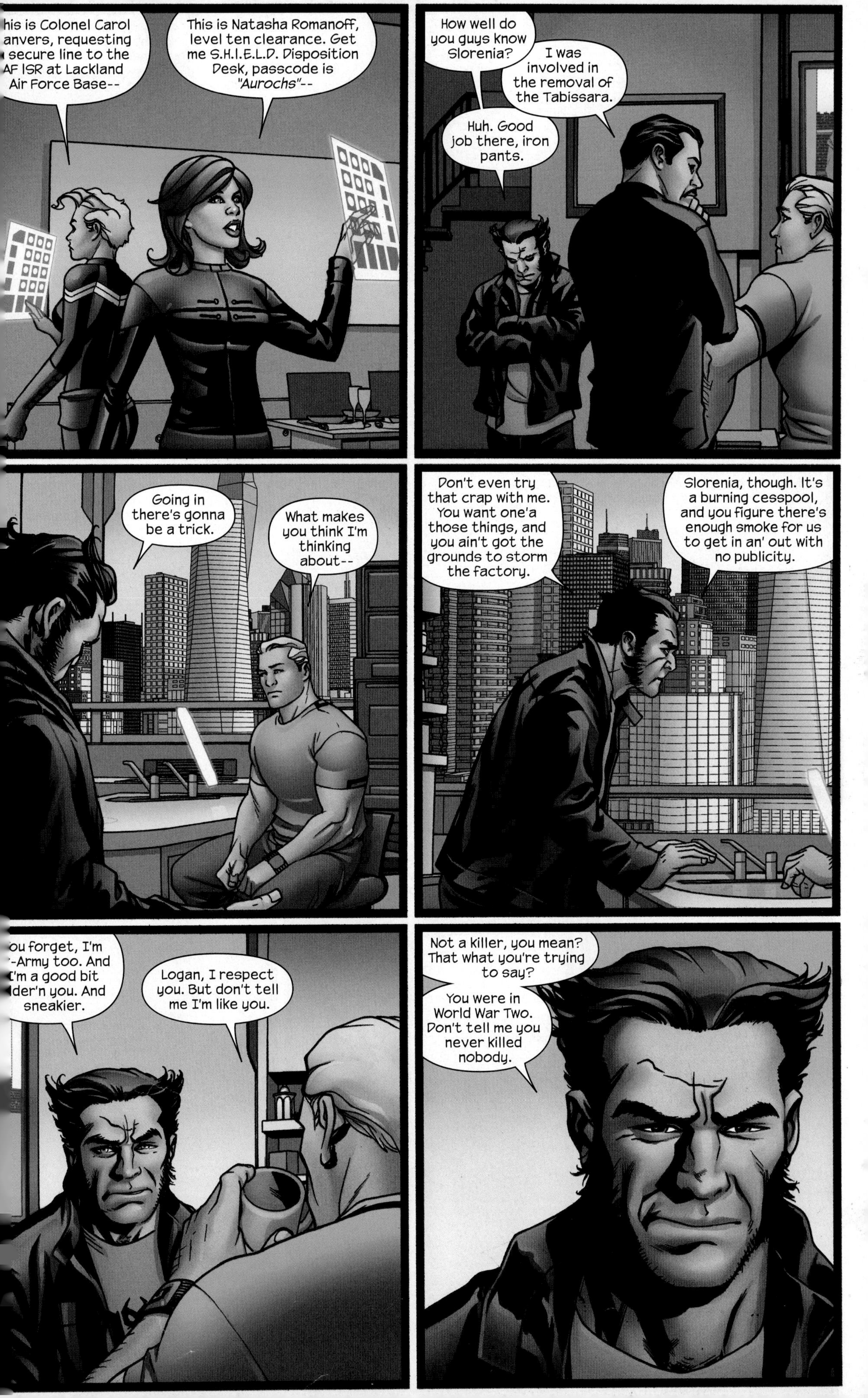

his is Colonel Carol anvers, requesting secure line to the AF ISR at Lackland Air Force Base--
This is Natasha Romanoff, level ten clearance. Get me S.H.I.E.L.D. Disposition Desk, passcode is "Aurochs"--
How well do you guys know Slorenia?
I was involved in the removal of the Tabissara.
Huh. Good job there, iron pants.
Going in there's gonna be a trick.
What makes you think I'm thinking about--
Don't even try that crap with me. You want one'a those things, and you ain't got the grounds to storm the factory.
Slorenia, though. It's a burning cesspool, and you figure there's enough smoke for us to get in an' out with no publicity.
ou forget, I'm -Army too. And I'm a good bit lder'n you. And sneakier.
Logan, I respect you. But don't tell me I'm like you.
Not a killer, you mean? That what you're trying to say?
You were in World War Two. Don't tell me you never killed nobody.

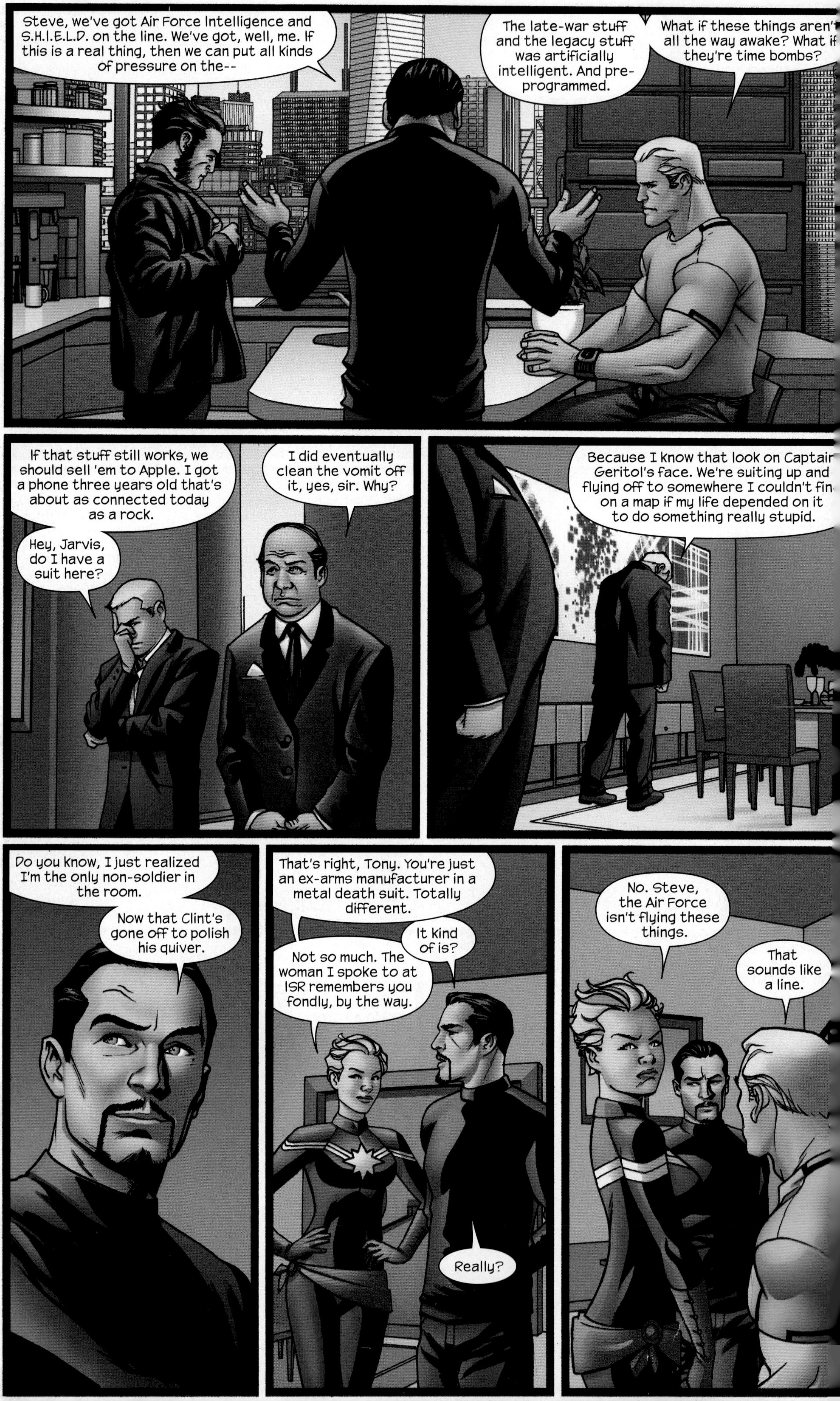
Steve, we've got Air Force Intelligence and S.H.I.E.L.D. on the line. We've got, well, me. If this is a real thing, then we can put all kinds of pressure on the--
The late-war stuff and the legacy stuff was artificially intelligent. And pre-programmed.
What if these things aren't all the way awake? What if they're time bombs?
If that stuff still works, we should sell 'em to Apple. I got a phone three years old that's about as connected today as a rock.
Hey, Jarvis, do I have a suit here?
I did eventually clean the vomit off it, yes, sir. Why?
Because I know that look on Captain Geritol's face. We're suiting up and flying off to somewhere I couldn't find on a map if my life depended on it to do something really stupid.
Do you know, I just realized I'm the only non-soldier in the room.
Now that Clint's gone off to polish his quiver.
That's right, Tony. You're just an ex-arms manufacturer in a metal death suit. Totally different.
It kind of is?
Not so much. The woman I spoke to at ISR remembers you fondly, by the way.
Really?
No. Steve, the Air Force isn't flying these things.
That sounds like a line.

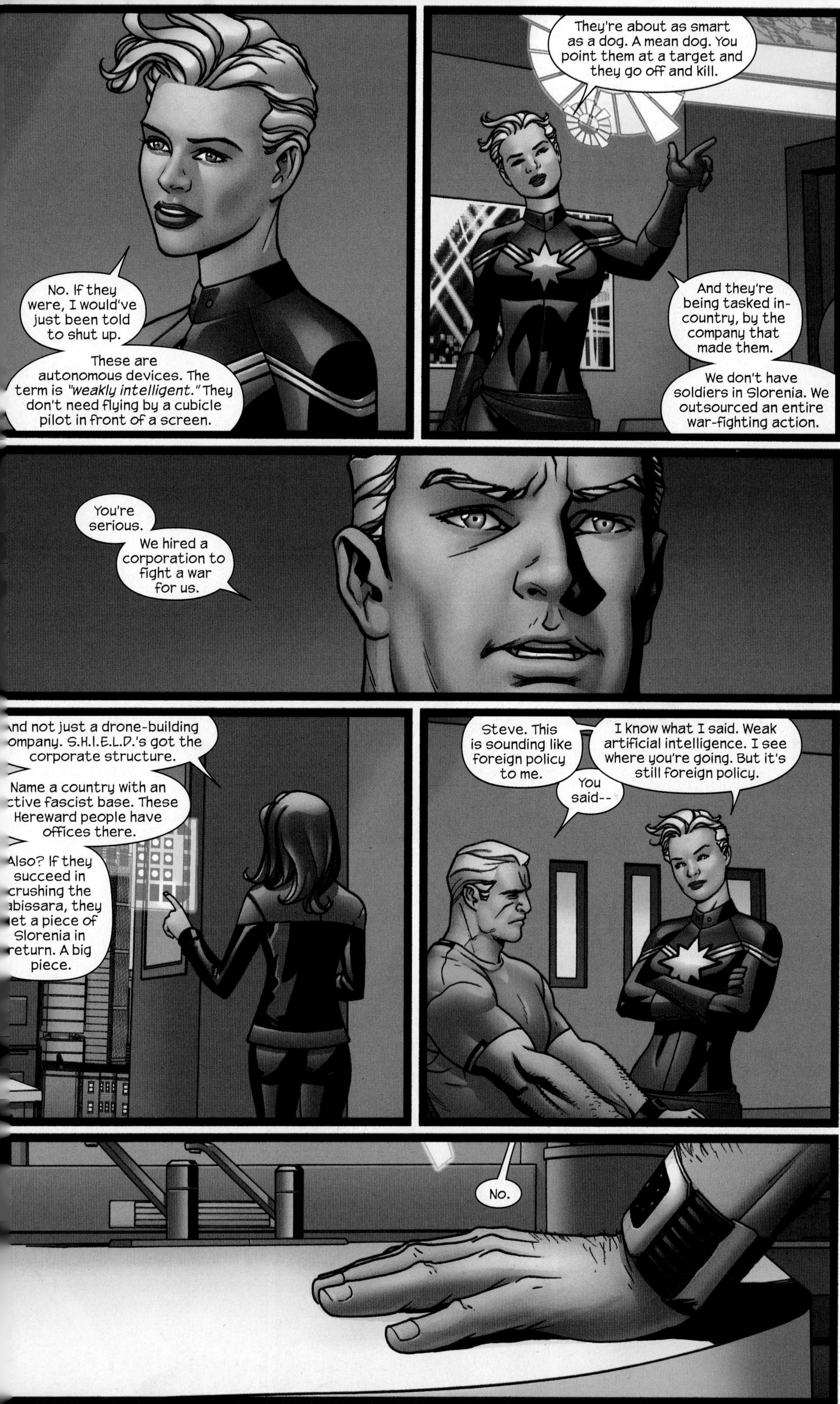

No. If they were, I would've just been told to shut up.
These are autonomous devices. The term is *"weakly intelligent."* They don't need flying by a cubicle pilot in front of a screen.
They're about as smart as a dog. A mean dog. You point them at a target and they go off and kill.
And they're being tasked in-country, by the company that made them.
We don't have soldiers in Slorenia. We outsourced an entire war-fighting action.
You're serious.
We hired a corporation to fight a war for us.
nd not just a drone-building ompany. S.H.I.E.L.D.'s got the corporate structure.
Name a country with an ctive fascist base. These Hereward people have offices there.
lso? If they succeed in crushing the abissara, they et a piece of Slorenia in eturn. A big piece.
Steve. This is sounding like foreign policy to me.
You said--
I know what I said. Weak artificial intelligence. I see where you're going. But it's still foreign policy.
No.

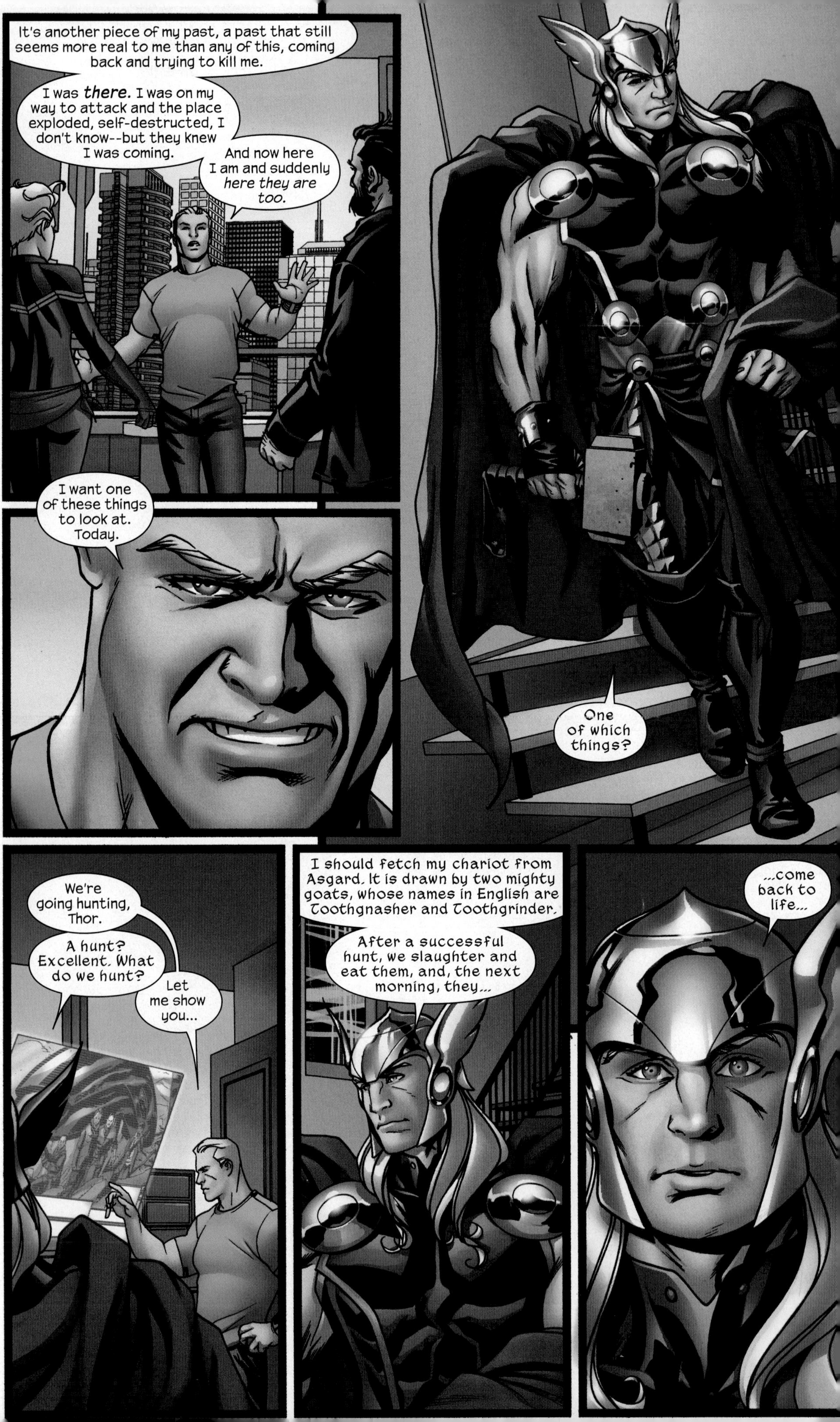
It's another piece of my past, a past that still seems more real to me than any of this, coming back and trying to kill me.
I was there. I was on my way to attack and the place exploded, self-destructed, I don't know--but they knew I was coming.
And now here I am and suddenly here they are too.
I want one of these things to look at. Today.
One of which things?
We're going hunting, Thor.
A hunt? Excellent. What do we hunt?
Let me show you...
I should fetch my chariot from Asgard. It is drawn by two mighty goats, whose names in English are Toothgnasher and Toothgrinder.
After a successful hunt, we slaughter and eat them, and, the next morning, they...
...come back to life...

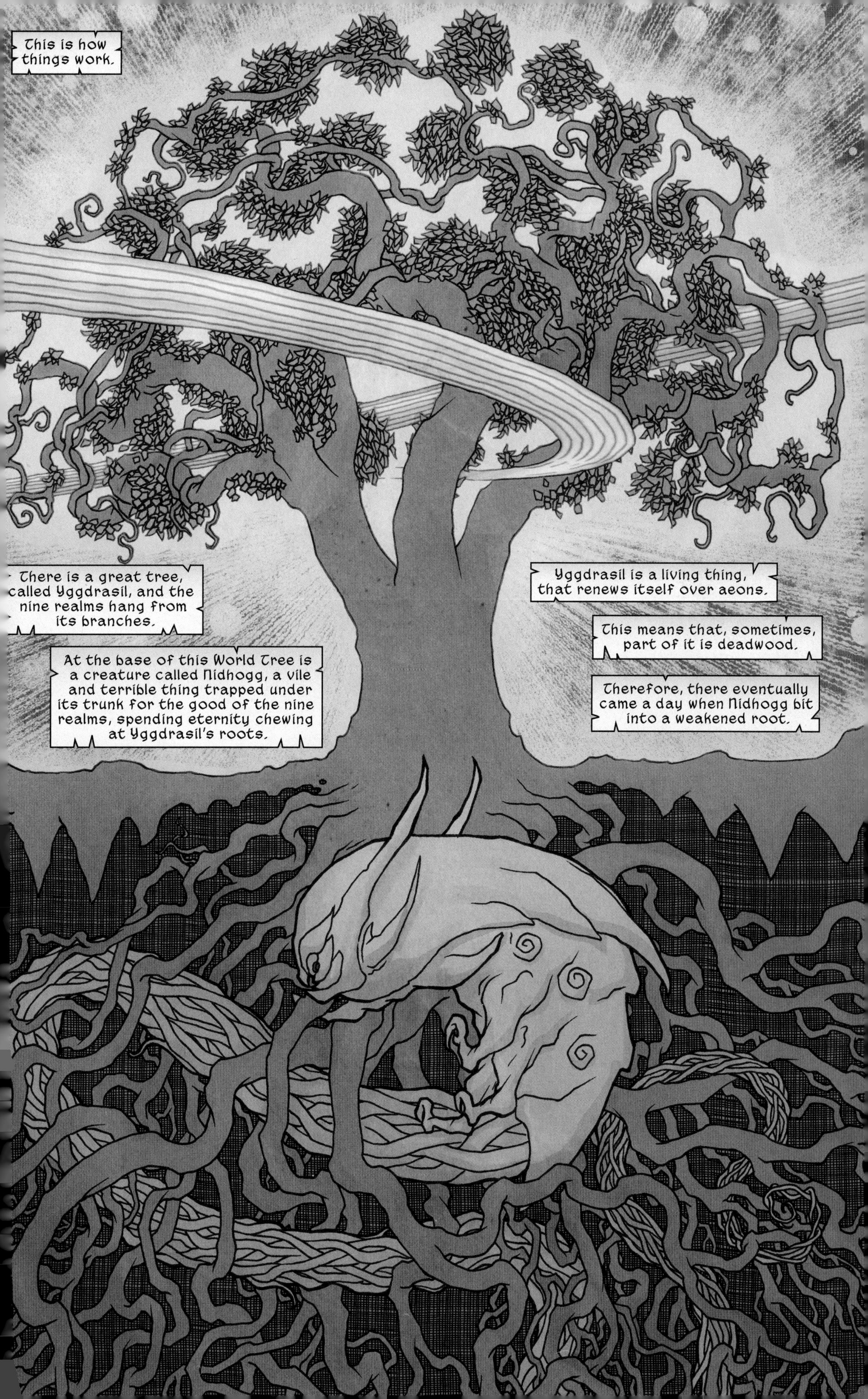
This is how things work.
There is a great tree, called Yggdrasil, and the nine realms hang from its branches.
At the base of this World Tree is a creature called Nidhogg, a vile and terrible thing trapped under its trunk for the good of the nine realms, spending eternity chewing at Yggdrasil's roots.
Yggdrasil is a living thing, that renews itself over aeons.
This means that, sometimes, part of it is deadwood.
Therefore, there eventually came a day when Nidhogg bit into a weakened root.

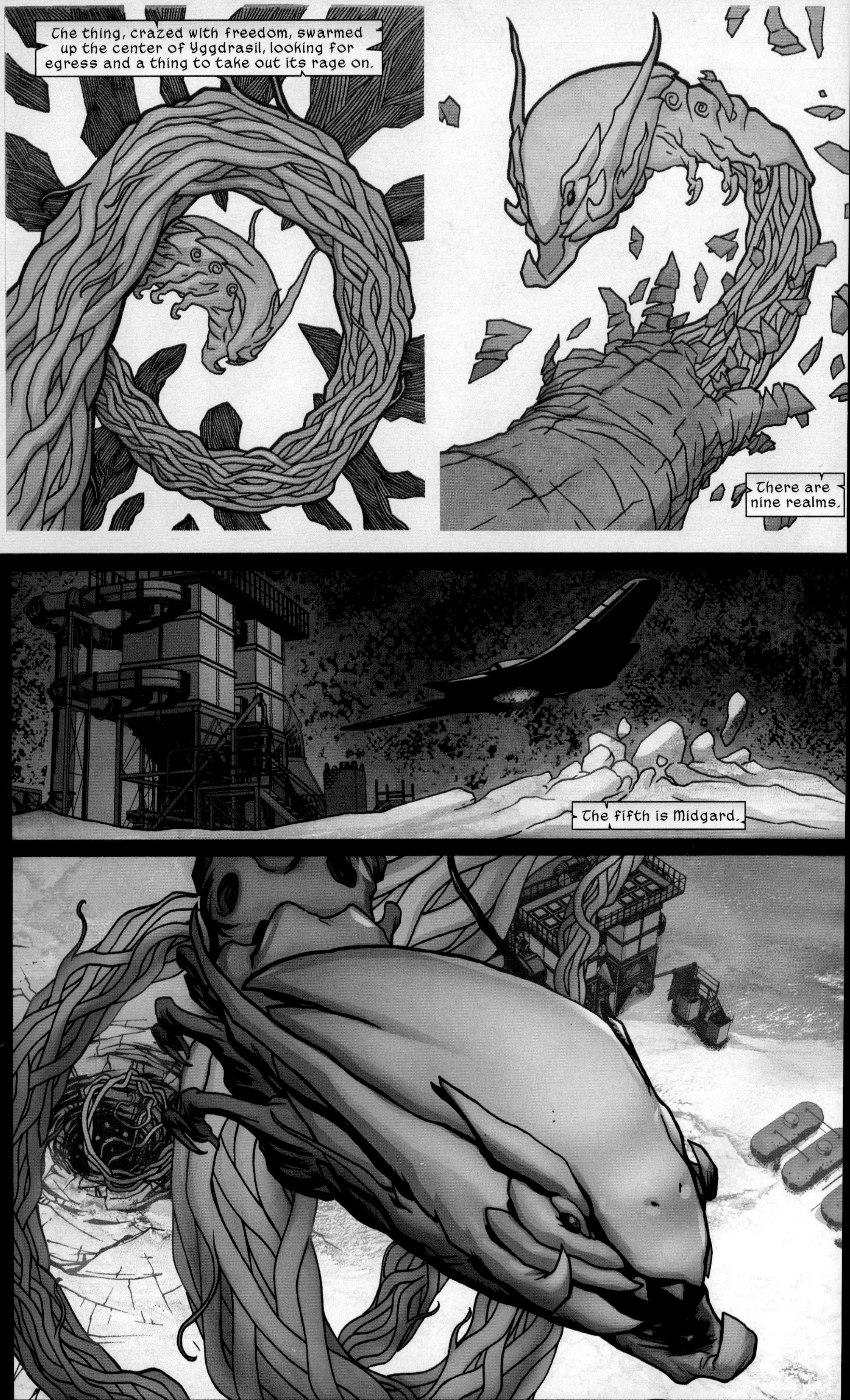
The thing, crazed with freedom, swarmed up the center of Yggdrasil, looking for egress and a thing to take out its rage on.
There are nine realms.
The fifth is Midgard.

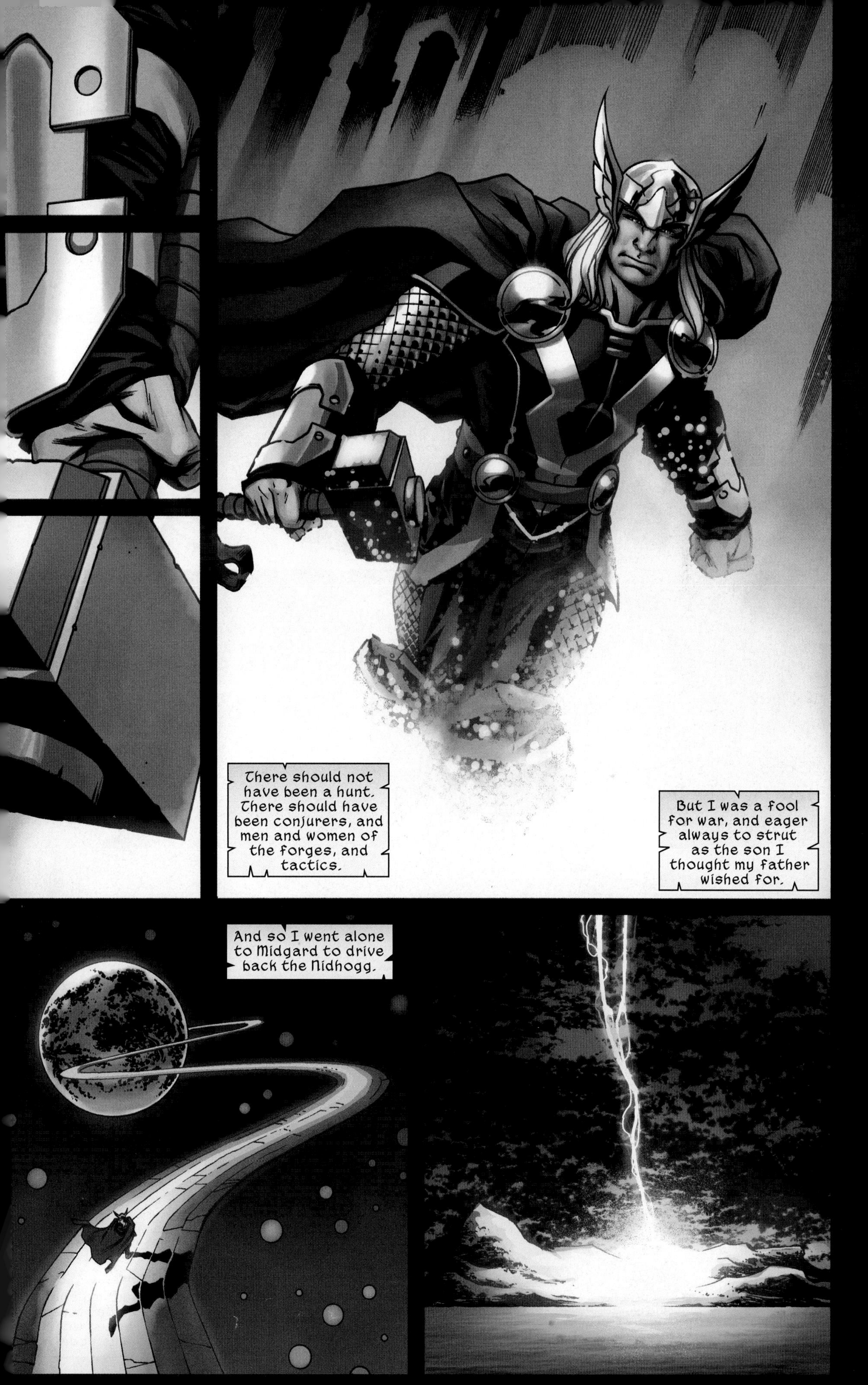
There should not have been a hunt. There should have been conjurers, and men and women of the forges, and tactics.
But I was a fool for war, and eager always to strut as the son I thought my father wished for.
And so I went alone to Midgard to drive back the Nidhogg.

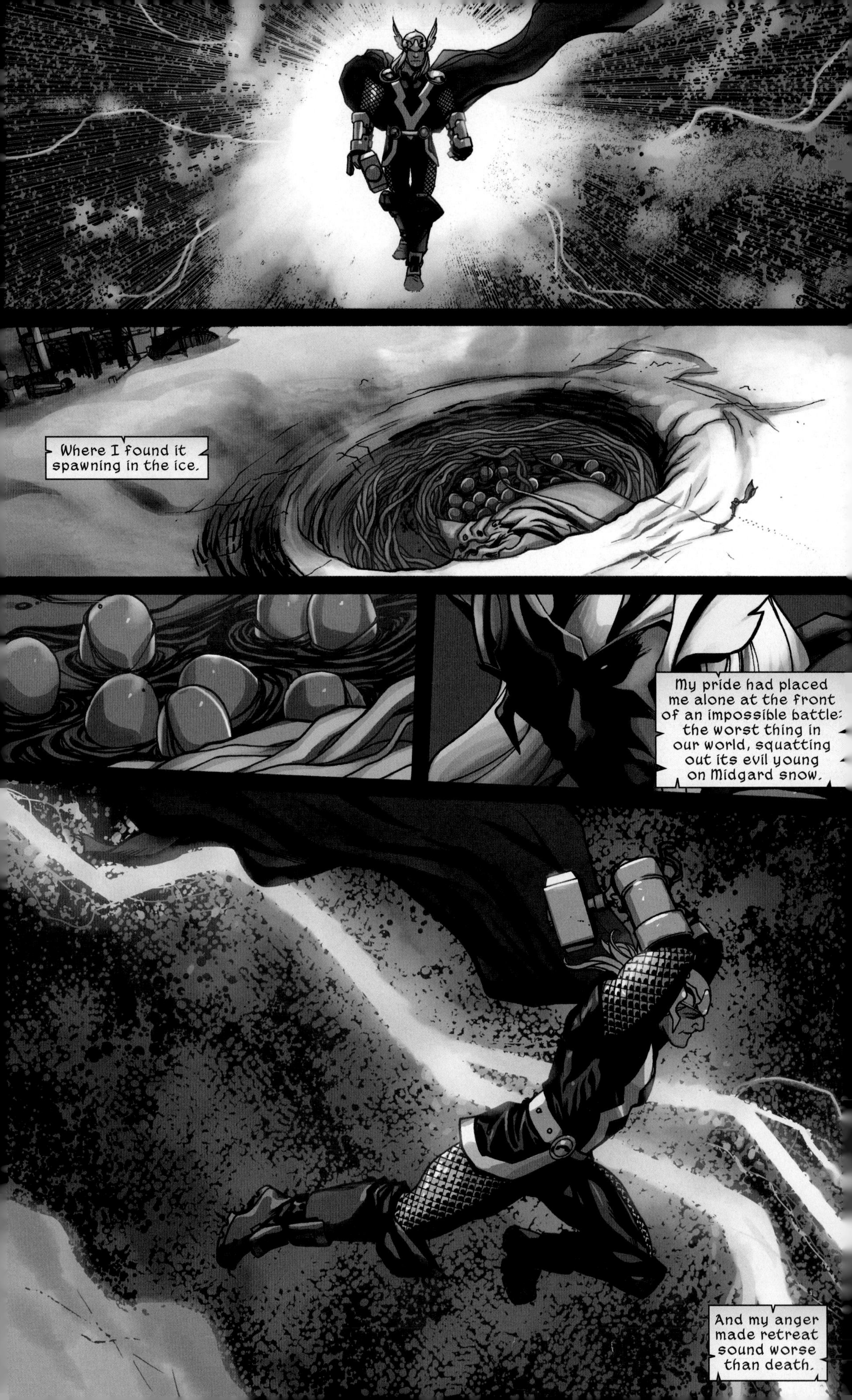
Where I found it spawning in the ice.
My pride had placed me alone at the front of an impossible battle: the worst thing in our world, squatting out its evil young on Midgard snow.
And my anger made retreat sound worse than death.

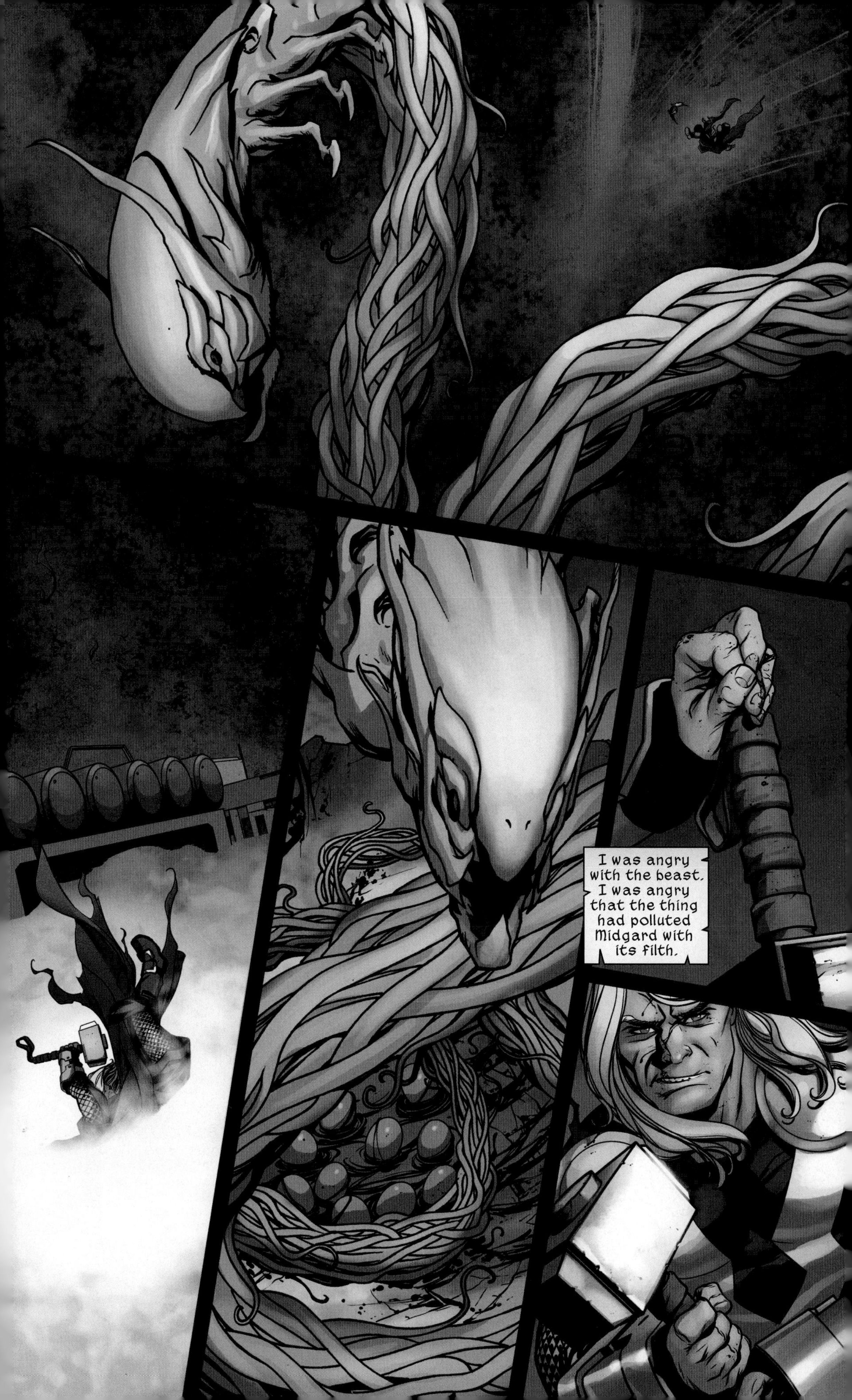
I was angry with the beast. I was angry that the thing had polluted Midgard with its filth.

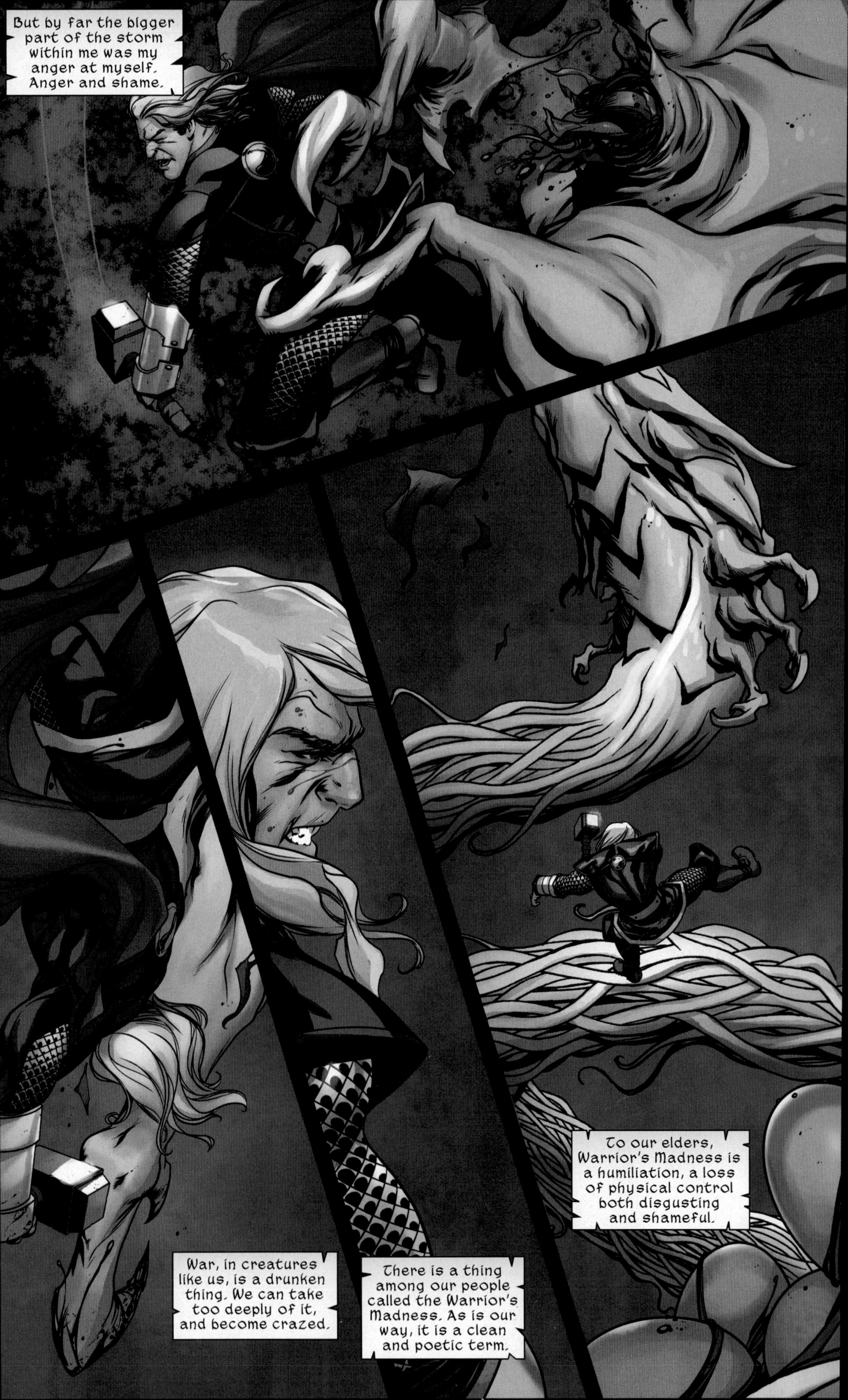
But by far the bigger part of the storm within me was my anger at myself. Anger and shame.
War, in creatures like us, is a drunken thing. We can take too deeply of it, and become crazed.
There is a thing among our people called the Warrior's Madness. As is our way, it is a clean and poetic term.
To our elders, Warrior's Madness is a humiliation, a loss of physical control both disgusting and shameful.

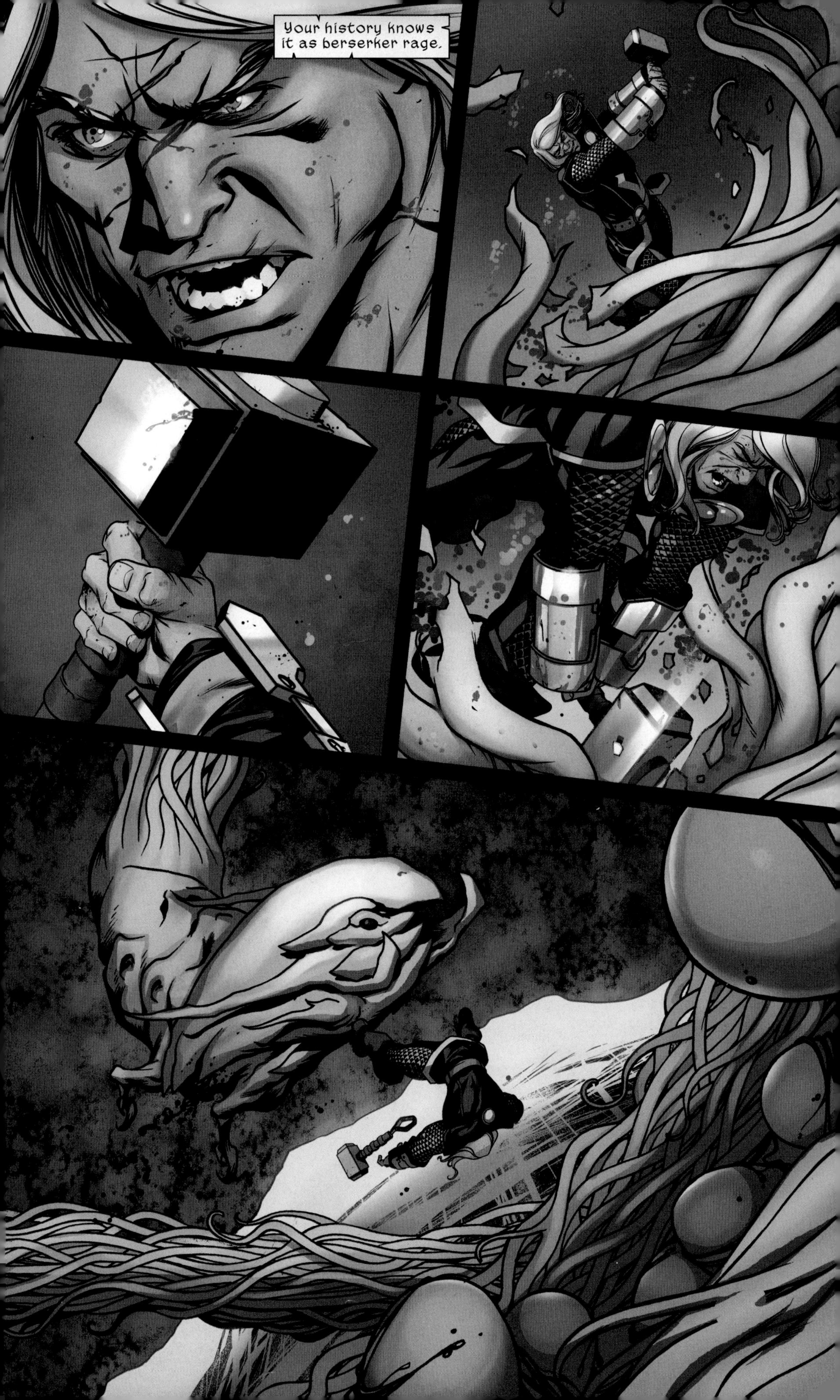
Your history knows it as berserker rage.

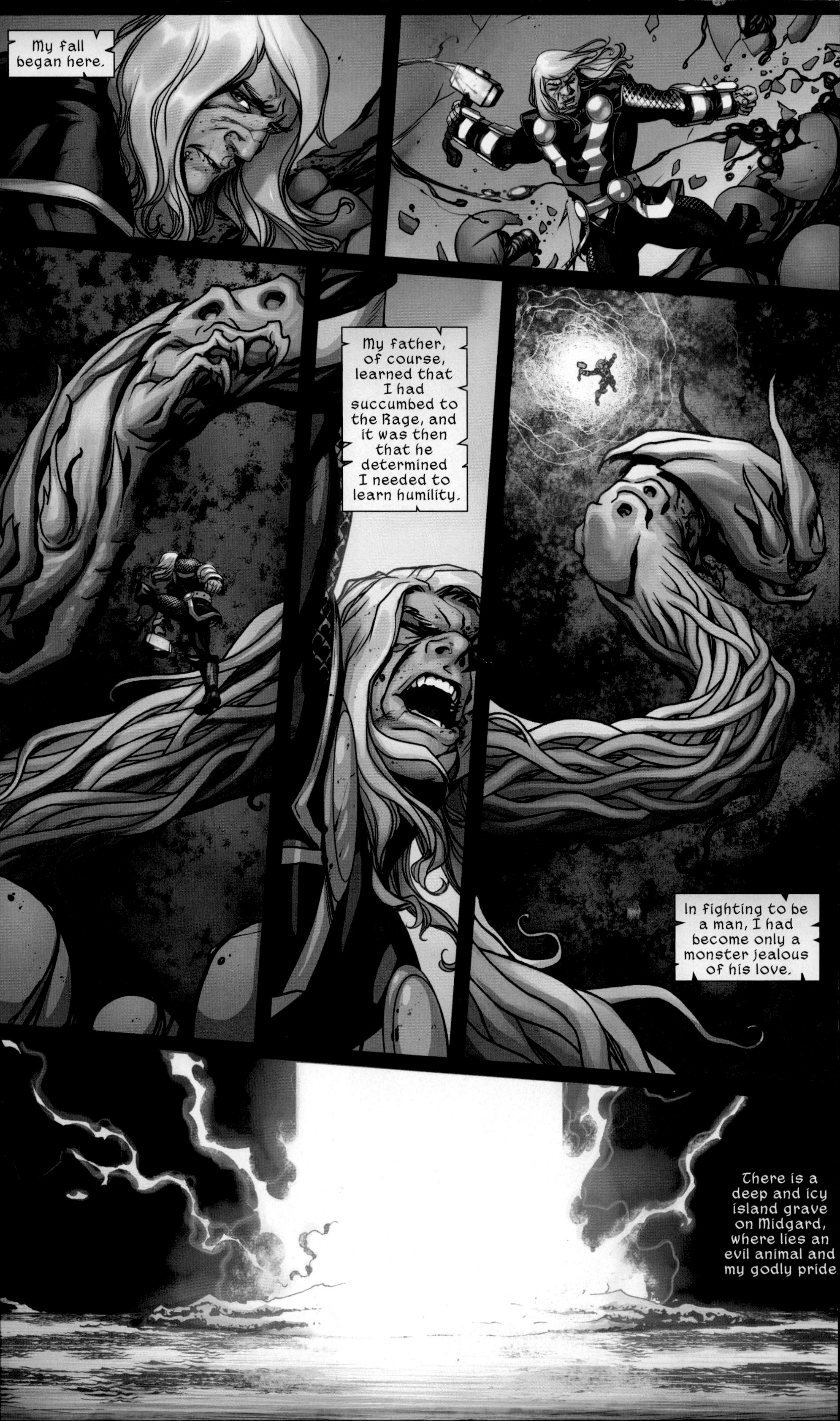

My fall began here.
My father, of course, learned that I had succumbed to the Rage, and it was then that he determined I needed to learn humility.
In fighting to be a man, I had become only a monster jealous of his love.
There is a deep and icy island grave on Midgard, where lies an evil animal and my godly pride

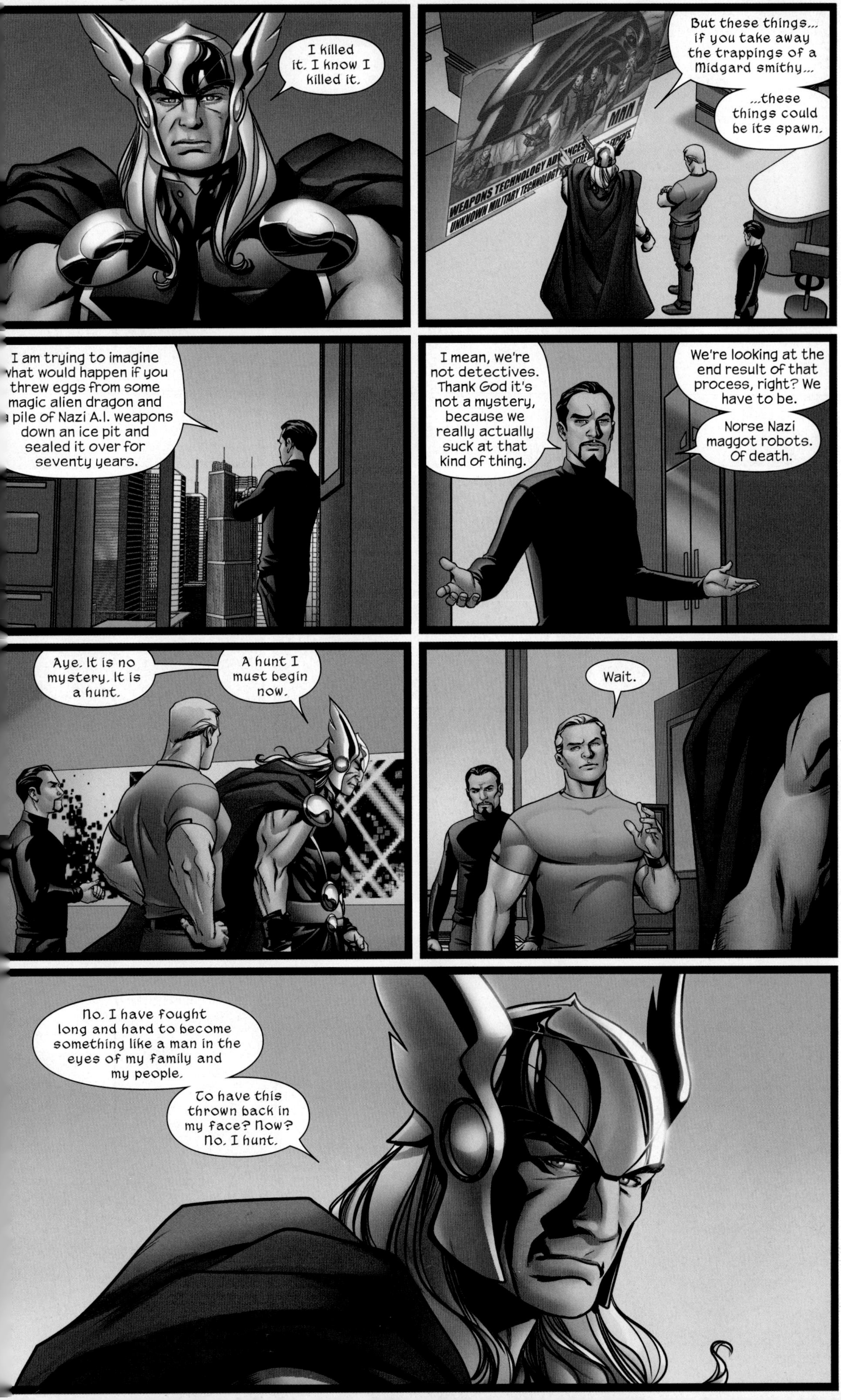
I killed it. I know I killed it.
But these things... if you take away the trappings of a Midgard smithy...
...these things could be its spawn.
I am trying to imagine what would happen if you threw eggs from some magic alien dragon and a pile of Nazi A.I. weapons down an ice pit and sealed it over for seventy years.
I mean, we're not detectives. Thank God it's not a mystery, because we really actually suck at that kind of thing.
We're looking at the end result of that process, right? We have to be.
Norse Nazi maggot robots. Of death.
Aye. It is no mystery. It is a hunt.
A hunt I must begin now.
Wait.
No. I have fought long and hard to become something like a man in the eyes of my family and my people.
To have this thrown back in my face? Now? No. I hunt.

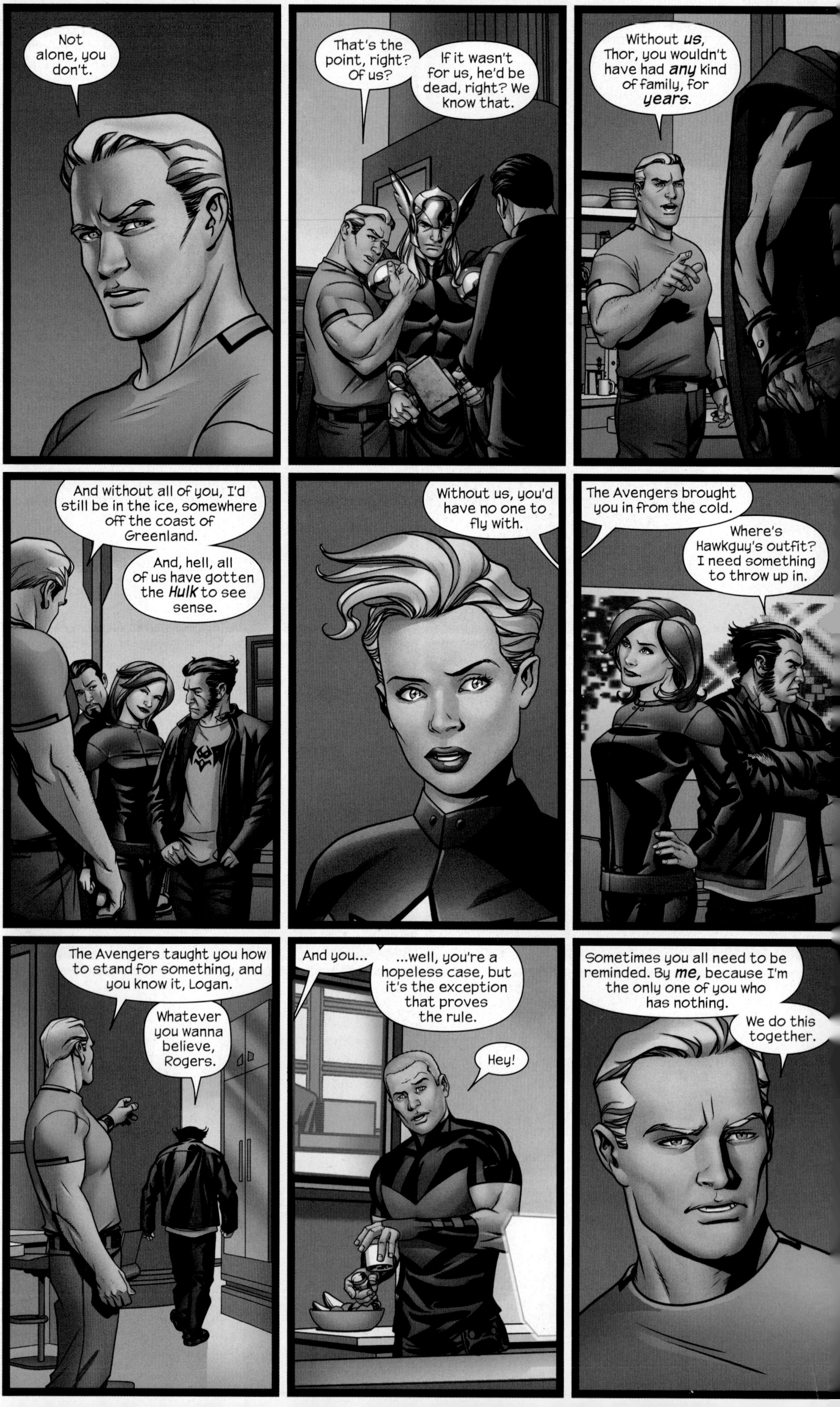
Not alone, you don't.
That's the point, right? Of us?
If it wasn't for us, he'd be dead, right? We know that.
Without us, Thor, you wouldn't have had any kind of family, for years.
And without all of you, I'd still be in the ice, somewhere off the coast of Greenland.
And, hell, all of us have gotten the Hulk to see sense.
Without us, you'd have no one to fly with.
The Avengers brought you in from the cold.
Where's Hawkguy's outfit? I need something to throw up in.
The Avengers taught you how to stand for something, and you know it, Logan.
Whatever you wanna believe, Rogers.
And you...
...well, you're a hopeless case, but it's the exception that proves the rule.
Hey!
Sometimes you all need to be reminded. By me, because I'm the only one of you who has nothing.
We do this together.

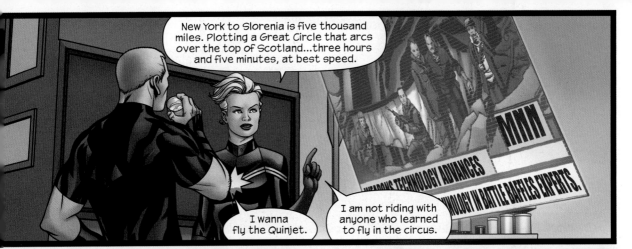

New York to Slorenia is five thousand miles. Plotting a Great Circle that arcs over the top of Scotland...three hours and five minutes, at best speed.

I wanna fly the Quinjet.

I am not riding with anyone who learned to fly in the circus.

WEAPONS TECHNOLOGY ADVANCES

...NOLOGY IN BATTLE BAFFLES EXPERTS.

We could just drop the Hulk on them.

I hear Bruce is doing really well over at S.H.I.E.L.D. Covered in Prozac skin patches, mind you, but...

He can hear them all, through walls and doors. Hear them talking about their normal world of brain drugs absorbed through skin and planes flying at sixteen hundred miles an hour.

He doesn't even know why he's doing this, really. Except that he has a need to confirm operation intelligence in person, boots on the ground...

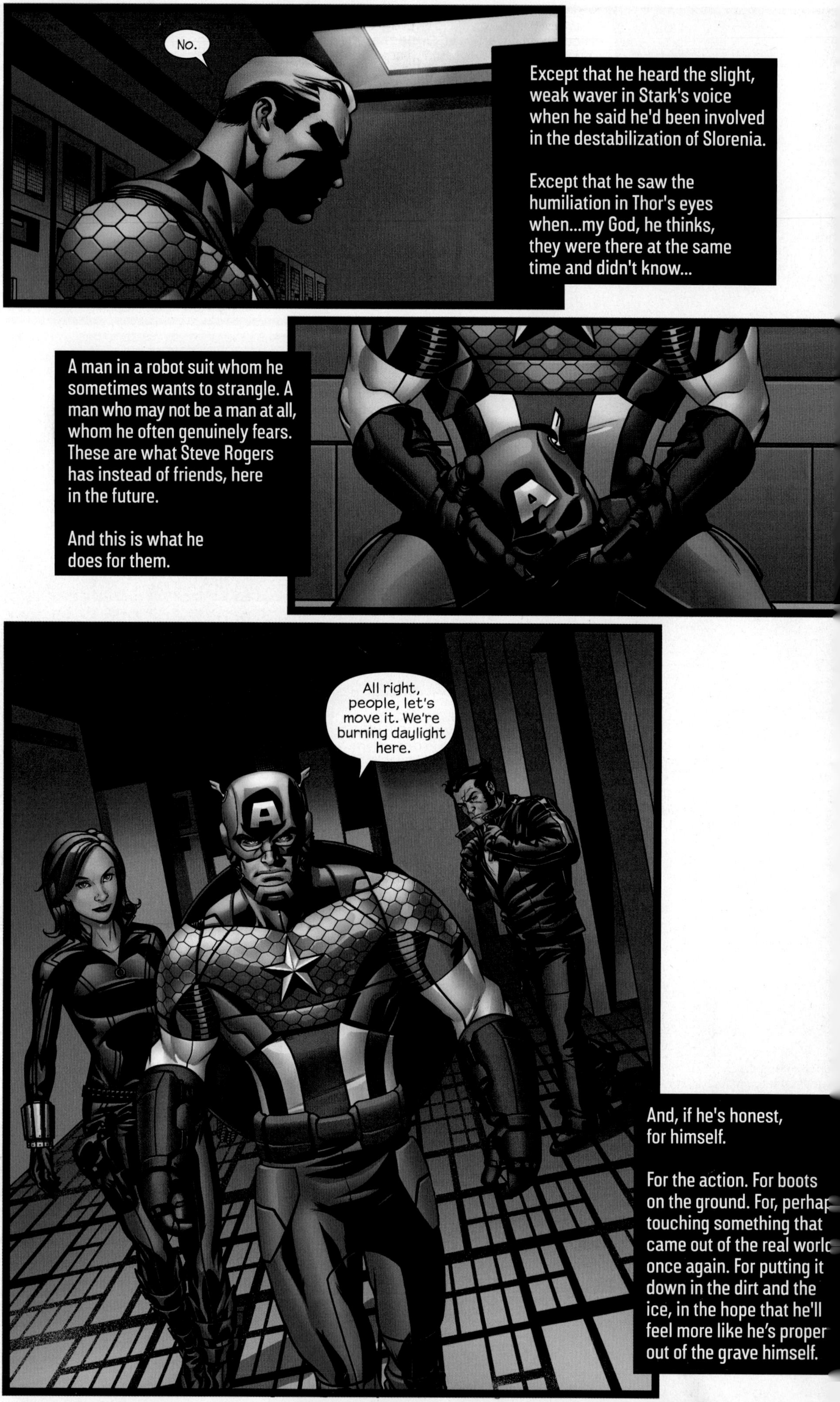
No.
Except that he heard the slight, weak waver in Stark's voice when he said he'd been involved in the destabilization of Slorenia.
Except that he saw the humiliation in Thor's eyes when...my God, he thinks, they were there at the same time and didn't know...
A man in a robot suit whom he sometimes wants to strangle. A man who may not be a man at all, whom he often genuinely fears. These are what Steve Rogers has instead of friends, here in the future.
And this is what he does for them.
All right, people, let's move it. We're burning daylight here.
And, if he's honest, for himself.
For the action. For boots on the ground. For, perhap touching something that came out of the real worl once again. For putting it down in the dirt and the ice, in the hope that he'll feel more like he's proper out of the grave himself.

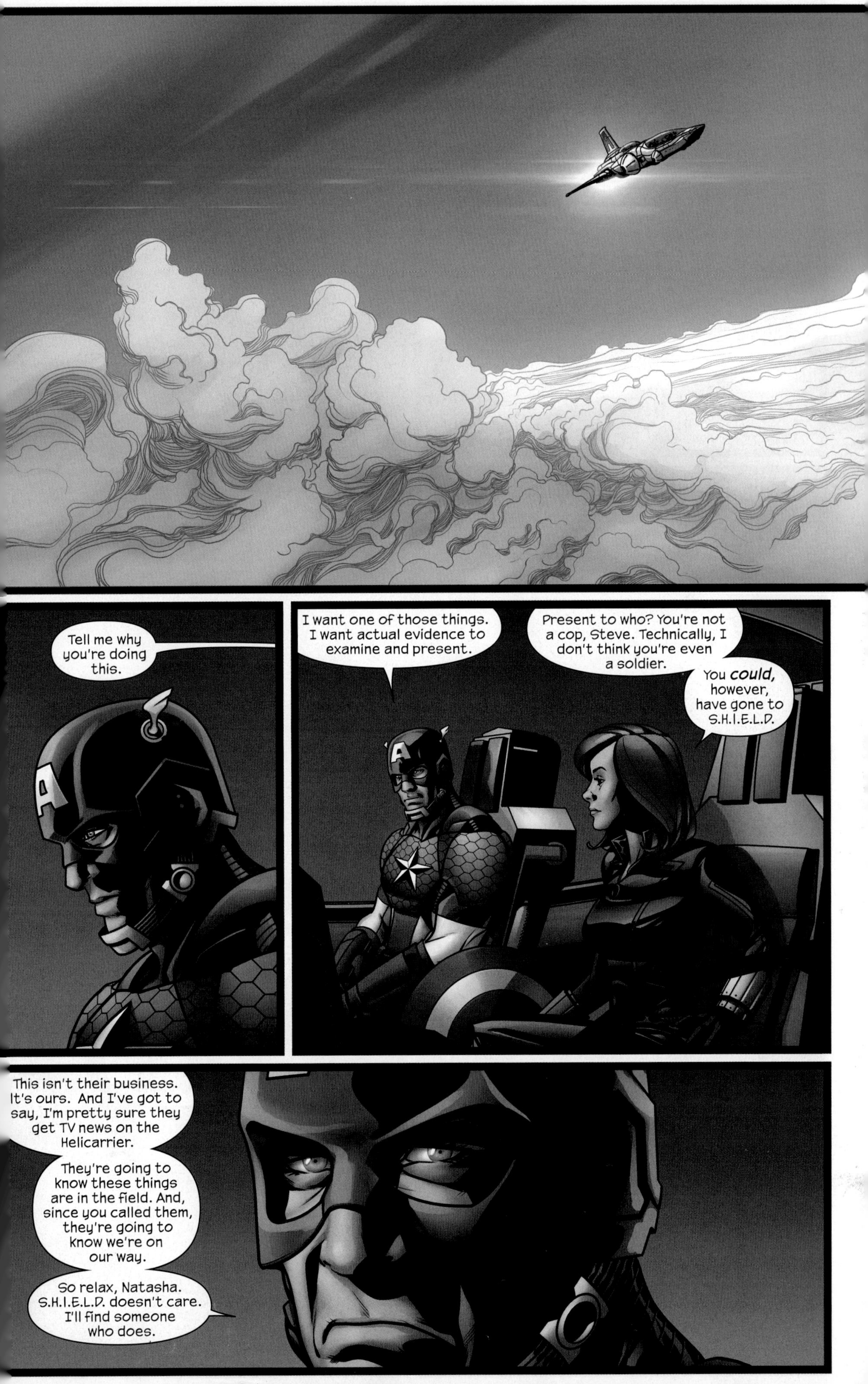
Tell me why you're doing this.
I want one of those things. I want actual evidence to examine and present.
Present to who? You're not a cop, Steve. Technically, I don't think you're even a soldier.
You *could,* however, have gone to S.H.I.E.L.D.
This isn't their business. It's ours. And I've got to say, I'm pretty sure they get TV news on the Helicarrier.
They're going to know these things are in the field. And, since you called them, they're going to know we're on our way.
So relax, Natasha. S.H.I.E.L.D. doesn't care. I'll find someone who does.

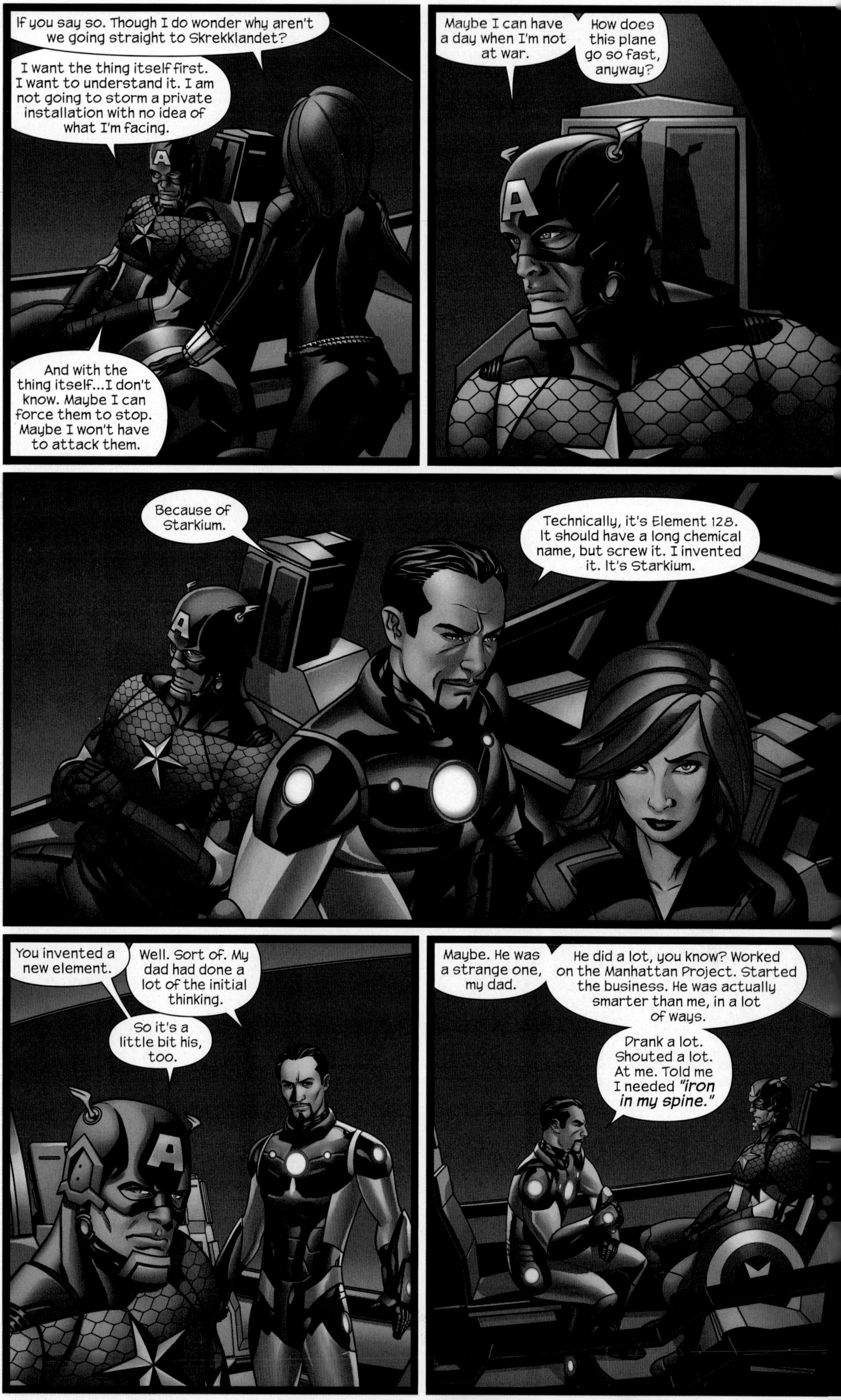

If you say so. Though I do wonder why aren't we going straight to Skrekklandet?
I want the thing itself first. I want to understand it. I am not going to storm a private installation with no idea of what I'm facing.
And with the thing itself...I don't know. Maybe I can force them to stop. Maybe I won't have to attack them.
Maybe I can have a day when I'm not at war.
How does this plane go so fast, anyway?
Because of Starkium.
Technically, it's Element 128. It should have a long chemical name, but screw it. I invented it. It's Starkium.
You invented a new element.
Well. Sort of. My dad had done a lot of the initial thinking.
So it's a little bit his, too.
Maybe. He was a strange one, my dad.
He did a lot, you know? Worked on the Manhattan Project. Started the business. He was actually smarter than me, in a lot of ways.
Drank a lot. Shouted a lot. At me. Told me I needed *"iron in my spine."*

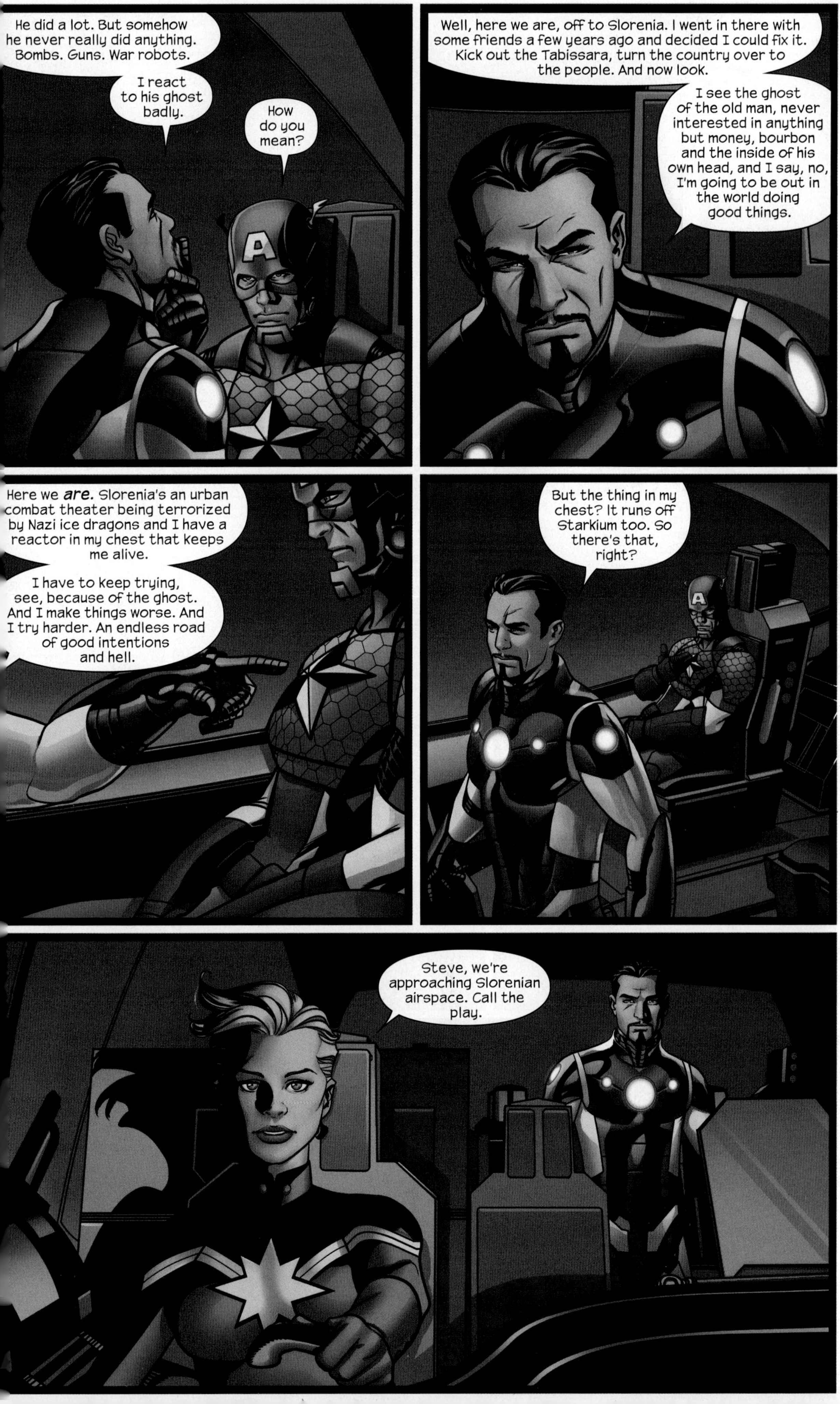
He did a lot. But somehow he never really did anything. Bombs. Guns. War robots.
I react to his ghost badly.
How do you mean?
Well, here we are, off to Slorenia. I went in there with some friends a few years ago and decided I could fix it. Kick out the Tabissara, turn the country over to the people. And now look.
I see the ghost of the old man, never interested in anything but money, bourbon and the inside of his own head, and I say, no, I'm going to be out in the world doing good things.
Here we *are*. Slorenia's an urban combat theater being terrorized by Nazi ice dragons and I have a reactor in my chest that keeps me alive.
I have to keep trying, see, because of the ghost. And I make things worse. And I try harder. An endless road of good intentions and hell.
But the thing in my chest? It runs off Starkium too. So there's that, right?
Steve, we're approaching Slorenian airspace. Call the play.

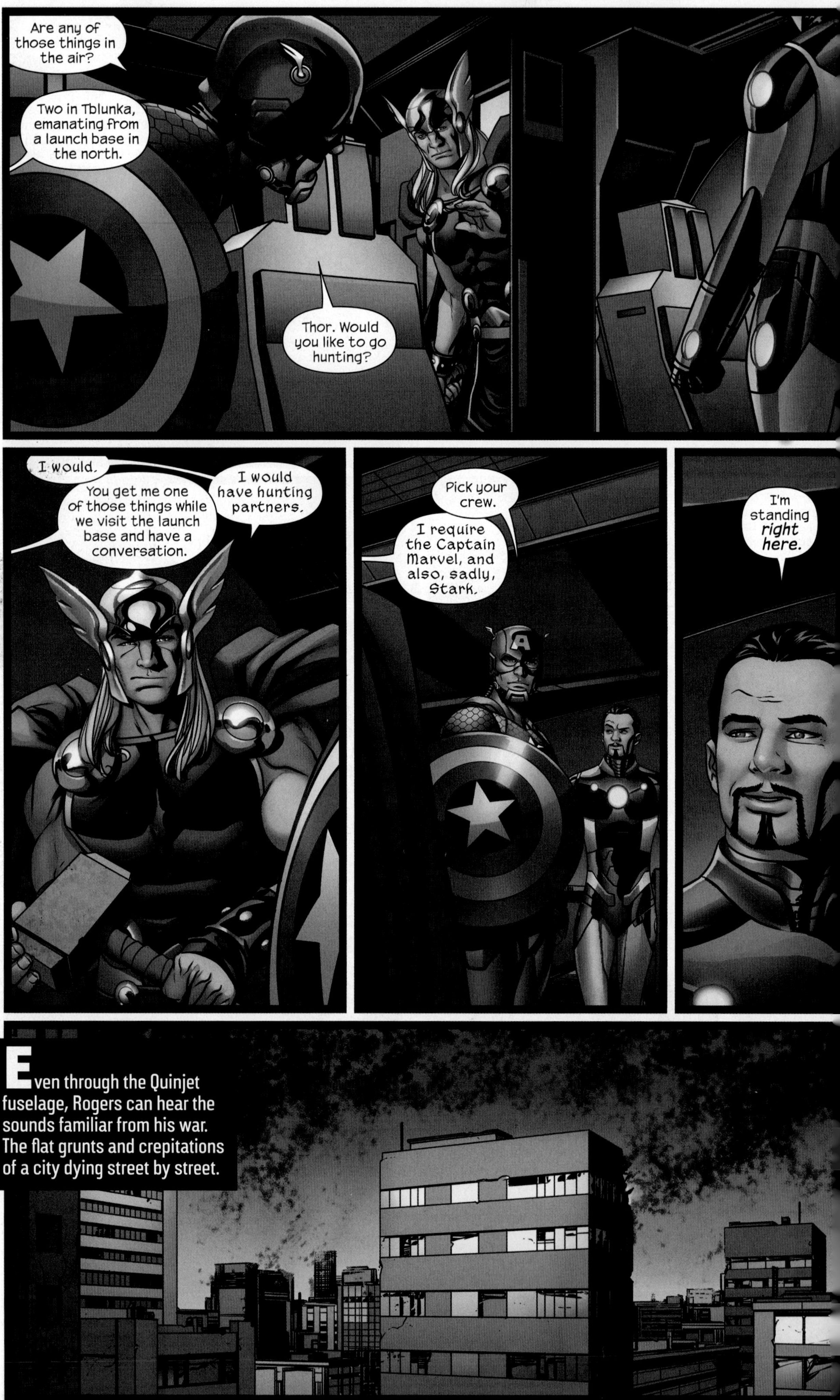

Are any of those things in the air?
Two in Tblunka, emanating from a launch base in the north.
Thor. Would you like to go hunting?
I would.
You get me one of those things while we visit the launch base and have a conversation.
I would have hunting partners.
Pick your crew.
I require the Captain Marvel, and also, sadly, Stark.
I'm standing *right here.*
Even through the Quinjet fuselage, Rogers can hear the sounds familiar from his war. The flat grunts and crepitations of a city dying street by street.

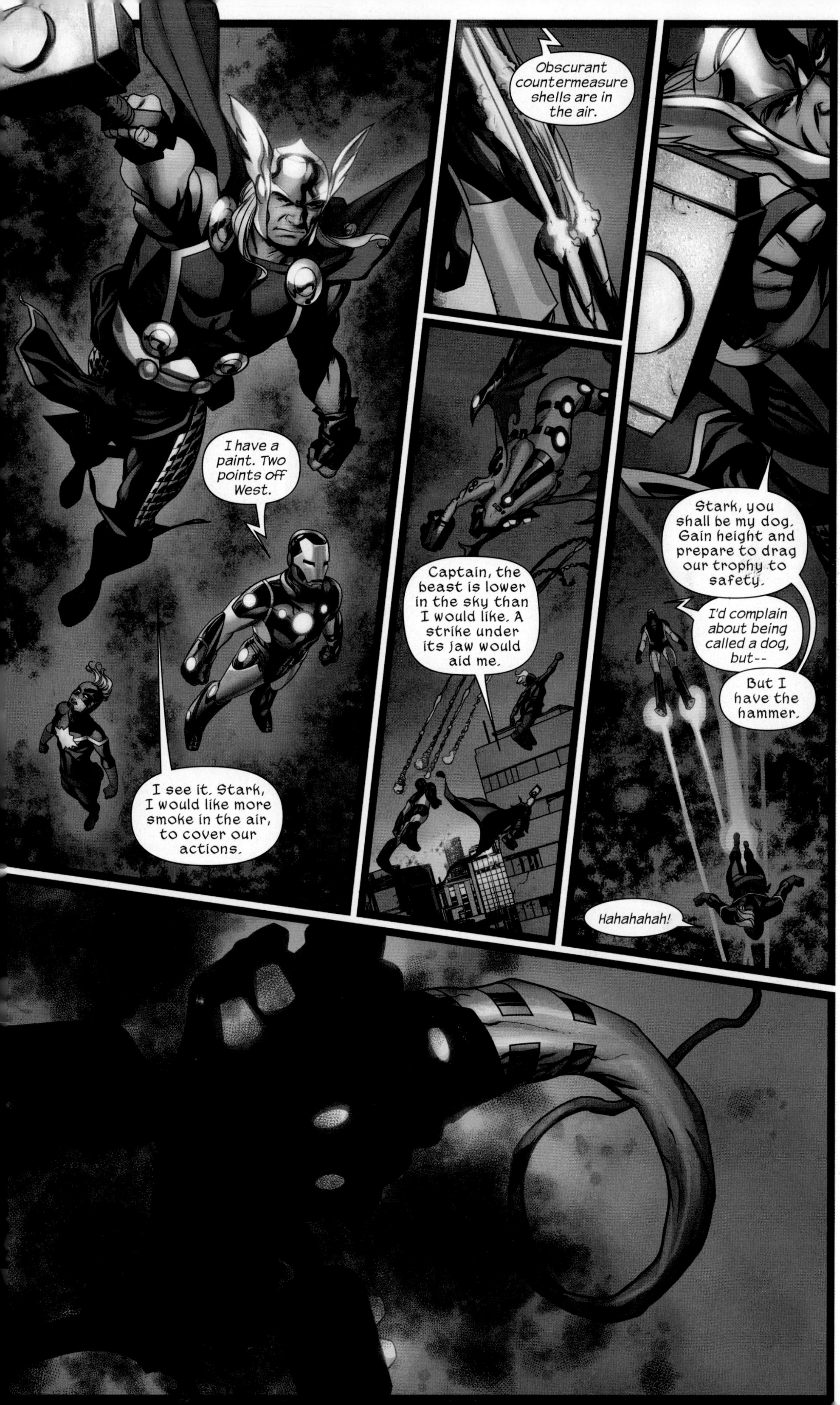
I have a paint. Two points off West.
I see it. Stark, I would like more smoke in the air, to cover our actions.
Obscurant countermeasure shells are in the air.
Captain, the beast is lower in the sky than I would like. A strike under its jaw would aid me.
Stark, you shall be my dog. Gain height and prepare to drag our trophy to safety.
I'd complain about being called a dog, but--
But I have the hammer.
Hahahahah!

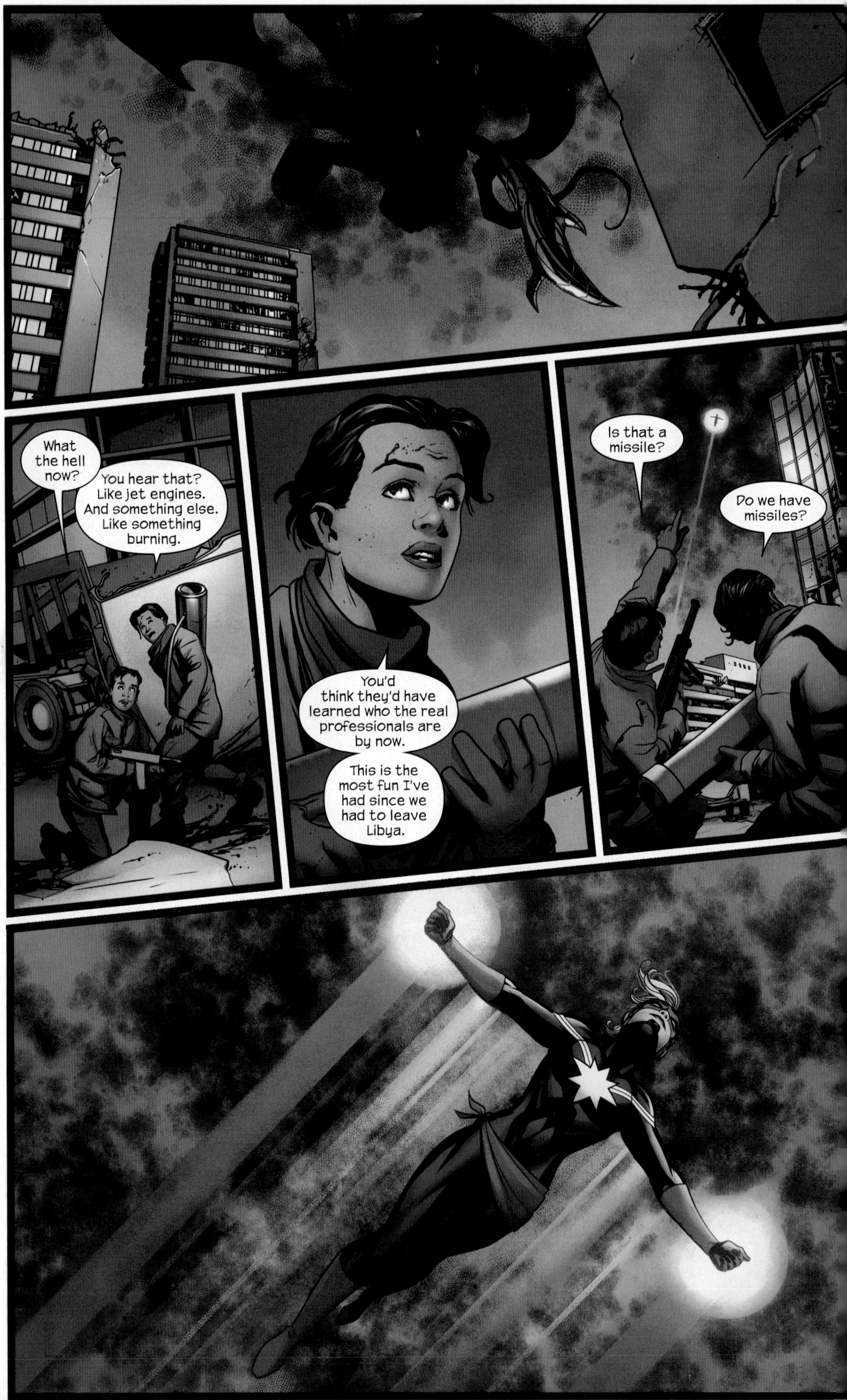
What the hell now?
You hear that? Like jet engines. And something else. Like something burning.
You'd think they'd have learned who the real professionals are by now.
This is the most fun I've had since we had to leave Libya.
Is that a missile?
Do we have missiles?

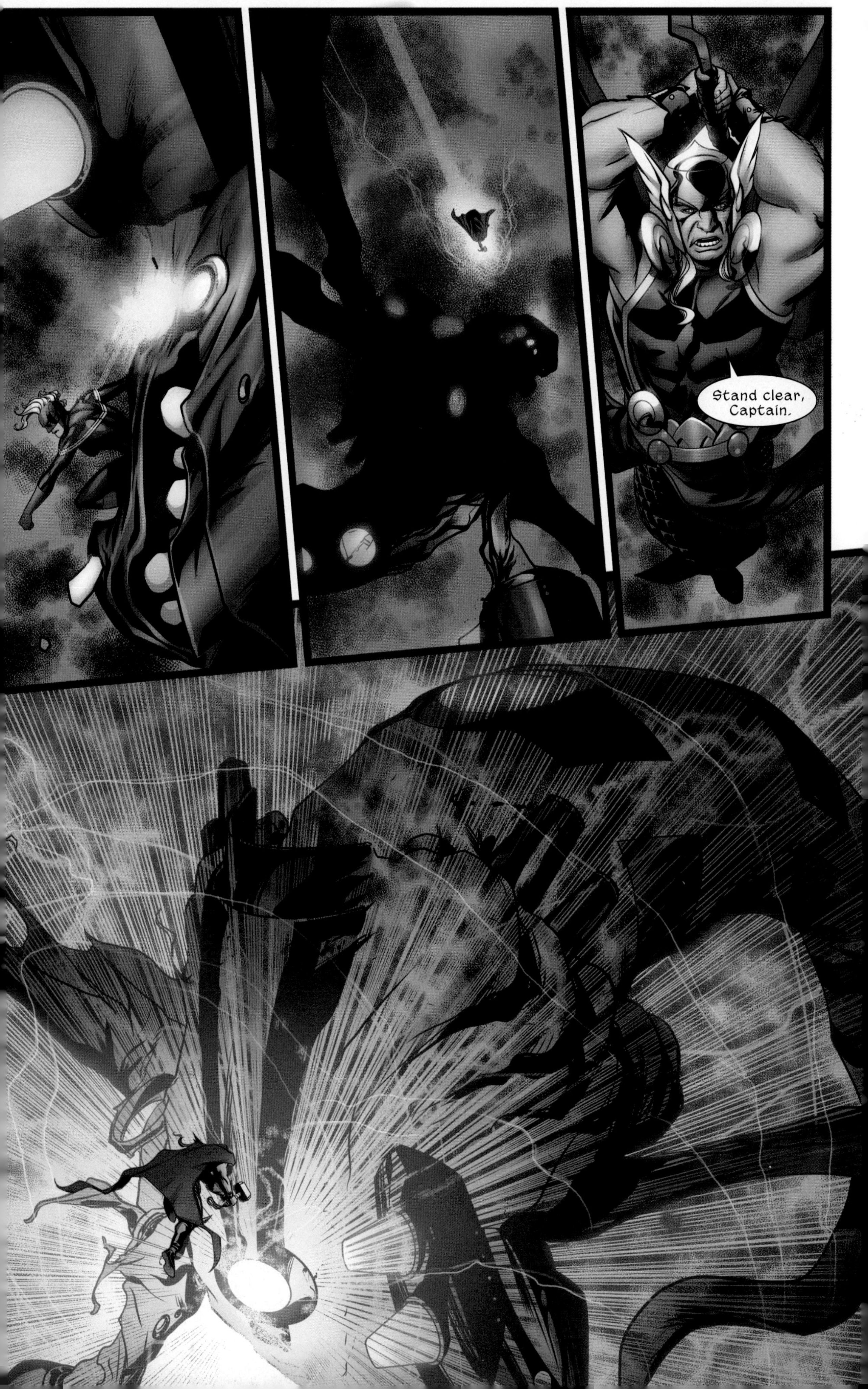
Stand clear, Captain.

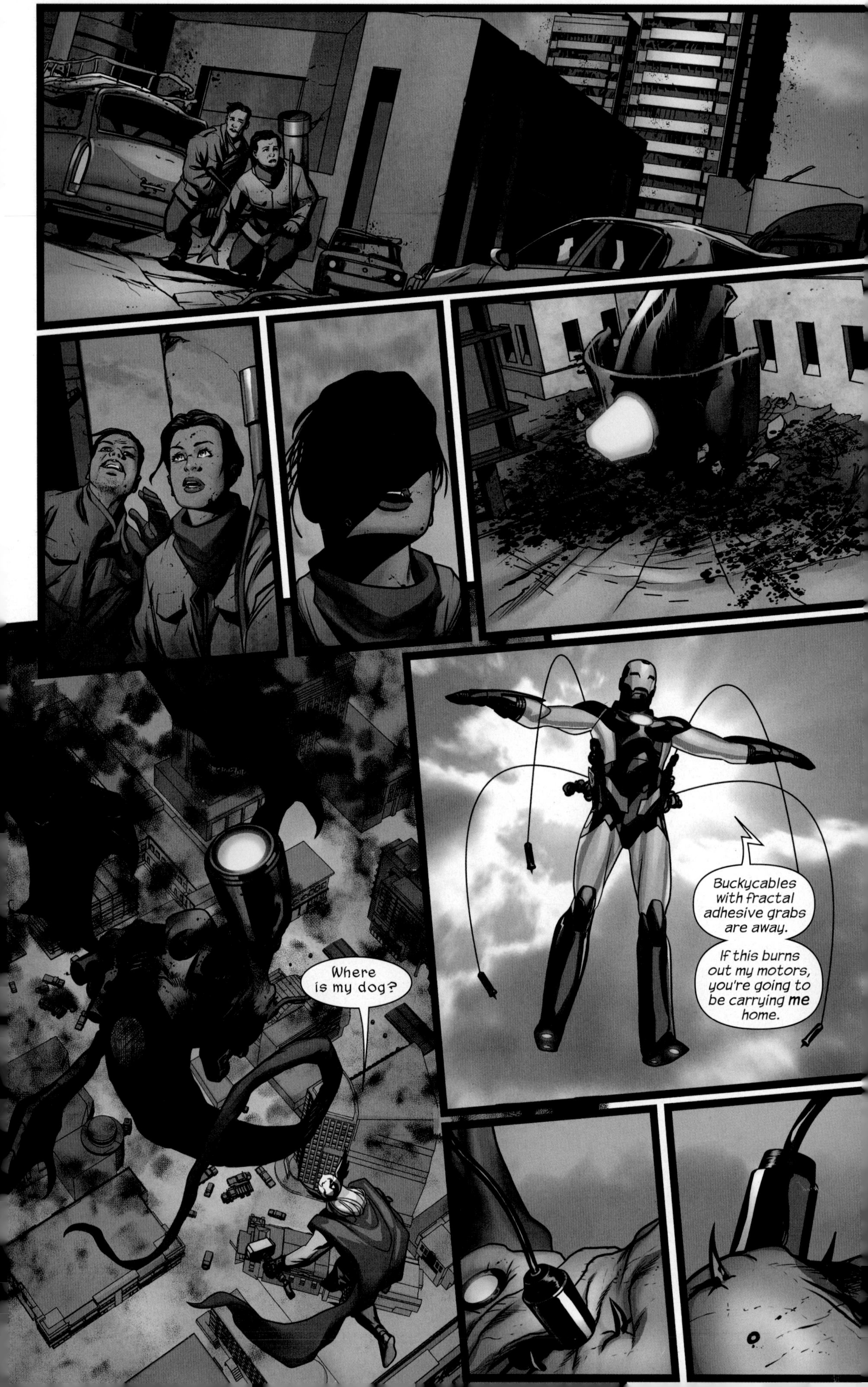
Buckycables with fractal adhesive grabs are away.
If this burns out my motors, you're going to be carrying **me** home.
Where is my dog?

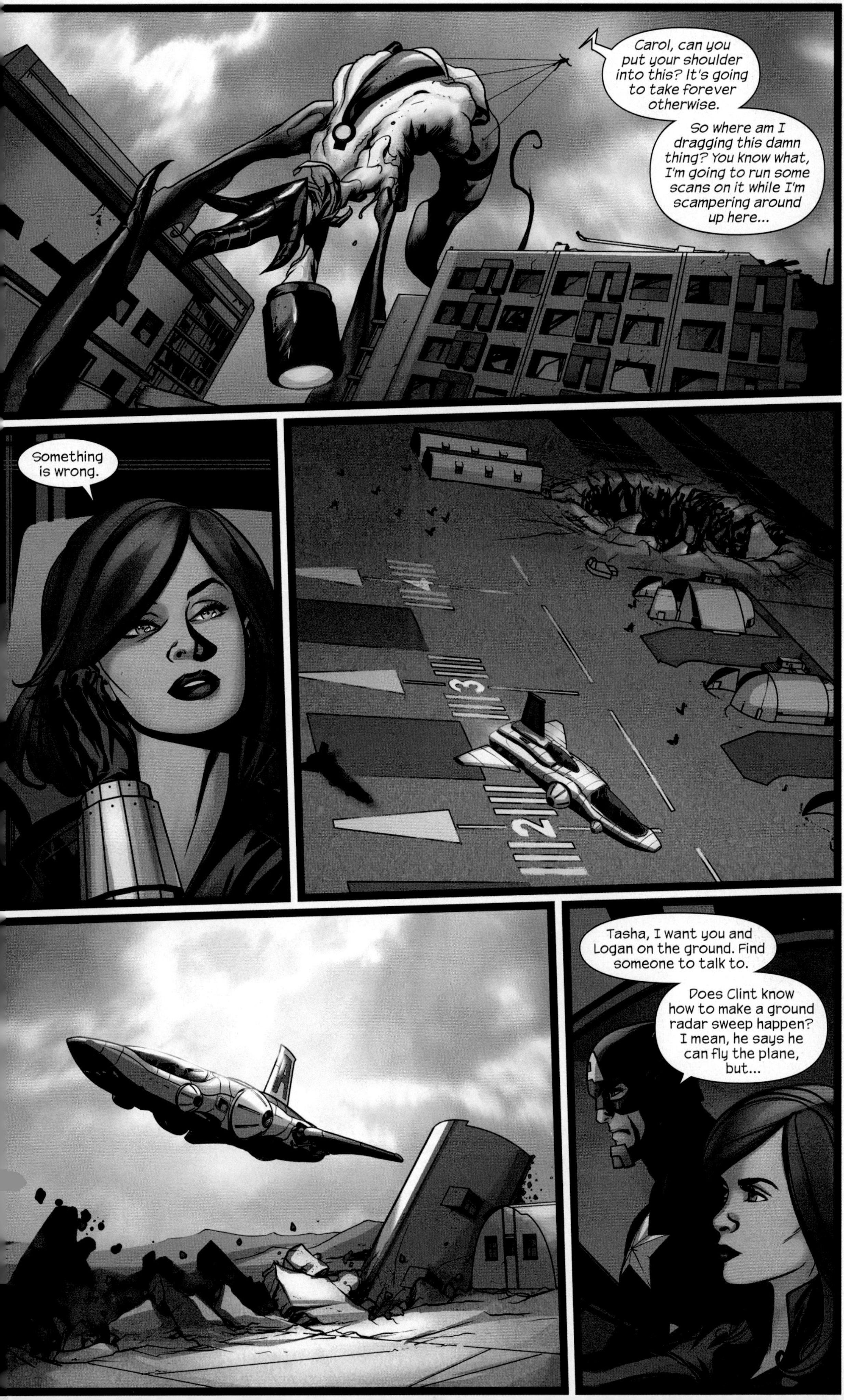
Carol, can you put your shoulder into this? It's going to take forever otherwise.
So where am I dragging this damn thing? You know what, I'm going to run some scans on it while I'm scampering around up here...
Something is wrong.
Tasha, I want you and Logan on the ground. Find someone to talk to.
Does Clint know how to make a ground radar sweep happen? I mean, he says he can fly the plane, but...

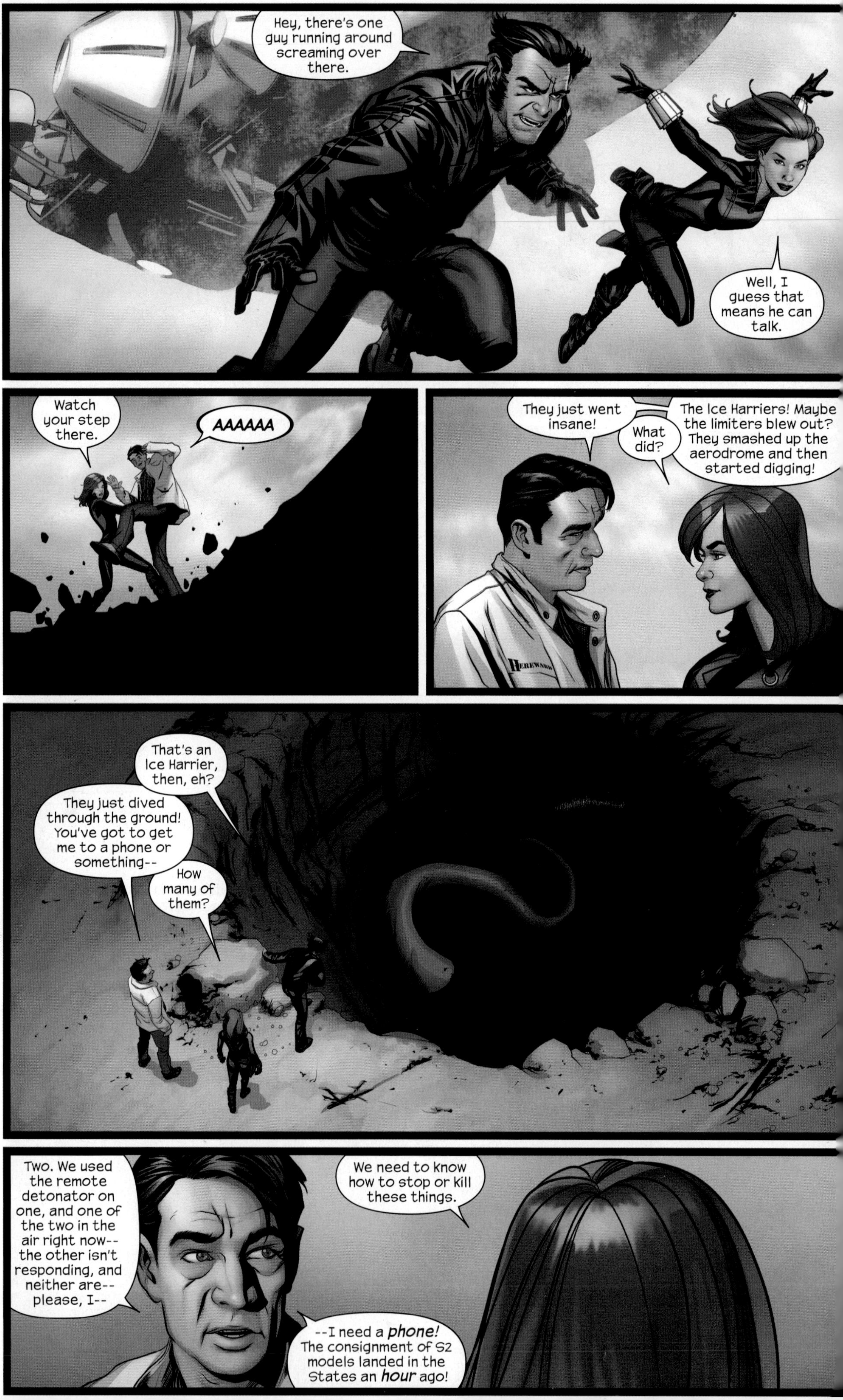
Hey, there's one guy running around screaming over there.
Well, I guess that means he can talk.
Watch your step there.
AAAAAA
They just went insane!
What did?
The Ice Harriers! Maybe the limiters blew out? They smashed up the aerodrome and then started digging!
That's an Ice Harrier, then, eh?
They just dived through the ground! You've got to get me to a phone or something--
How many of them?
Two. We used the remote detonator on one, and one of the two in the air right now-- the other isn't responding, and neither are-- please, I--
We need to know how to stop or kill these things.
--I need a *phone!* The consignment of S2 models landed in the States an *hour* ago!

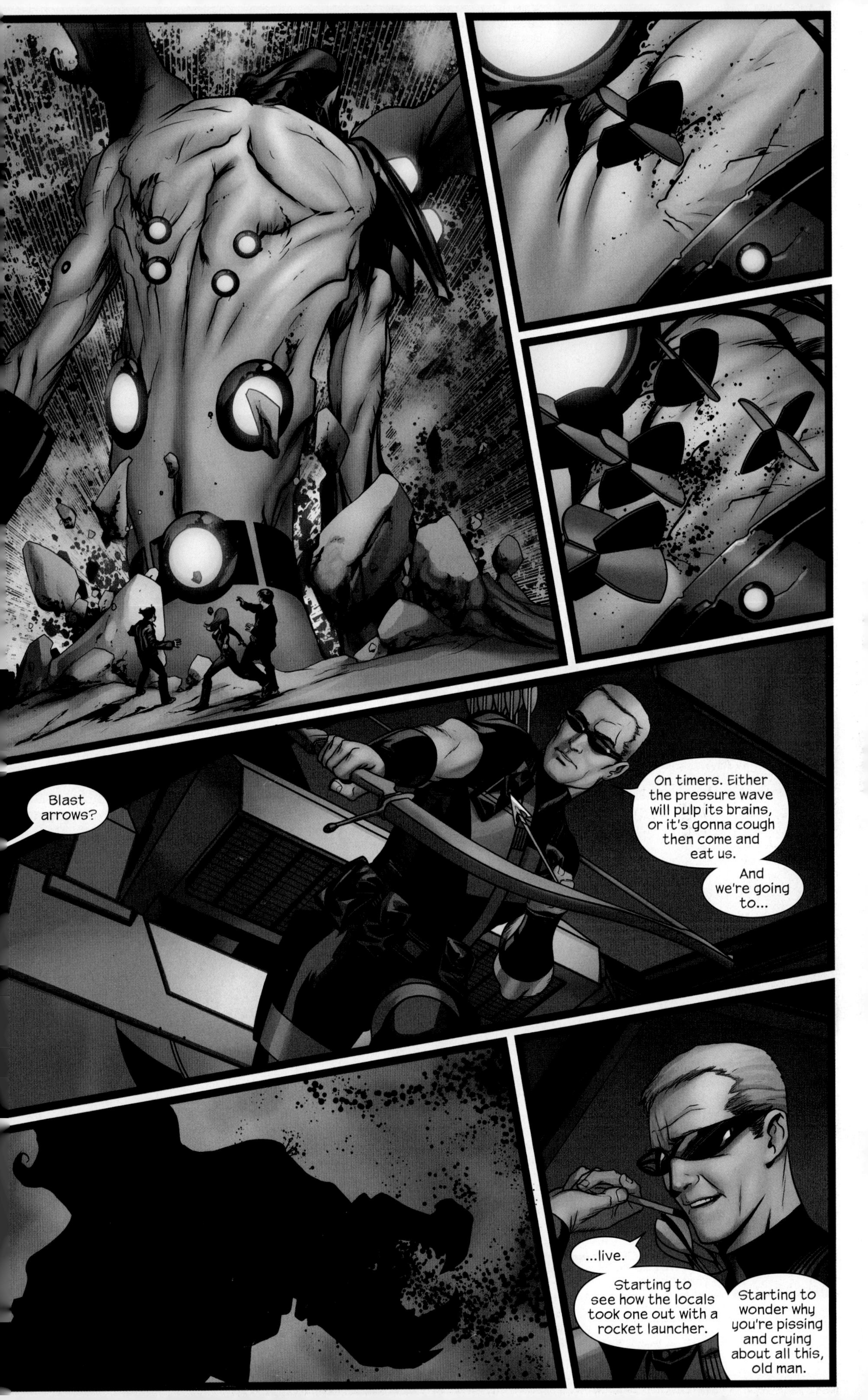
Blast arrows?
On timers. Either the pressure wave will pulp its brains, or it's gonna cough then come and eat us.
And we're going to...
...live.
Starting to see how the locals took one out with a rocket launcher.
Starting to wonder why you're pissing and crying about all this, old man.

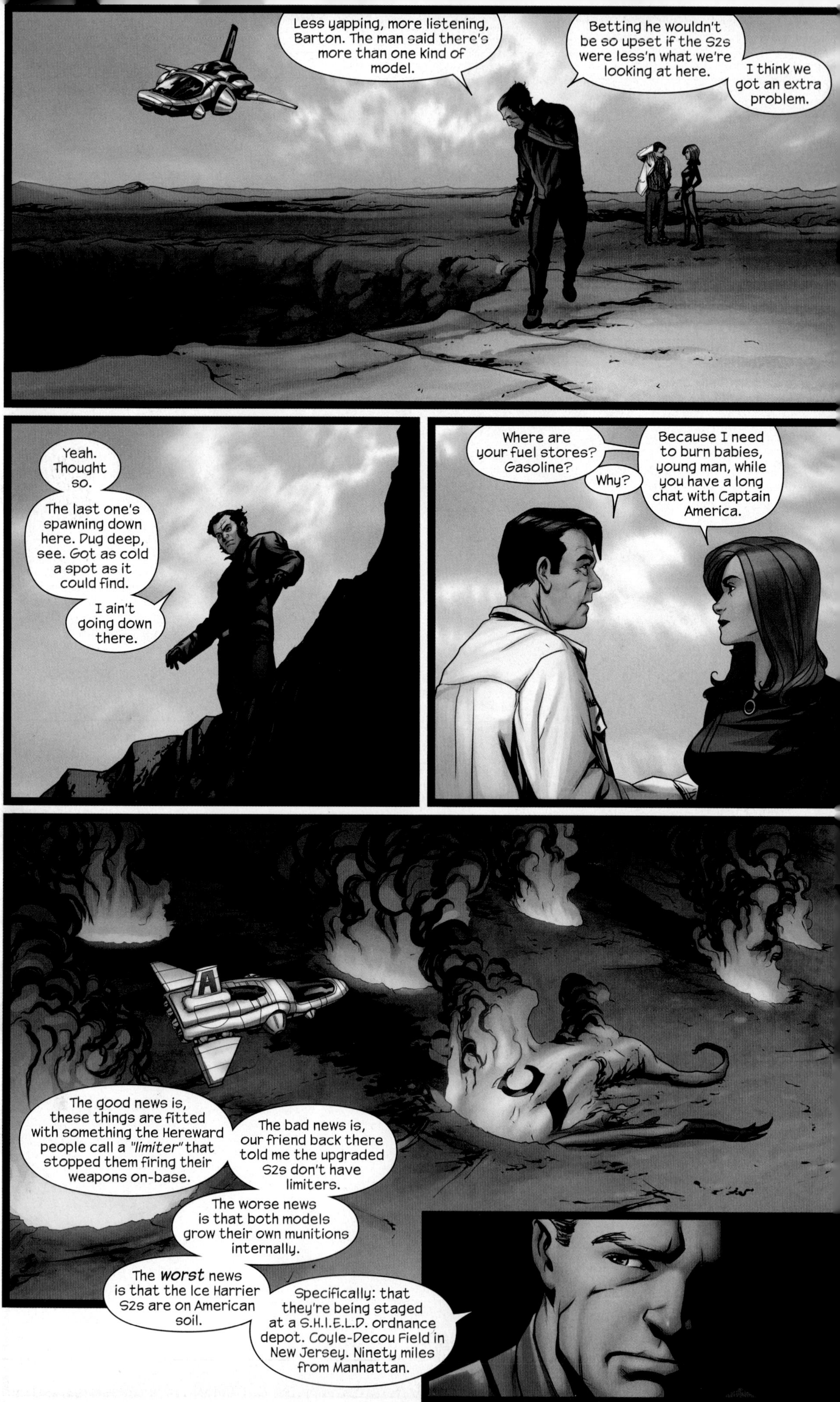
Less yapping, more listening, Barton. The man said there's more than one kind of model.
Betting he wouldn't be so upset if the S2s were less'n what we're looking at here.
I think we got an extra problem.
Yeah. Thought so.
The last one's spawning down here. Dug deep, see. Got as cold a spot as it could find.
I ain't going down there.
Where are your fuel stores? Gasoline?
Why?
Because I need to burn babies, young man, while you have a long chat with Captain America.
The good news is, these things are fitted with something the Hereward people call a "limiter" that stopped them firing their weapons on-base.
The bad news is, our friend back there told me the upgraded S2s don't have limiters.
The worse news is that both models grow their own munitions internally.
The worst news is that the Ice Harrier S2s are on American soil.
Specifically: that they're being staged at a S.H.I.E.L.D. ordnance depot. Coyle-Decou Field in New Jersey. Ninety miles from Manhattan.

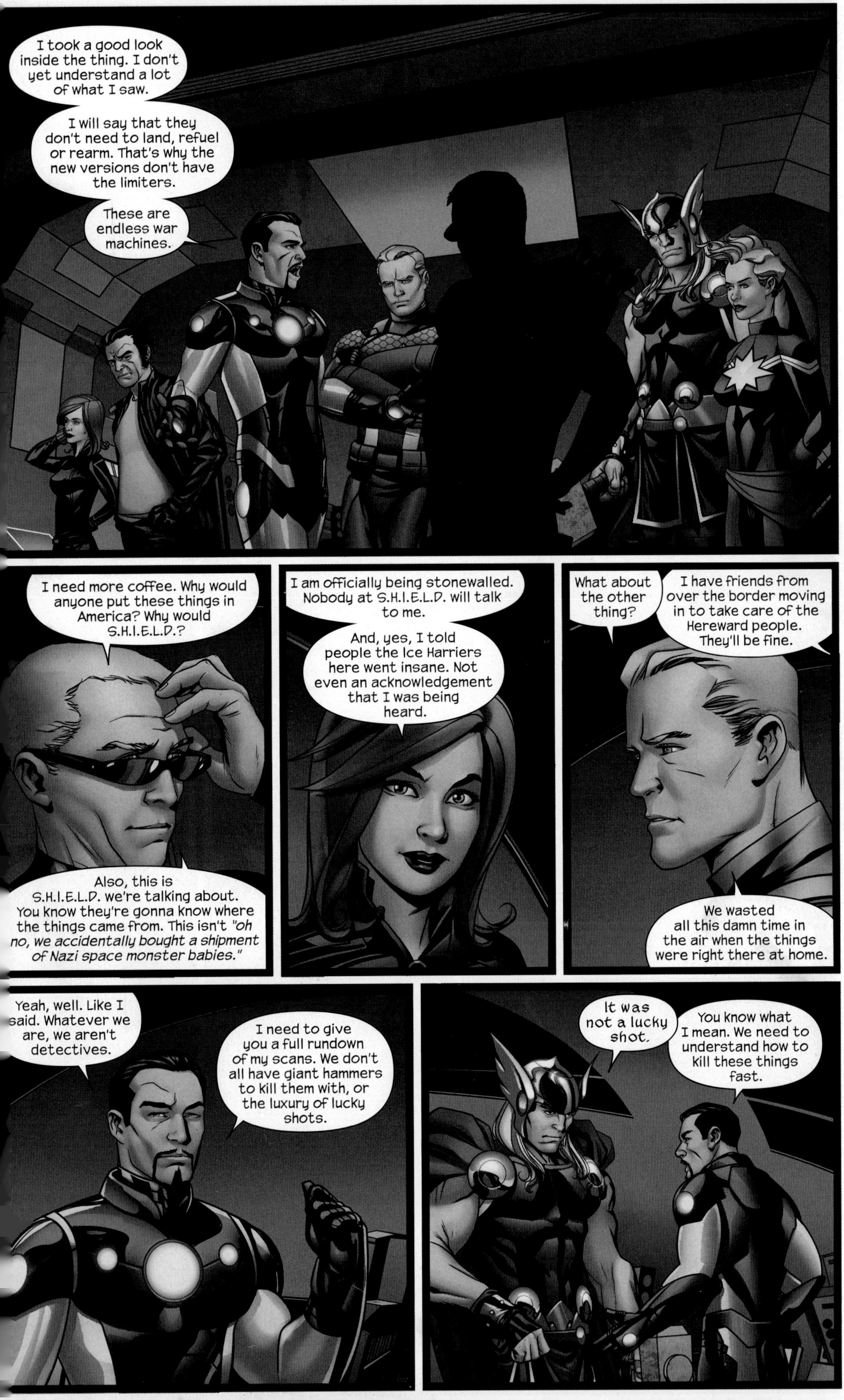
I took a good look inside the thing. I don't yet understand a lot of what I saw.
I will say that they don't need to land, refuel or rearm. That's why the new versions don't have the limiters.
These are endless war machines.
I need more coffee. Why would anyone put these things in America? Why would S.H.I.E.L.D.?
Also, this is S.H.I.E.L.D. we're talking about. You know they're gonna know where the things came from. This isn't *"oh no, we accidentally bought a shipment of Nazi space monster babies."*
I am officially being stonewalled. Nobody at S.H.I.E.L.D. will talk to me.
And, yes, I told people the Ice Harriers here went insane. Not even an acknowledgement that I was being heard.
What about the other thing?
I have friends from over the border moving in to take care of the Hereward people. They'll be fine.
We wasted all this damn time in the air when the things were right there at home.
Yeah, well. Like I said. Whatever we are, we aren't detectives.
I need to give you a full rundown of my scans. We don't all have giant hammers to kill them with, or the luxury of lucky shots.
It was not a lucky shot.
You know what I mean. We need to understand how to kill these things fast.

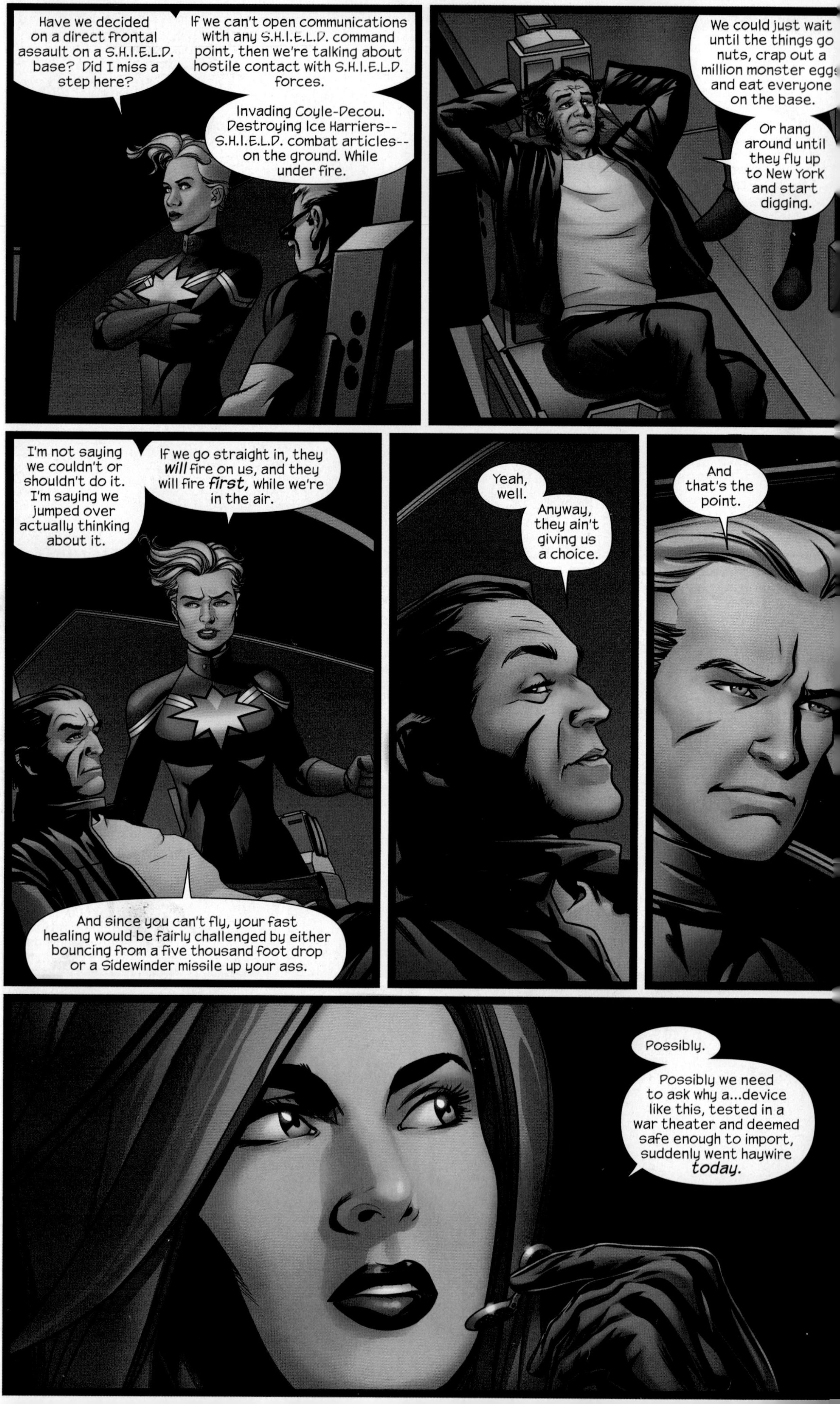

Have we decided on a direct frontal assault on a S.H.I.E.L.D. base? Did I miss a step here?
If we can't open communications with any S.H.I.E.L.D. command point, then we're talking about hostile contact with S.H.I.E.L.D. forces.
Invading Coyle-Decou. Destroying Ice Harriers--S.H.I.E.L.D. combat articles--on the ground. While under fire.
We could just wait until the things go nuts, crap out a million monster eggs and eat everyone on the base.
Or hang around until they fly up to New York and start digging.
I'm not saying we couldn't or shouldn't do it. I'm saying we jumped over actually thinking about it.
If we go straight in, they *will* fire on us, and they will fire ***first,*** while we're in the air.
And since you can't fly, your fast healing would be fairly challenged by either bouncing from a five thousand foot drop or a Sidewinder missile up your ass.
Yeah, well.
Anyway, they ain't giving us a choice.
And that's the point.
Possibly.
Possibly we need to ask why a...device like this, tested in a war theater and deemed safe enough to import, suddenly went haywire ***today.***

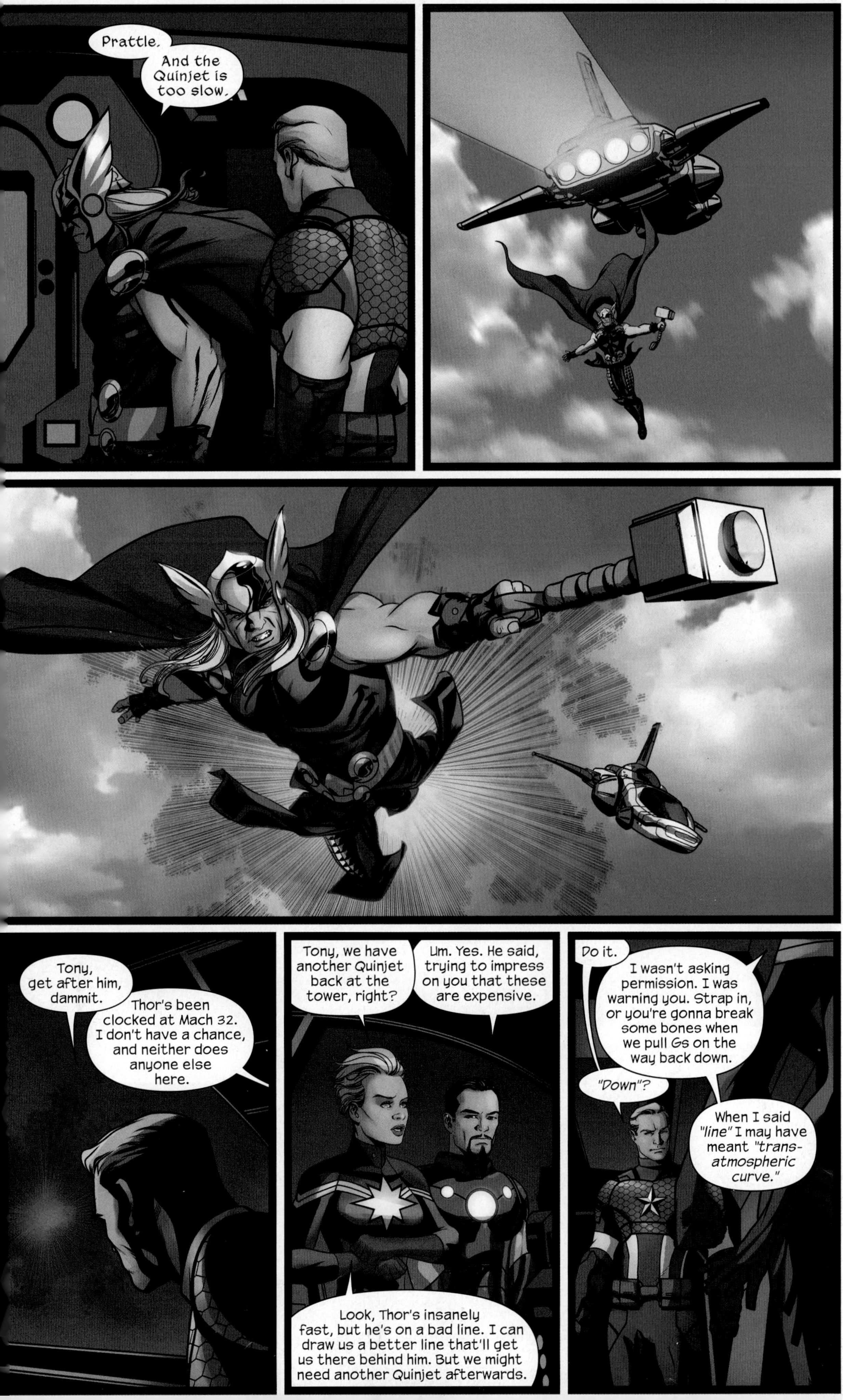
Prattle.
And the Quinjet is too slow.
Tony, get after him, dammit.
Thor's been clocked at Mach 32. I don't have a chance, and neither does anyone else here.
Tony, we have another Quinjet back at the tower, right?
Um. Yes. He said, trying to impress on you that these are expensive.
Look, Thor's insanely fast, but he's on a bad line. I can draw us a better line that'll get us there behind him. But we might need another Quinjet afterwards.
Do it.
I wasn't asking permission. I was warning you. Strap in, or you're gonna break some bones when we pull Gs on the way back down.
"Down"?
When I said "line" I may have meant "trans-atmospheric curve."

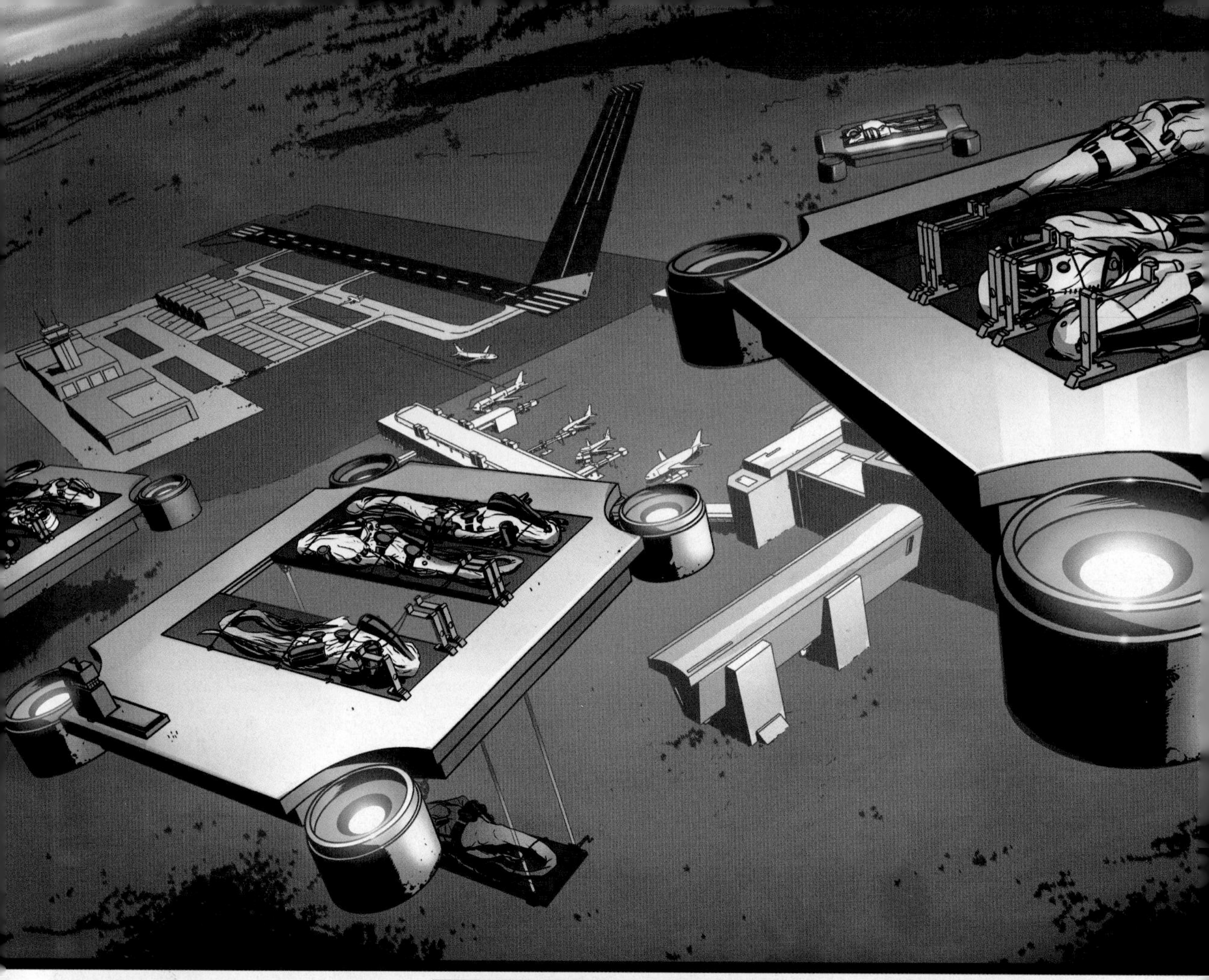

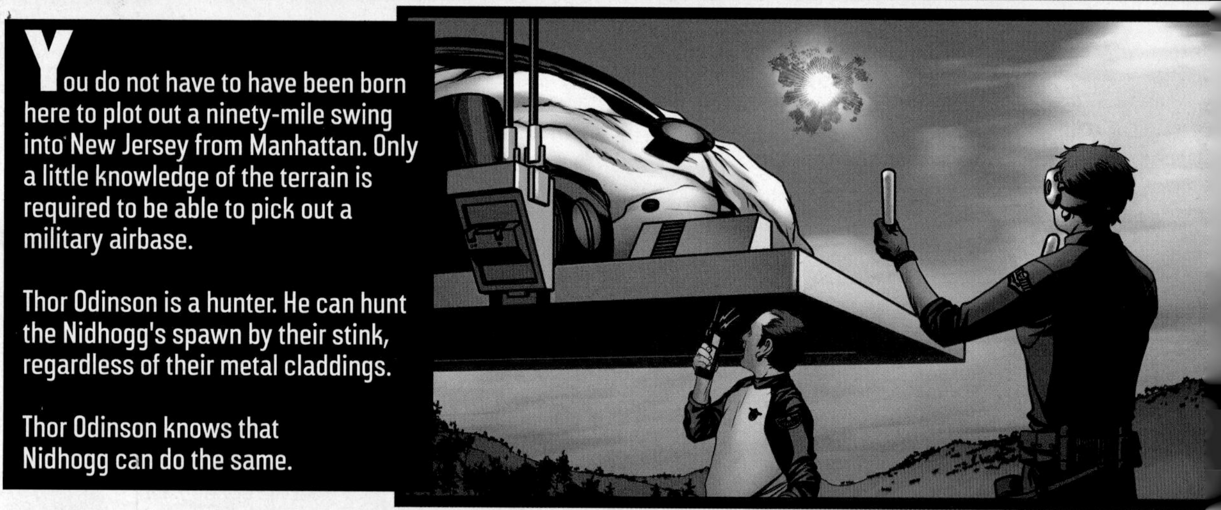
You do not have to have been born here to plot out a ninety-mile swing into New Jersey from Manhattan. Only a little knowledge of the terrain is required to be able to pick out a military airbase.
Thor Odinson is a hunter. He can hunt the Nidhogg's spawn by their stink, regardless of their metal claddings.
Thor Odinson knows that Nidhogg can do the same.

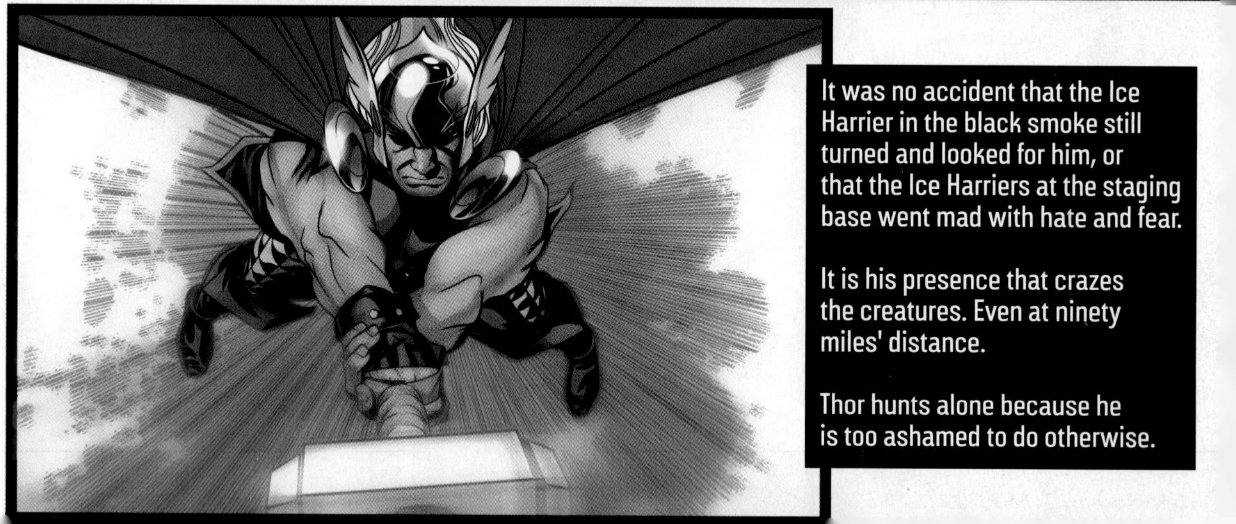
It was no accident that the Ice Harrier in the black smoke still turned and looked for him, or that the Ice Harriers at the staging base went mad with hate and fear.
It is his presence that crazes the creatures. Even at ninety miles' distance.
Thor hunts alone because he is too ashamed to do otherwise.

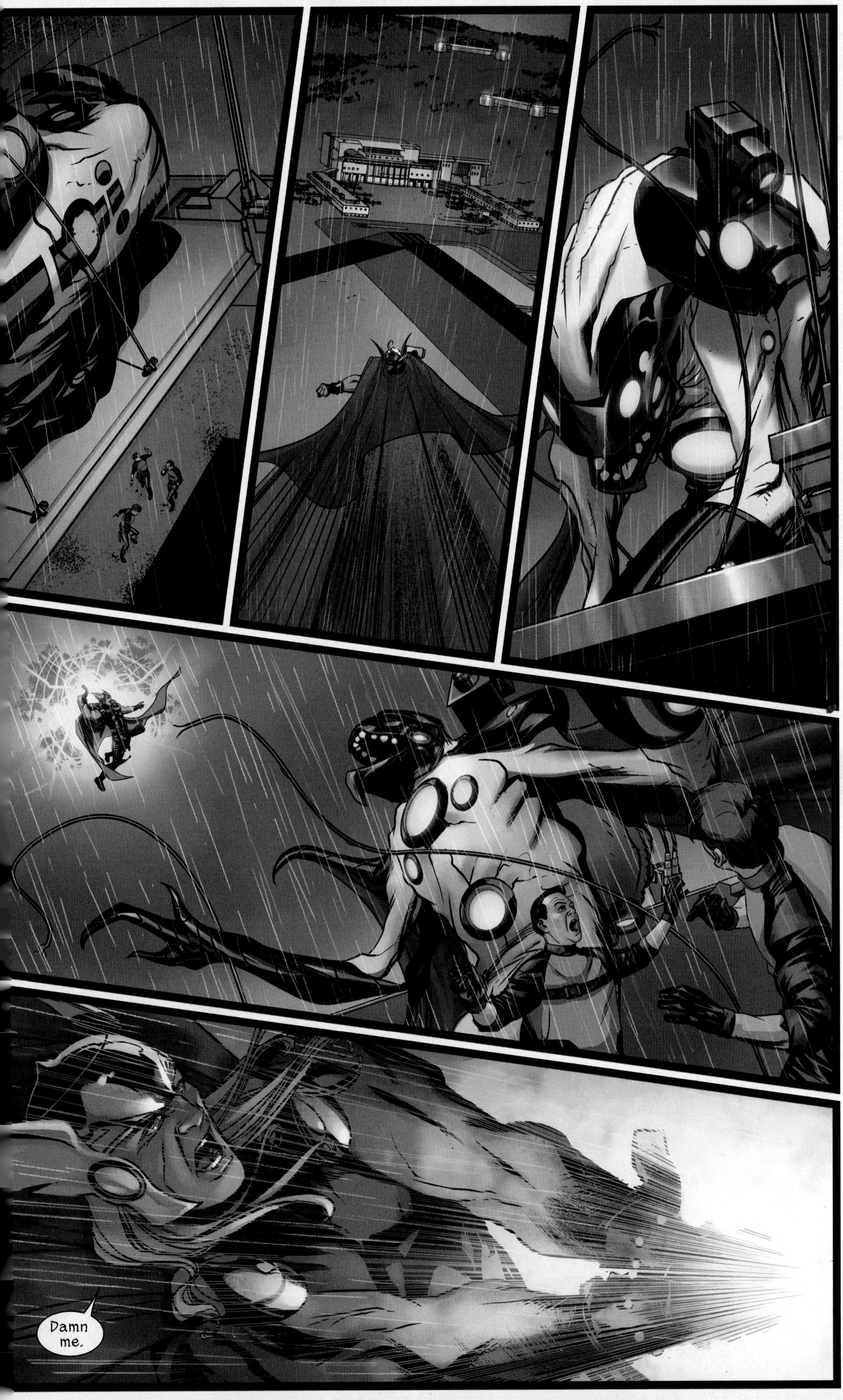
Damn me.

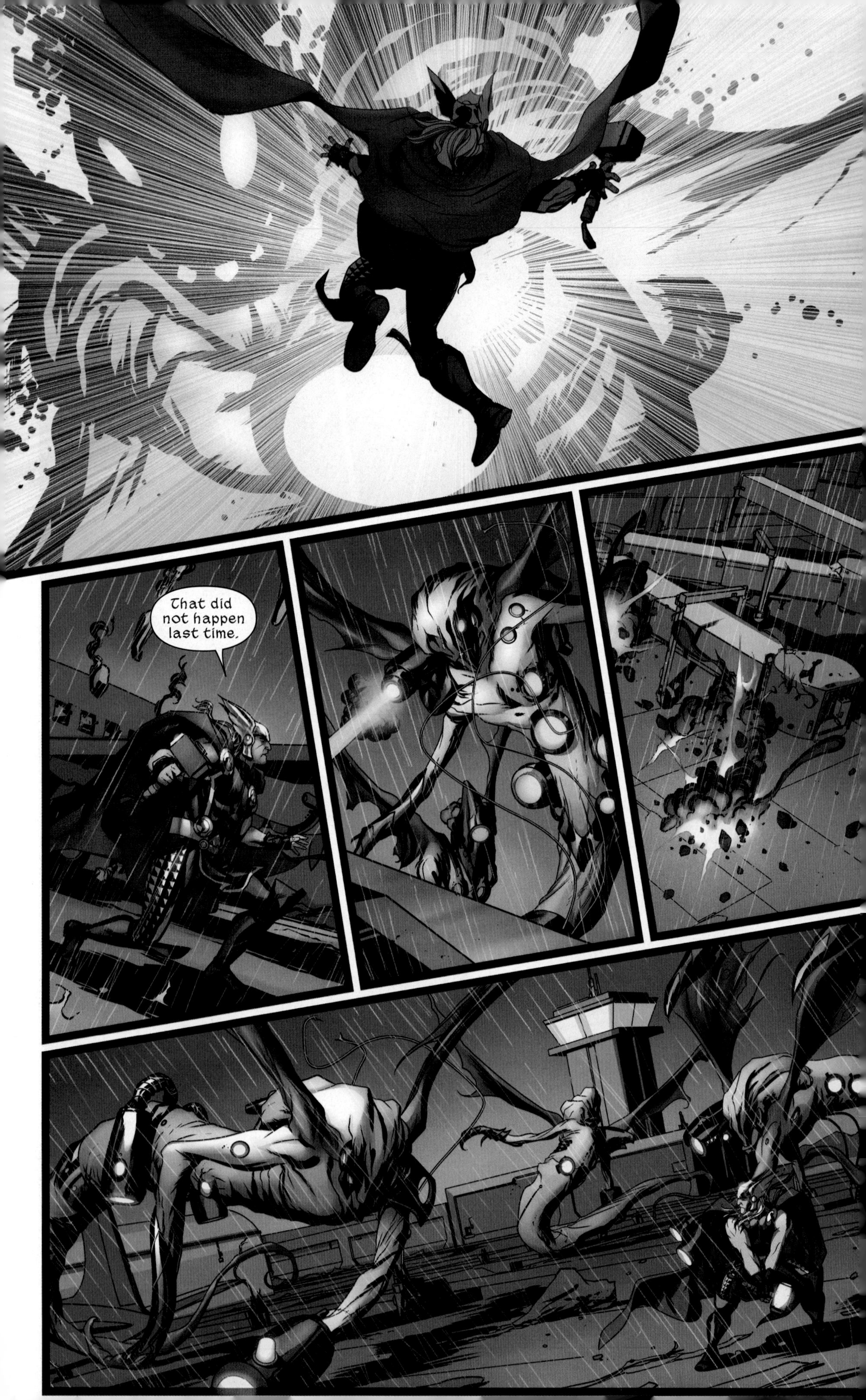
That did not happen last time.

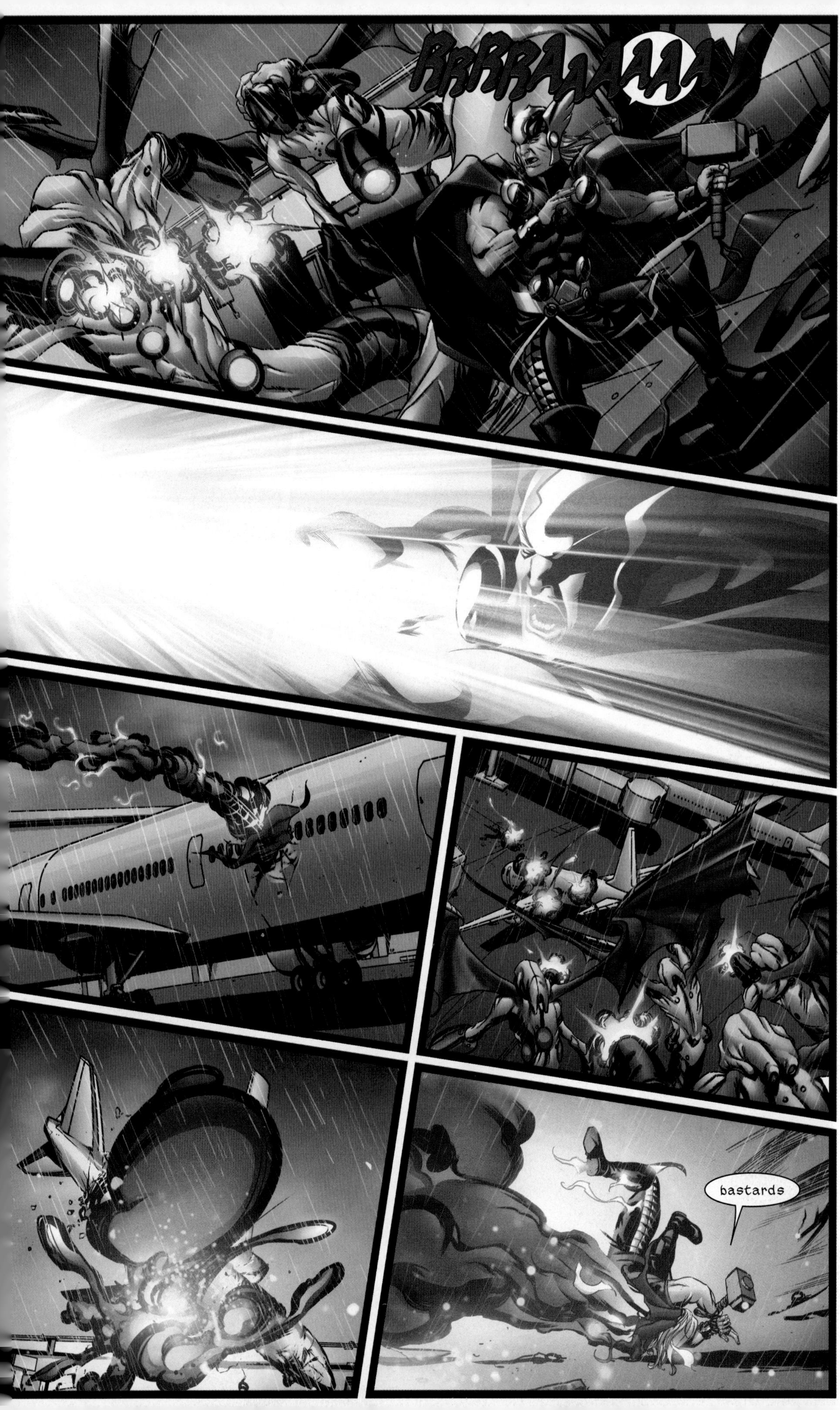
BRRRAAAAAA
bastards

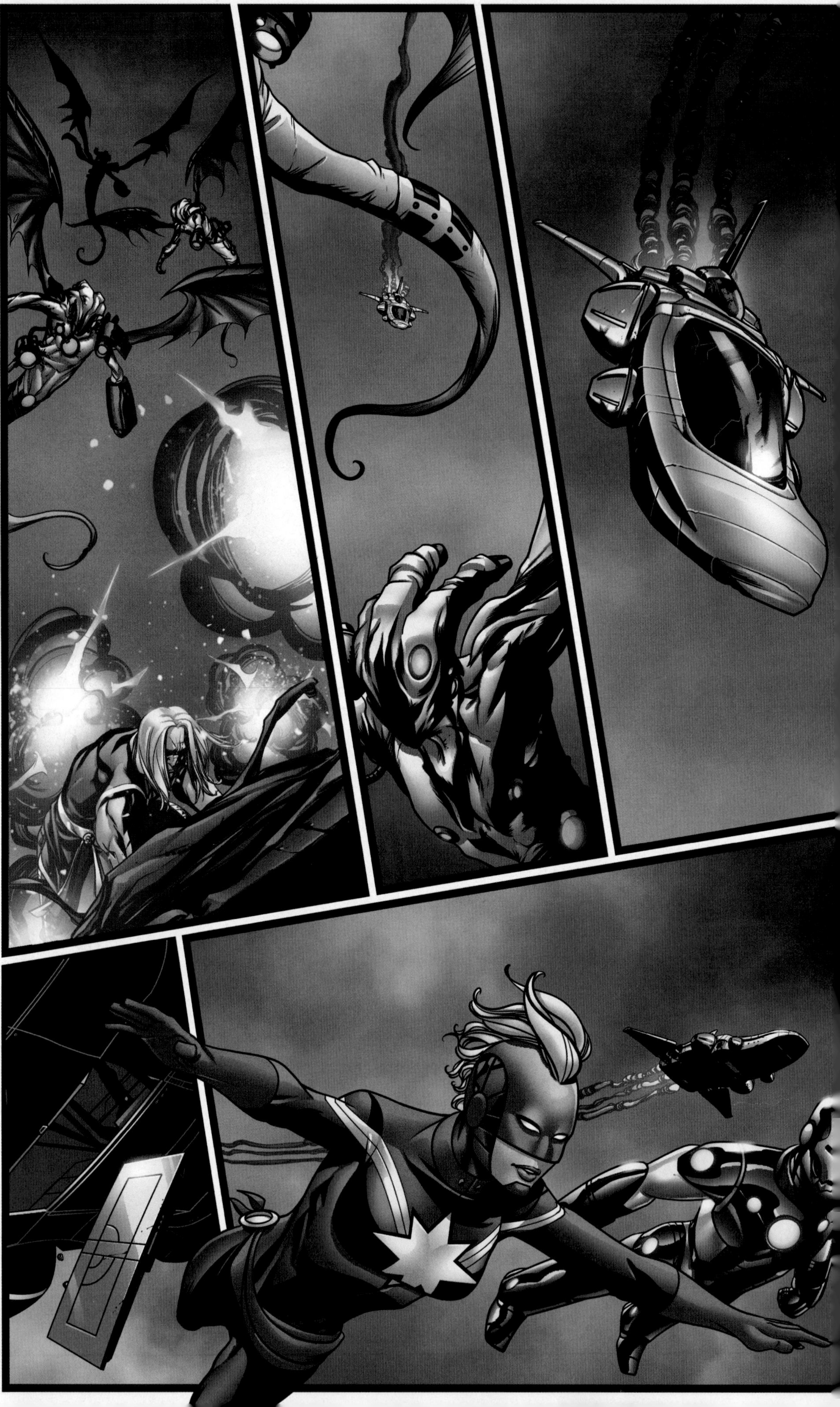

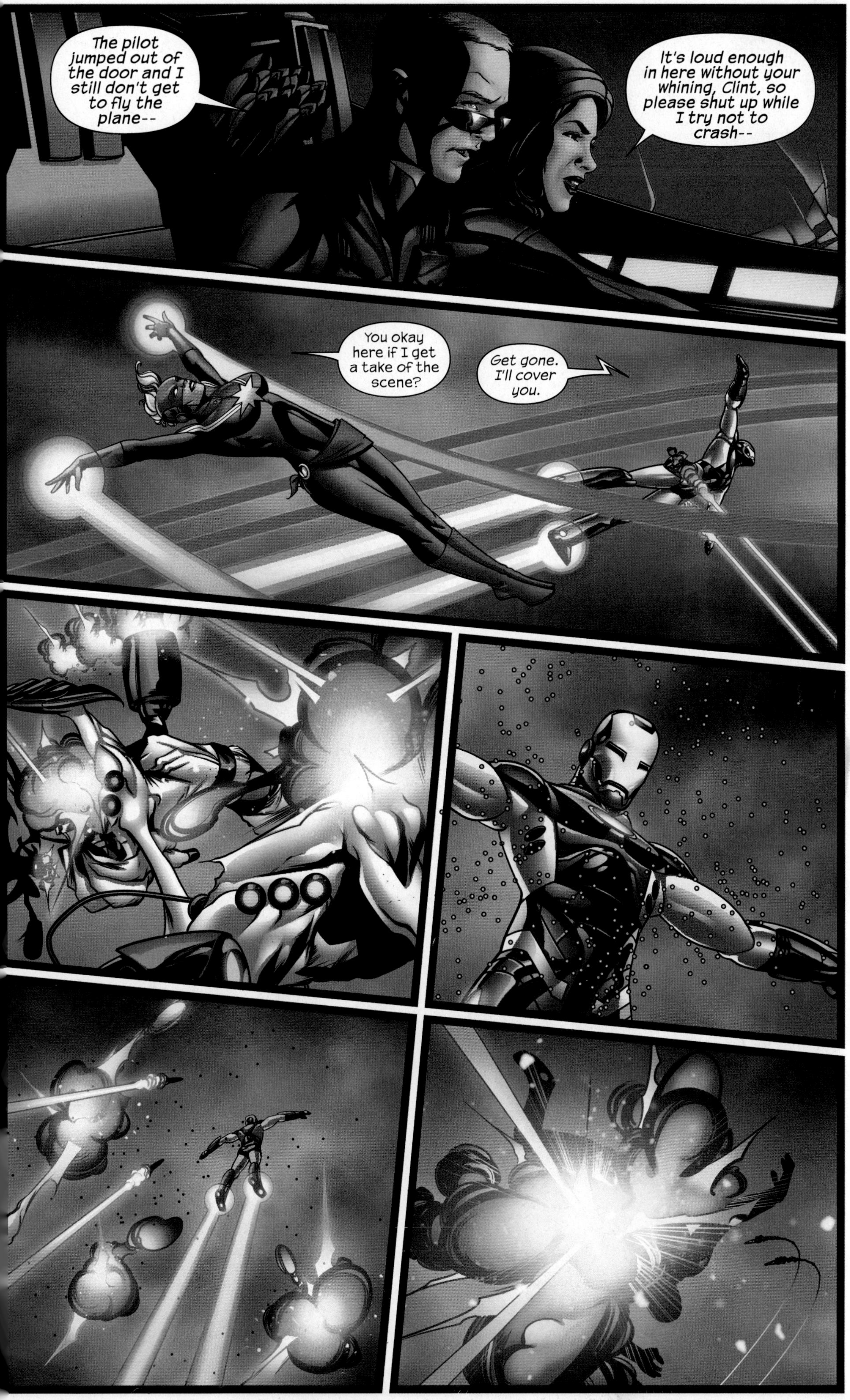
The pilot jumped out of the door and I still don't get to fly the plane--
It's loud enough in here without your whining, Clint, so please shut up while I try not to crash--
You okay here if I get a take of the scene?
Get gone. I'll cover you.

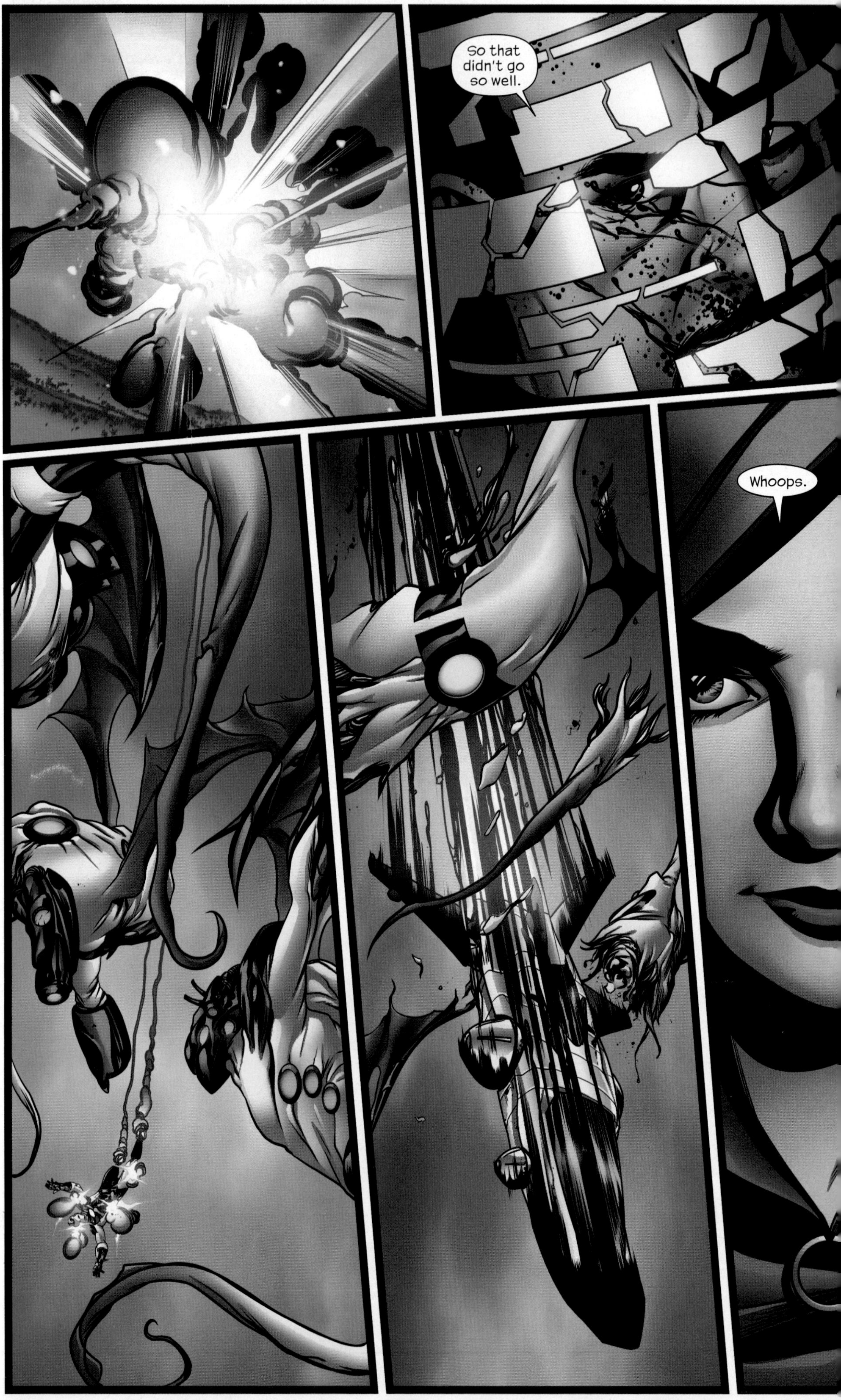
So that didn't go so well.
Whoops.

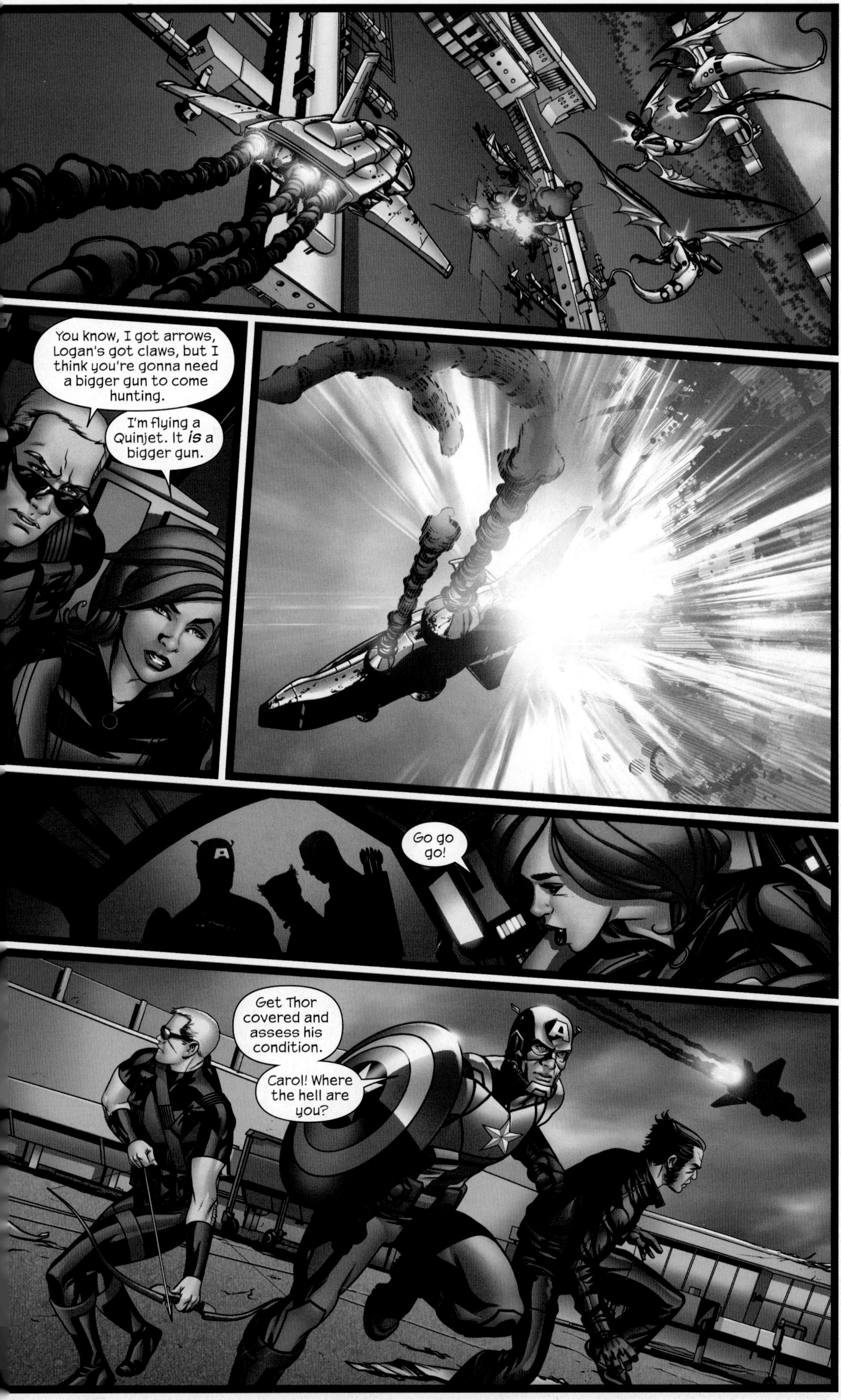
You know, I got arrows, Logan's got claws, but I think you're gonna need a bigger gun to come hunting.
I'm flying a Quinjet. It *is* a bigger gun.
Go go go!
Get Thor covered and assess his condition.
Carol! Where the hell are you?

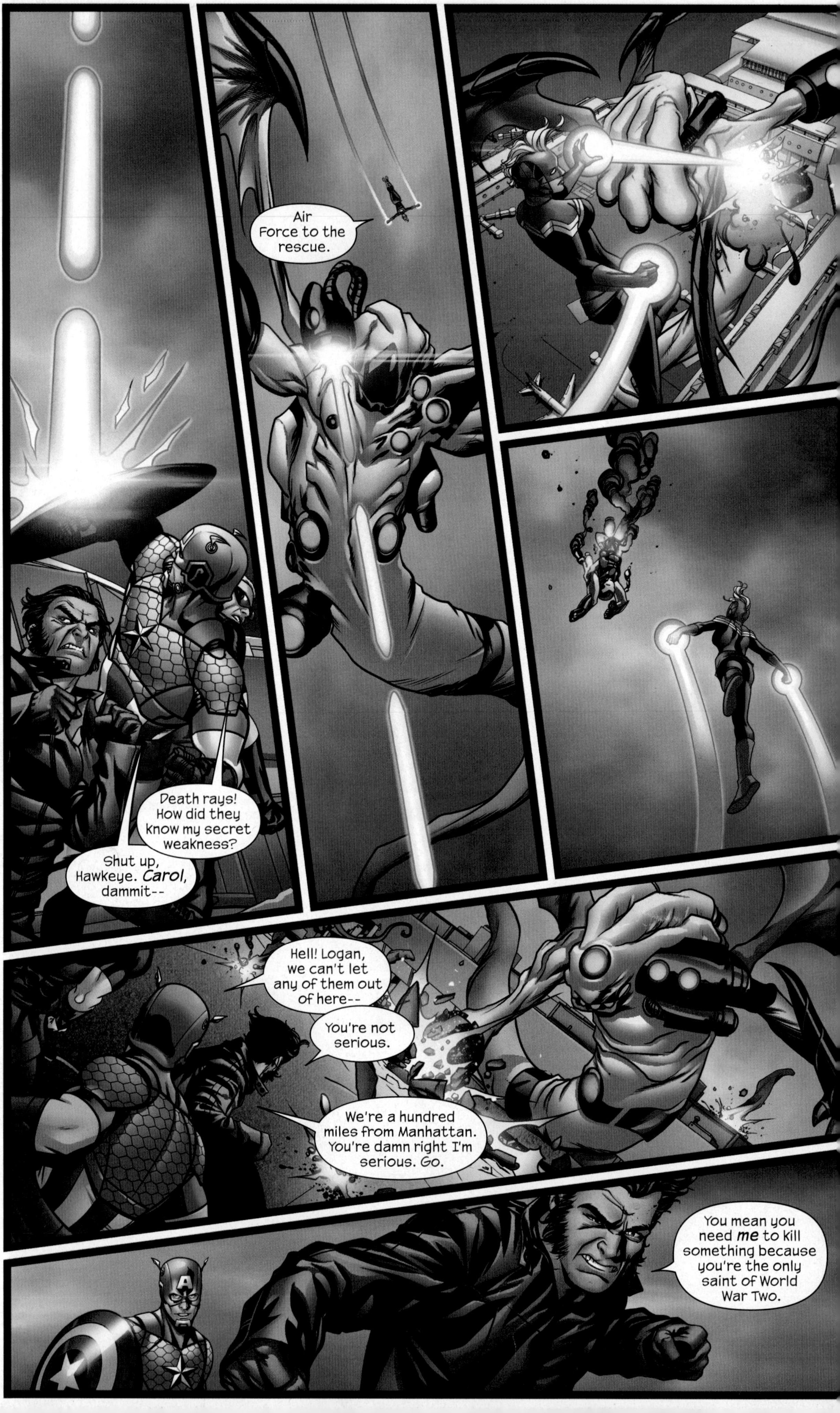
Air Force to the rescue.
Death rays! How did they know my secret weakness?
Shut up, Hawkeye. *Carol*, dammit--
Hell! Logan, we can't let any of them out of here--
You're not serious.
We're a hundred miles from Manhattan. You're damn right I'm serious. Go.
You mean you need *me* to kill something because you're the only saint of World War Two.

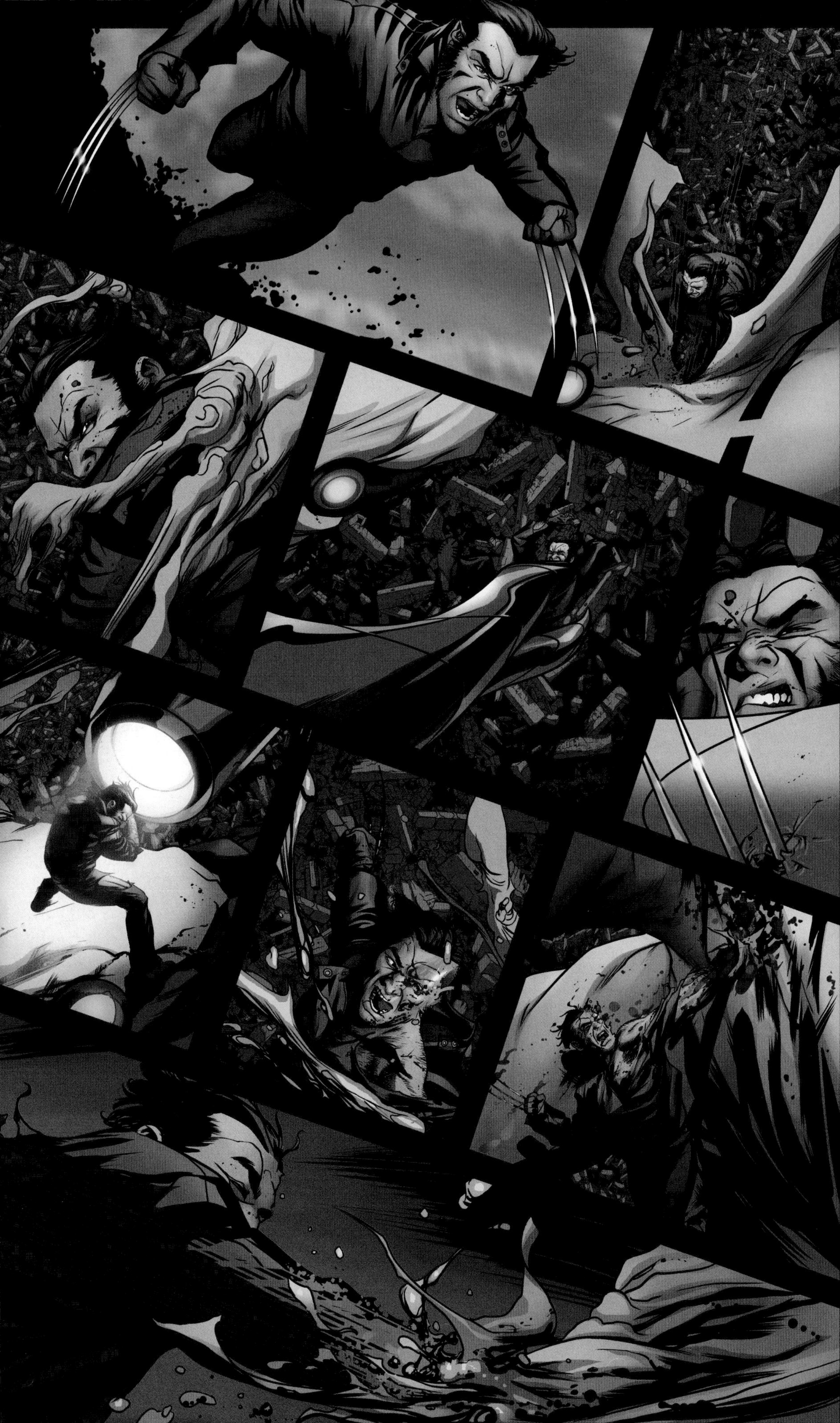

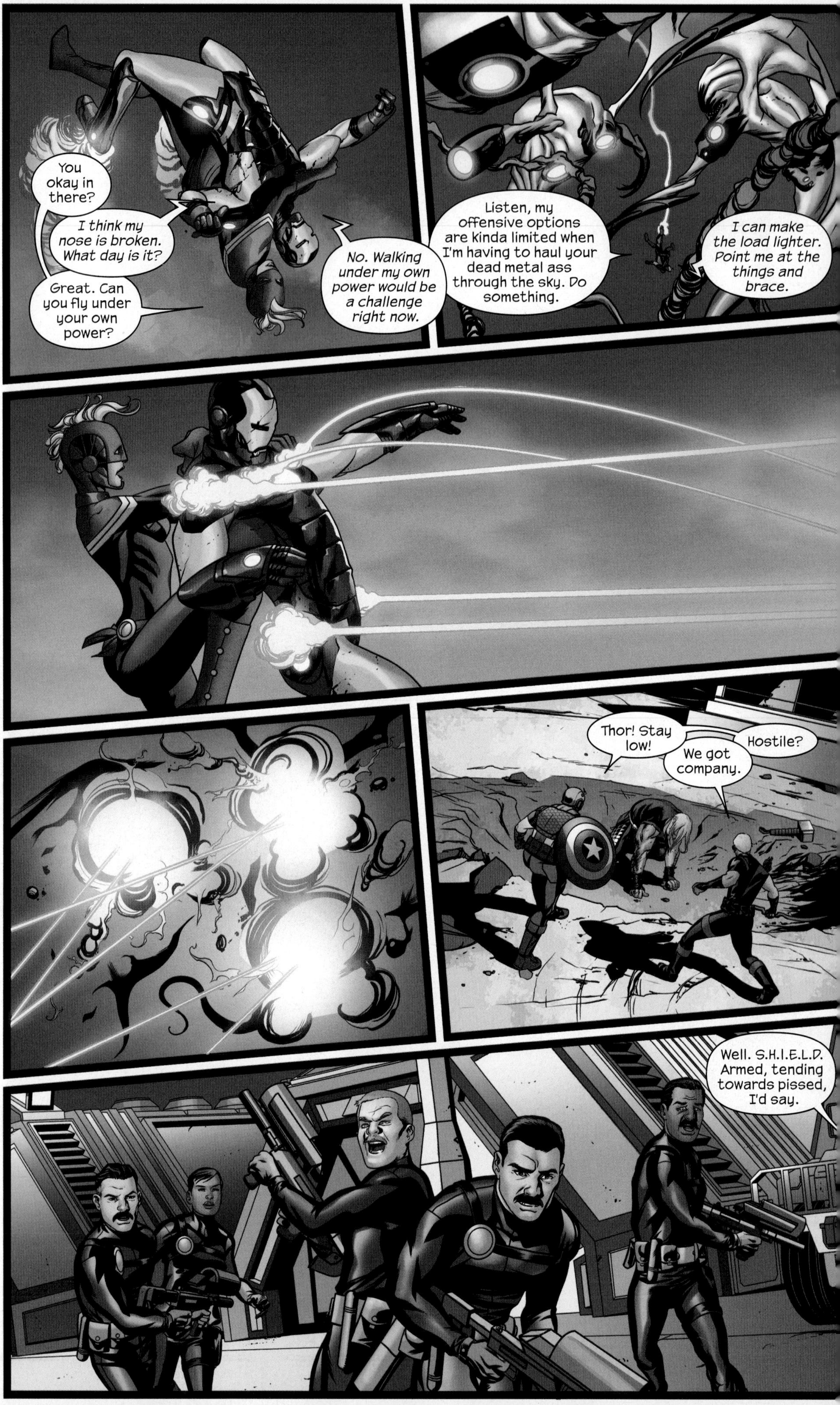
You okay in there?
I think my nose is broken. What day is it?
Great. Can you fly under your own power?
No. Walking under my own power would be a challenge right now.
Listen, my offensive options are kinda limited when I'm having to haul your dead metal ass through the sky. Do something.
I can make the load lighter. Point me at the things and brace.
Thor! Stay low!
Hostile?
We got company.
Well. S.H.I.E.L.D. Armed, tending towards pissed, I'd say.

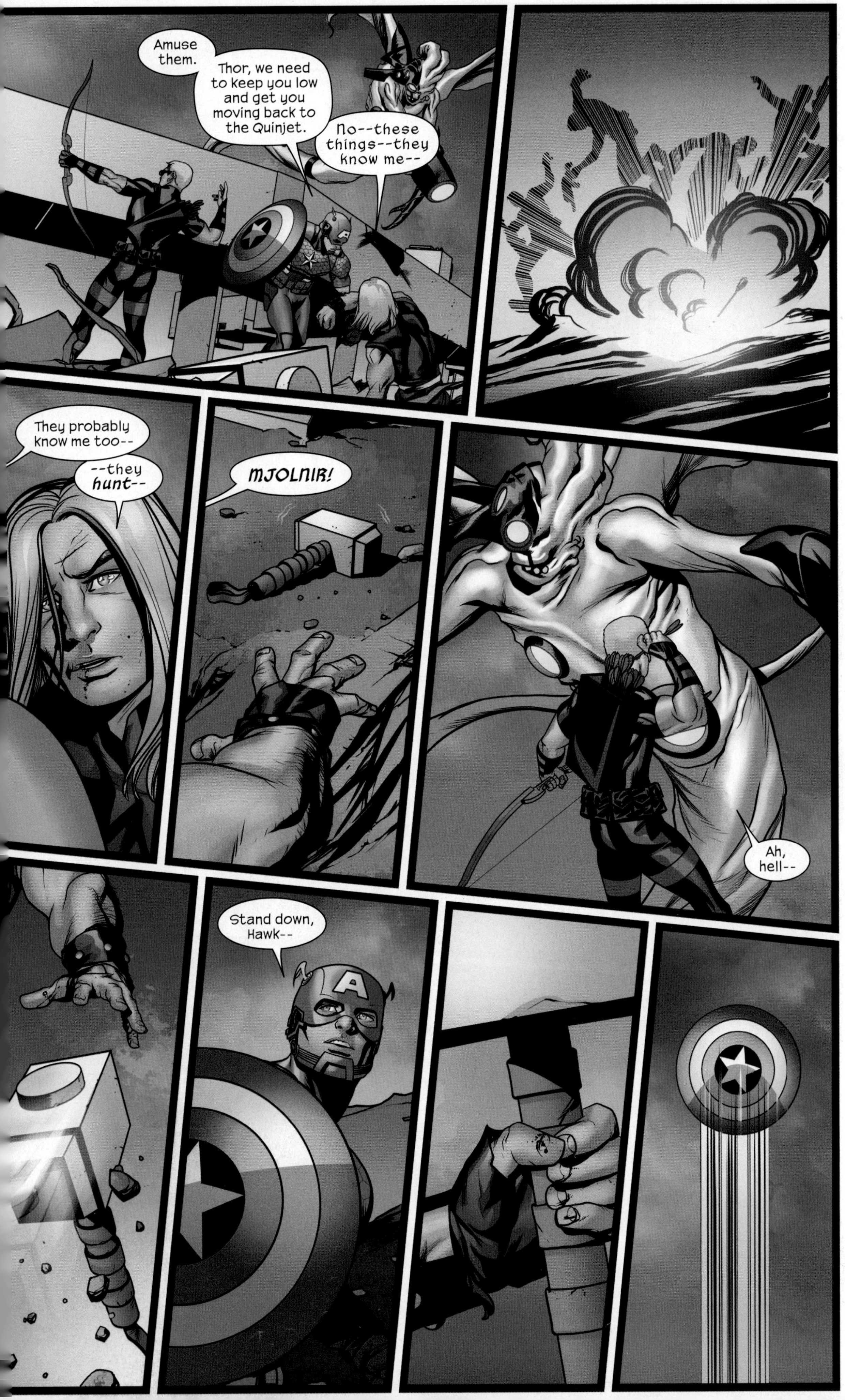
Amuse them.
Thor, we need to keep you low and get you moving back to the Quinjet.
No--these things--they know me--
They probably know me too--
--they *hunt*--
MJOLNIR!
Ah, hell--
Stand down, Hawk--

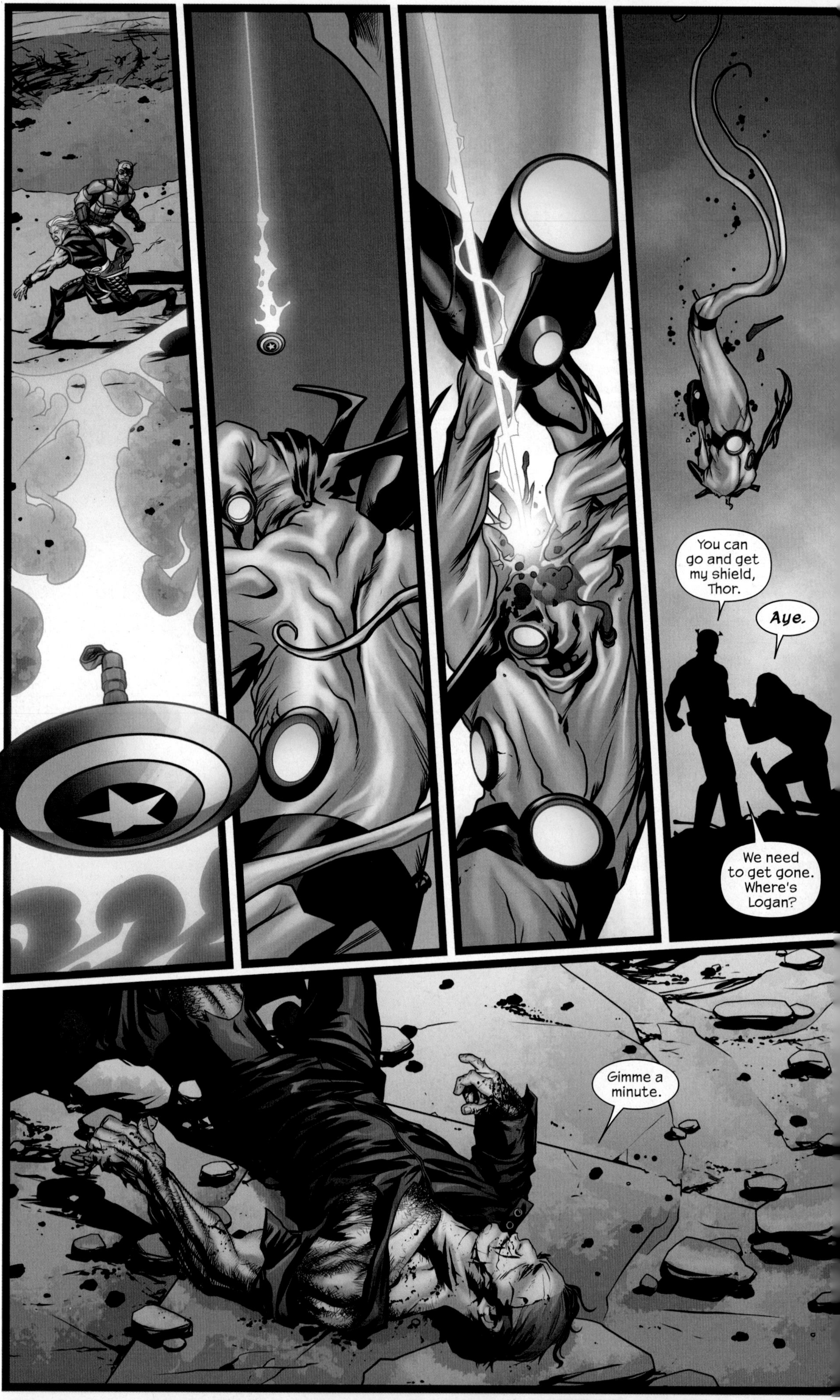
You can go and get my shield, Thor.
Aye.
We need to get gone. Where's Logan?
Gimme a minute.

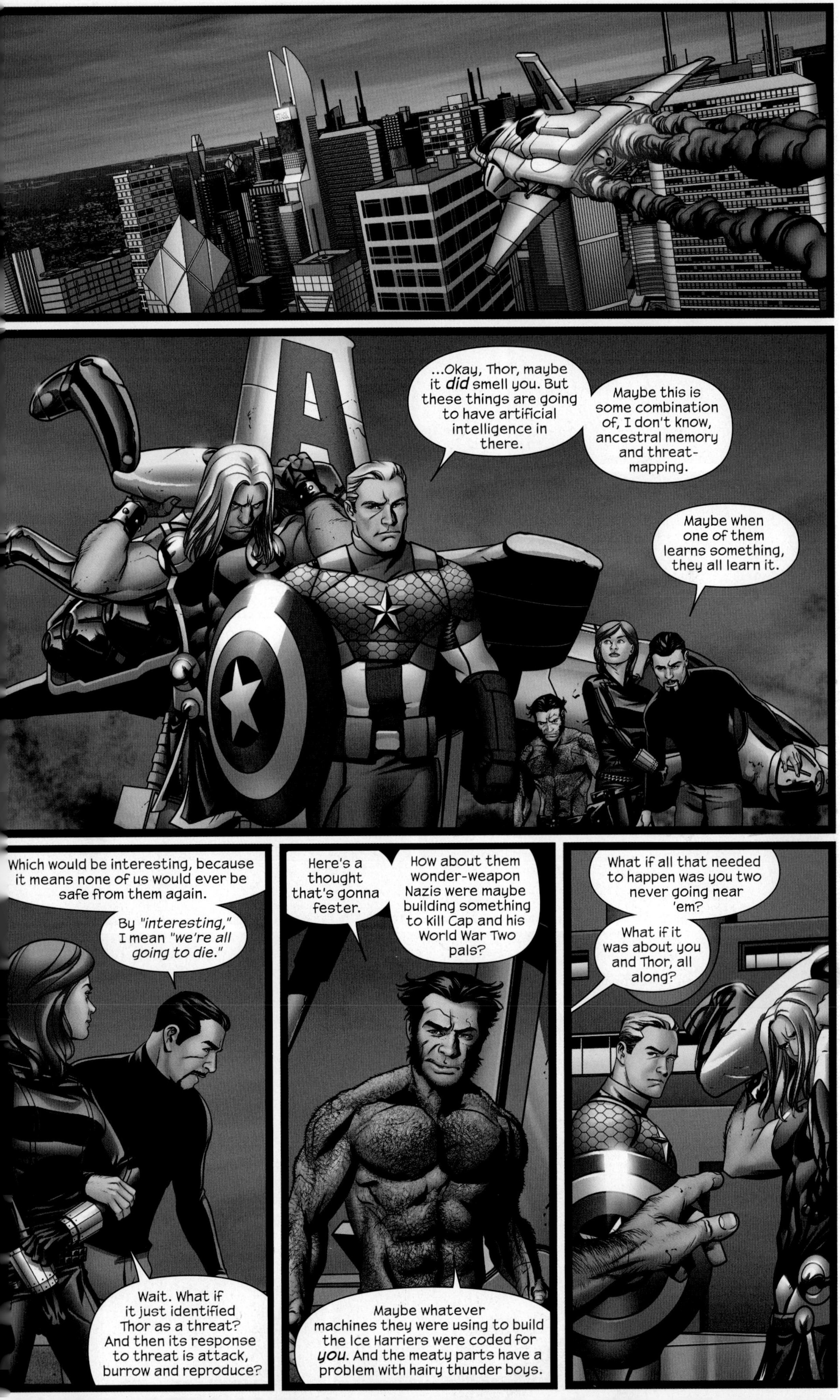
...Okay, Thor, maybe it *did* smell you. But these things are going to have artificial intelligence in there.
Maybe this is some combination of, I don't know, ancestral memory and threat-mapping.
Maybe when one of them learns something, they all learn it.
Which would be interesting, because it means none of us would ever be safe from them again.
By *"interesting,"* I mean *"we're all going to die."*
Wait. What if it just identified Thor as a threat? And then its response to threat is attack, burrow and reproduce?
Here's a thought that's gonna fester.
How about them wonder-weapon Nazis were maybe building something to kill Cap and his World War Two pals?
Maybe whatever machines they were using to build the Ice Harriers were coded for *you*. And the meaty parts have a problem with hairy thunder boys.
What if all that needed to happen was you two never going near 'em?
What if it was about you and Thor, all along?

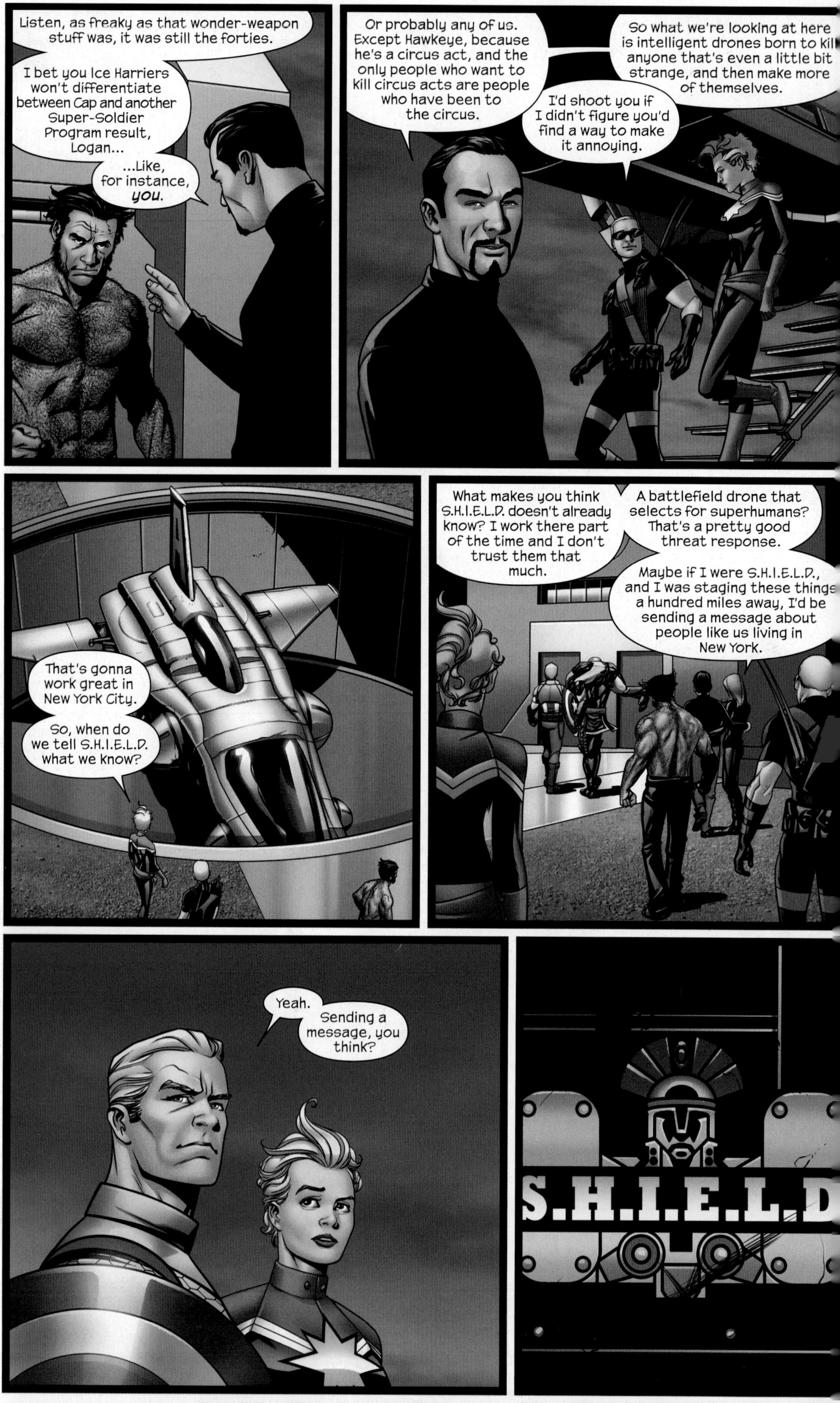
Listen, as freaky as that wonder-weapon stuff was, it was still the forties.
I bet you Ice Harriers won't differentiate between Cap and another Super-Soldier Program result, Logan...
...Like, for instance, *you*.
Or probably any of us. Except Hawkeye, because he's a circus act, and the only people who want to kill circus acts are people who have been to the circus.
So what we're looking at here is intelligent drones born to kil anyone that's even a little bit strange, and then make more of themselves.
I'd shoot you if I didn't figure you'd find a way to make it annoying.
That's gonna work great in New York City.
So, when do we tell S.H.I.E.L.D. what we know?
What makes you think S.H.I.E.L.D. doesn't already know? I work there part of the time and I don't trust them that much.
A battlefield drone that selects for superhumans? That's a pretty good threat response.
Maybe if I were S.H.I.E.L.D., and I was staging these things a hundred miles away, I'd be sending a message about people like us living in New York.
Yeah.
Sending a message, you think?
S.H.I.E.L.D

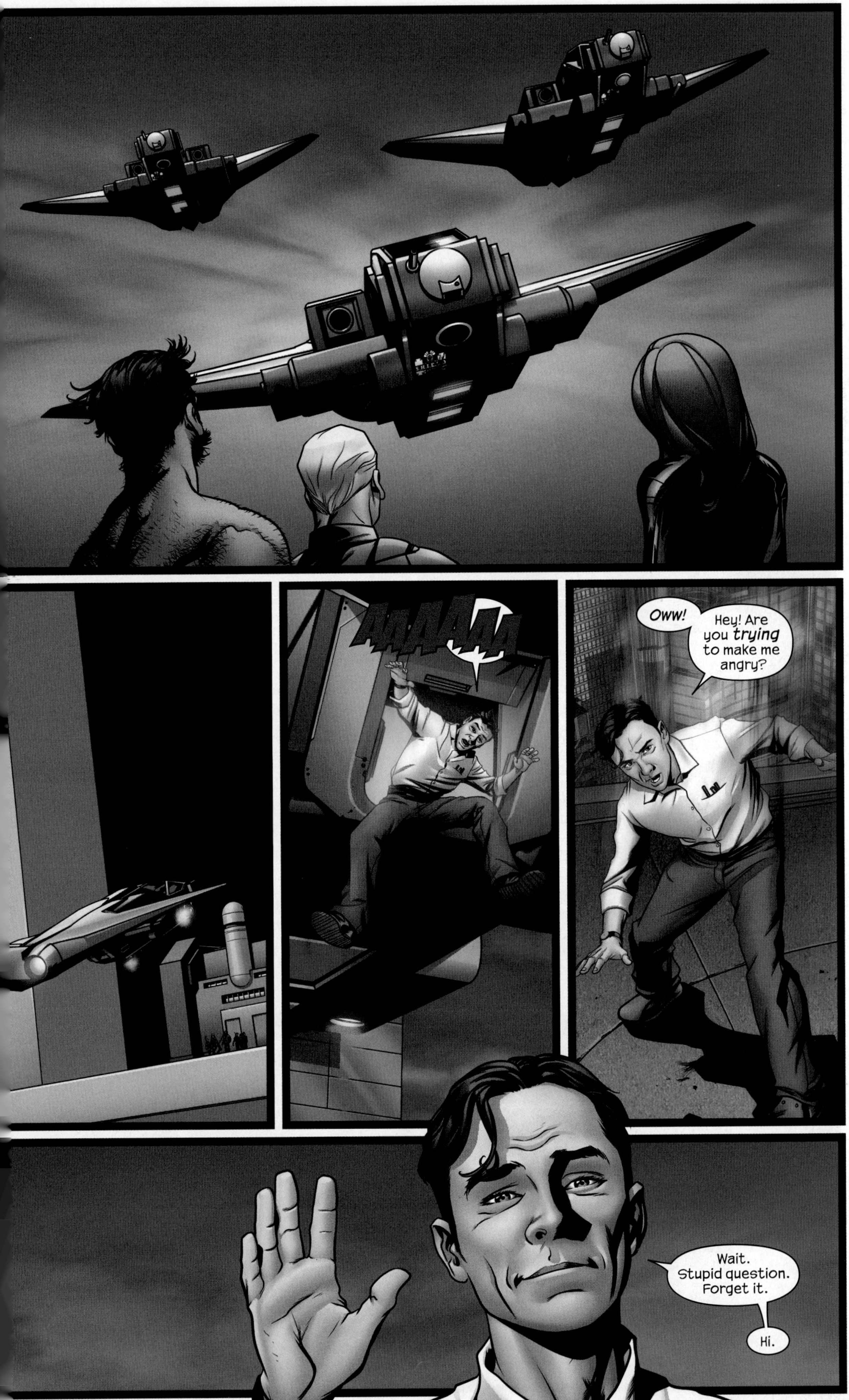
AAAAAA
Oww!
Hey! Are you *trying* to make me angry?
Wait. Stupid question. Forget it.
Hi.

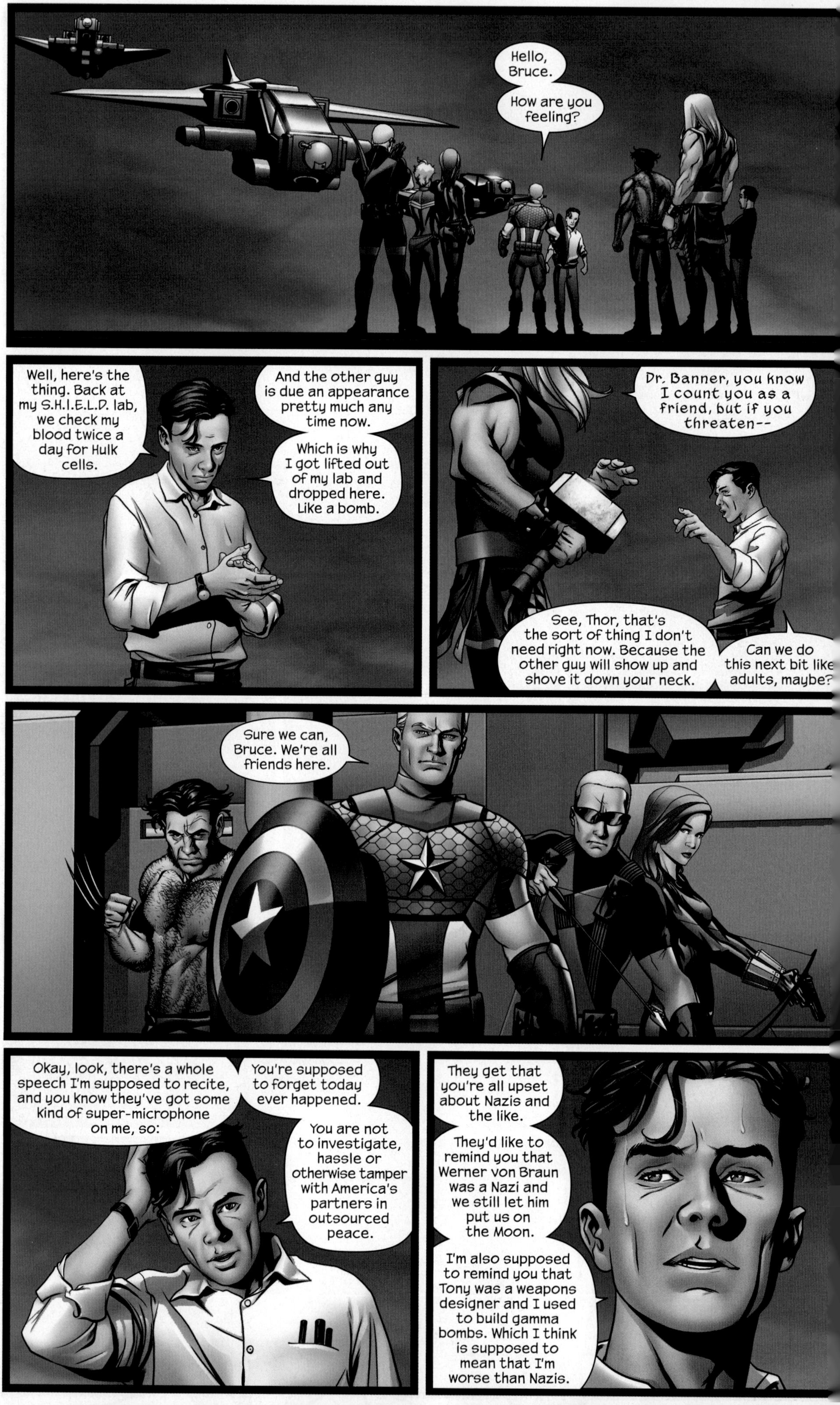

Hello, Bruce.
How are you feeling?
Well, here's the thing. Back at my S.H.I.E.L.D. lab, we check my blood twice a day for Hulk cells.
And the other guy is due an appearance pretty much any time now.
Which is why I got lifted out of my lab and dropped here. Like a bomb.
Dr. Banner, you know I count you as a friend, but if you threaten--
See, Thor, that's the sort of thing I don't need right now. Because the other guy will show up and shove it down your neck.
Can we do this next bit like adults, maybe?
Sure we can, Bruce. We're all friends here.
Okay, look, there's a whole speech I'm supposed to recite, and you know they've got some kind of super-microphone on me, so:
You're supposed to forget today ever happened.
You are not to investigate, hassle or otherwise tamper with America's partners in outsourced peace.
They get that you're all upset about Nazis and the like.
They'd like to remind you that Werner von Braun was a Nazi and we still let him put us on the Moon.
I'm also supposed to remind you that Tony was a weapons designer and I used to build gamma bombs. Which I think is supposed to mean that I'm worse than Nazis.

I'm supposed to say this: that the Avengers bring more trouble to New York City than they solve, and that you not being here isn't always good for Manhattan either.

They can't work on the basis that you'll always be here to save the city or fix your own messes.

So...these drones. S.H.I.E.L.D.'s New York City defense system.

You're kidding me. The things go nuts at a moment's notice.

I mean, if you're gonna bring up that I was a weaponeer, you can at least listen to my expert testimony.

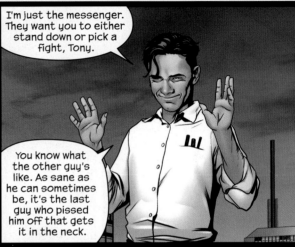

I'm just the messenger. They want you to either stand down or pick a fight, Tony.

You know what the other guy's like. As sane as he can sometimes be, it's the last guy who pissed him off that gets it in the neck.

So that's the deal. We walk away, or you stand in front of us 'til the bomb goes off?

Something like that. How bad are these things, anyway? The drones they're talking about?

They can't be controlled. This whole action is about massacre prevention.

Huh. So how do you do that? Deal with it, I mean?

We go to where they're being manufactured and shut them down.

Um, Bruce. I don't want to annoy you, but it looks a lot like you're taking your clothes off.

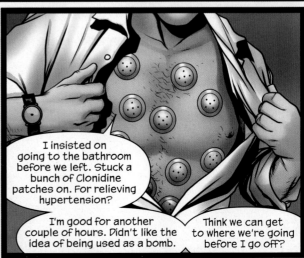

I insisted on going to the bathroom before we left. Stuck a bunch of Clonidine patches on. For relieving hypertension?

I'm good for another couple of hours. Didn't like the idea of being used as a bomb.

Think we can get to where we're going before I go off?

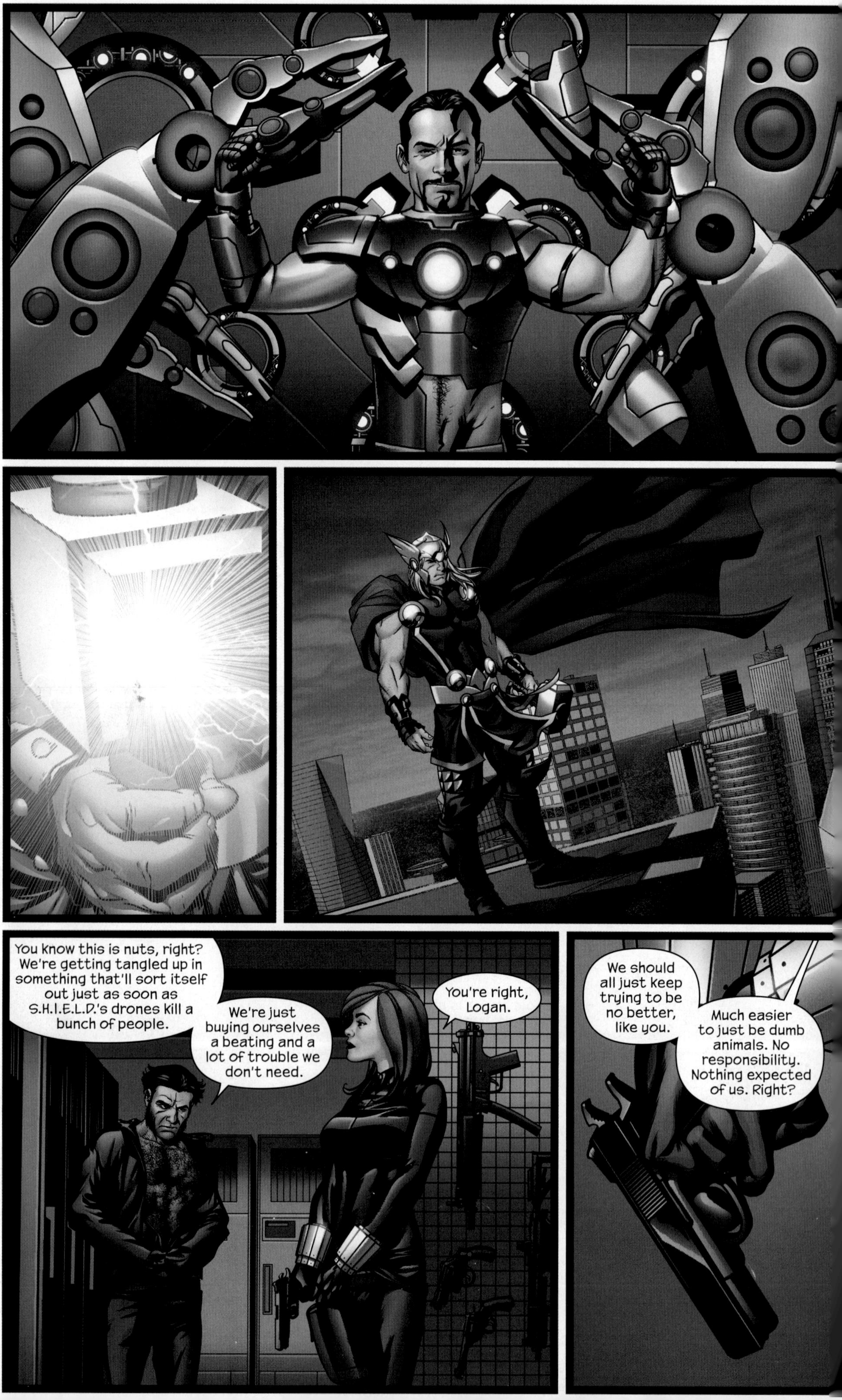
You know this is nuts, right? We're getting tangled up in something that'll sort itself out just as soon as S.H.I.E.L.D.'s drones kill a bunch of people.
We're just buying ourselves a beating and a lot of trouble we don't need.
You're right, Logan.
We should all just keep trying to be no better, like you.
Much easier to just be dumb animals. No responsibility. Nothing expected of us. Right?

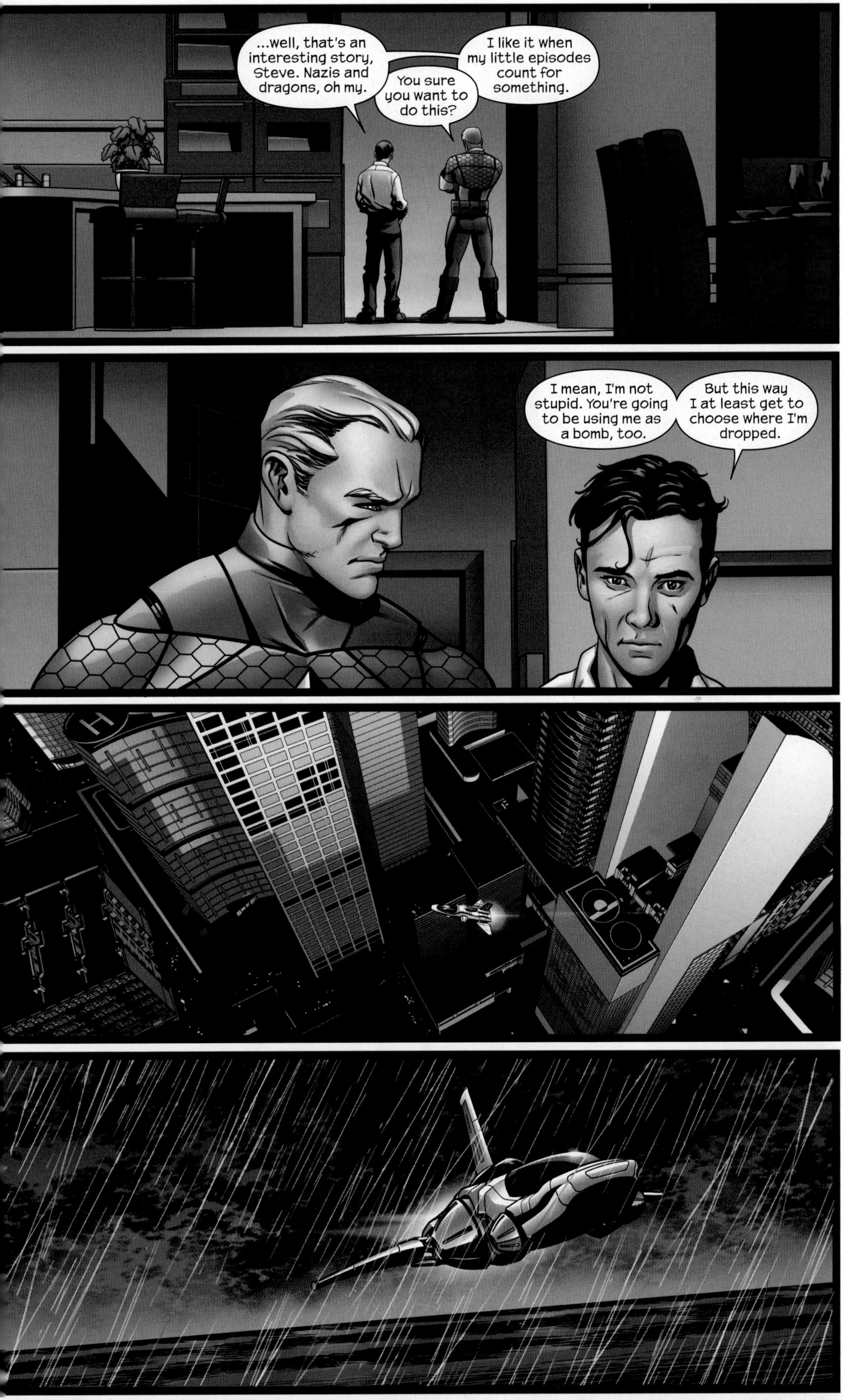
...well, that's an interesting story, Steve. Nazis and dragons, oh my.
You sure you want to do this?
I like it when my little episodes count for something.
I mean, I'm not stupid. You're going to be using me as a bomb, too.
But this way I at least get to choose where I'm dropped.

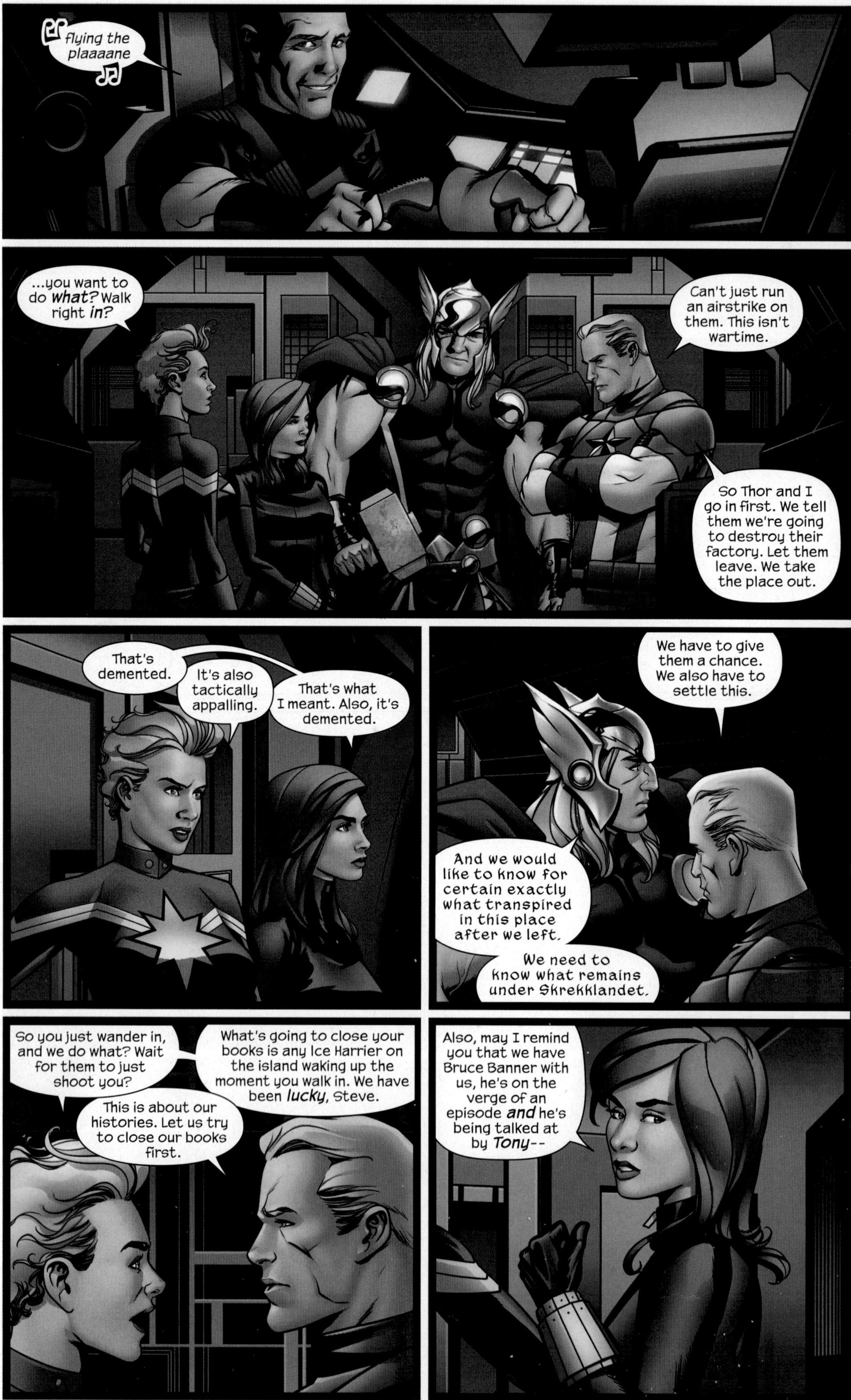
flying the plaaaane
...you want to do what? Walk right in?
Can't just run an airstrike on them. This isn't wartime.
So Thor and I go in first. We tell them we're going to destroy their factory. Let them leave. We take the place out.
That's demented.
It's also tactically appalling.
That's what I meant. Also, it's demented.
We have to give them a chance. We also have to settle this.
And we would like to know for certain exactly what transpired in this place after we left.
We need to know what remains under Skrekklandet.
So you just wander in, and we do what? Wait for them to just shoot you?
What's going to close your books is any Ice Harrier on the island waking up the moment you walk in. We have been lucky, Steve.
This is about our histories. Let us try to close our books first.
Also, may I remind you that we have Bruce Banner with us, he's on the verge of an episode and he's being talked at by Tony--

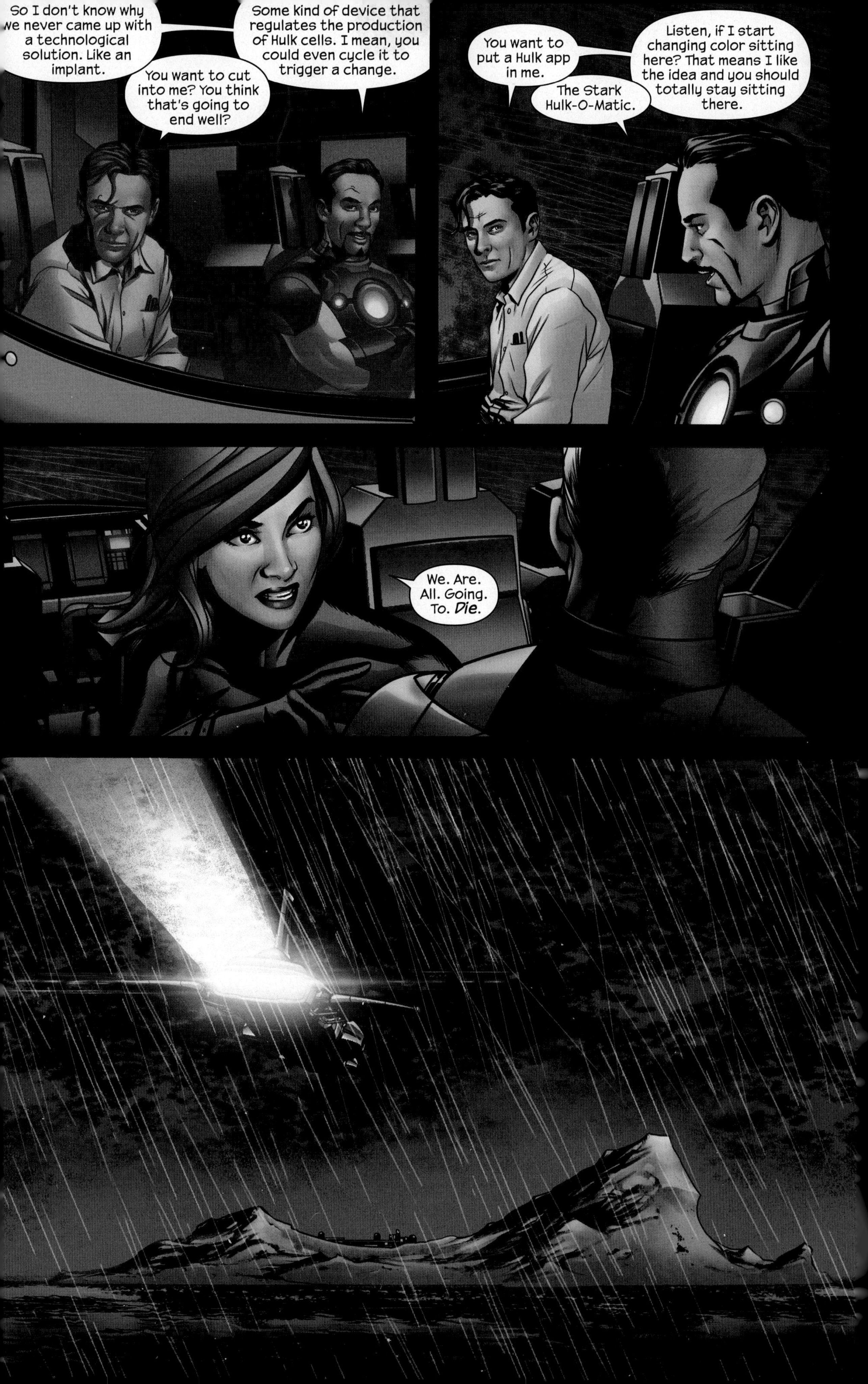
So I don't know why we never came up with a technological solution. Like an implant.
Some kind of device that regulates the production of Hulk cells. I mean, you could even cycle it to trigger a change.
You want to cut into me? You think that's going to end well?
You want to put a Hulk app in me.
The Stark Hulk-O-Matic.
Listen, if I start changing color sitting here? That means I like the idea and you should totally stay sitting there.
We. Are. All. Going. To. *Die*.

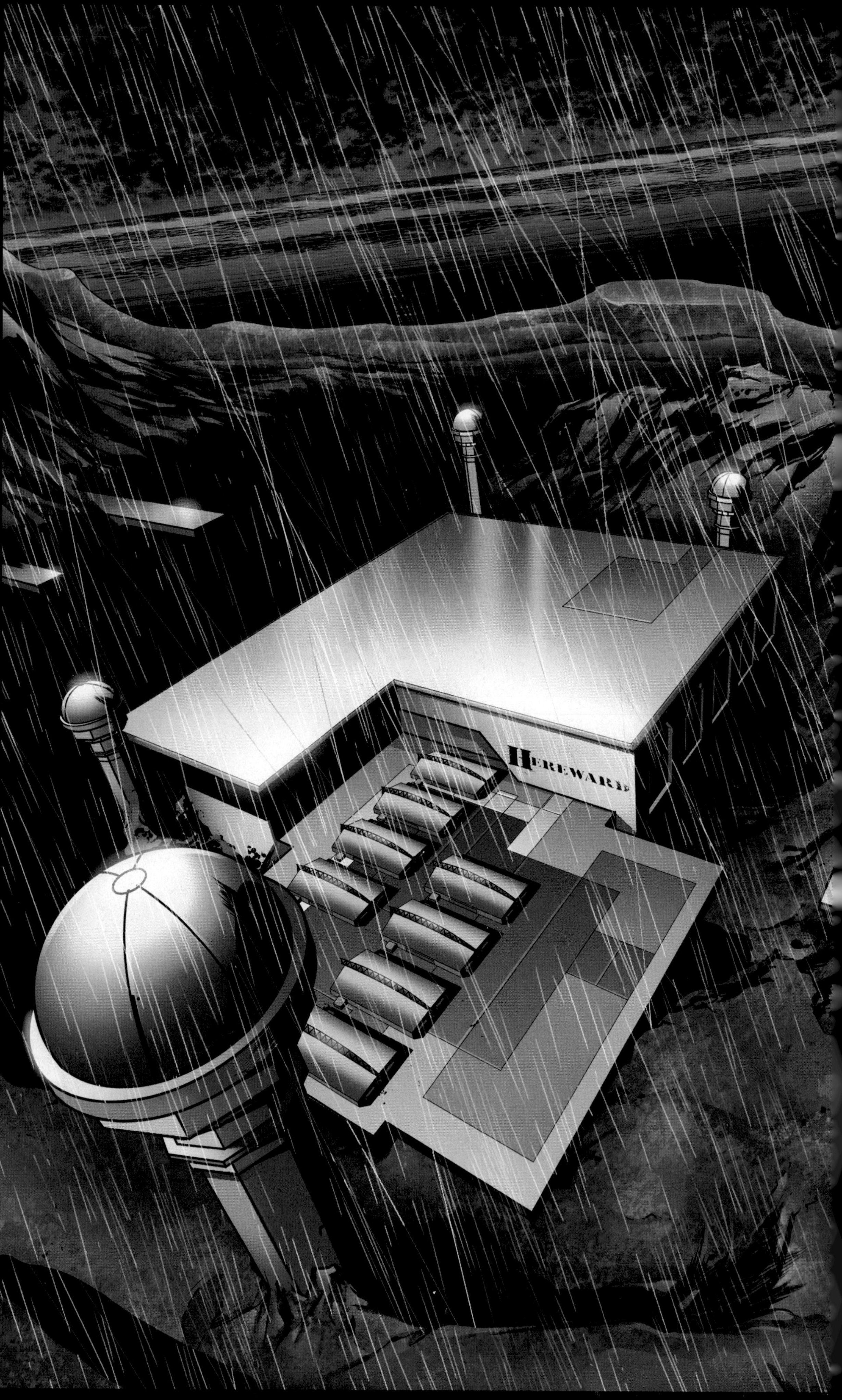
HEREWARD

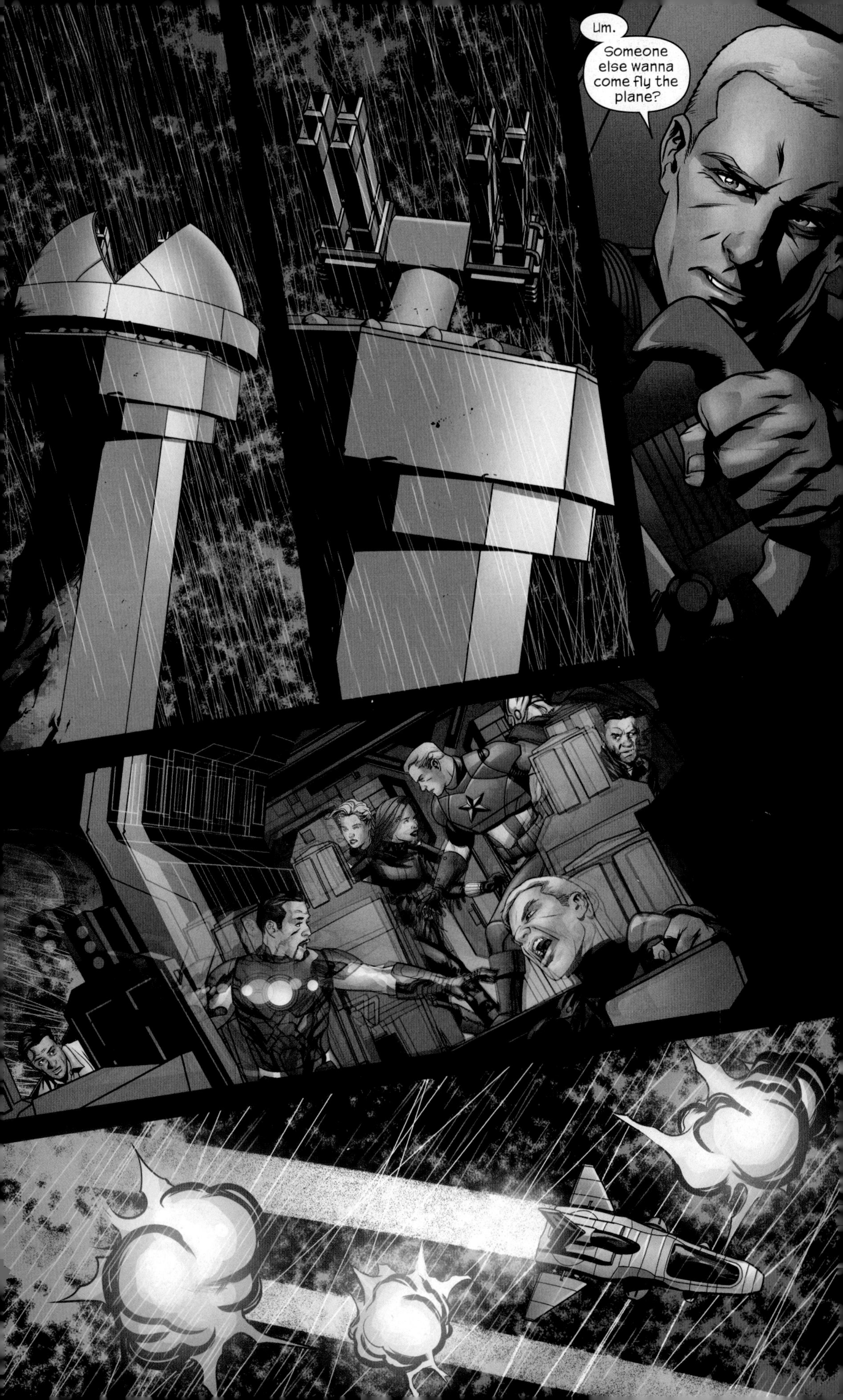
Um.
Someone else wanna come fly the plane?

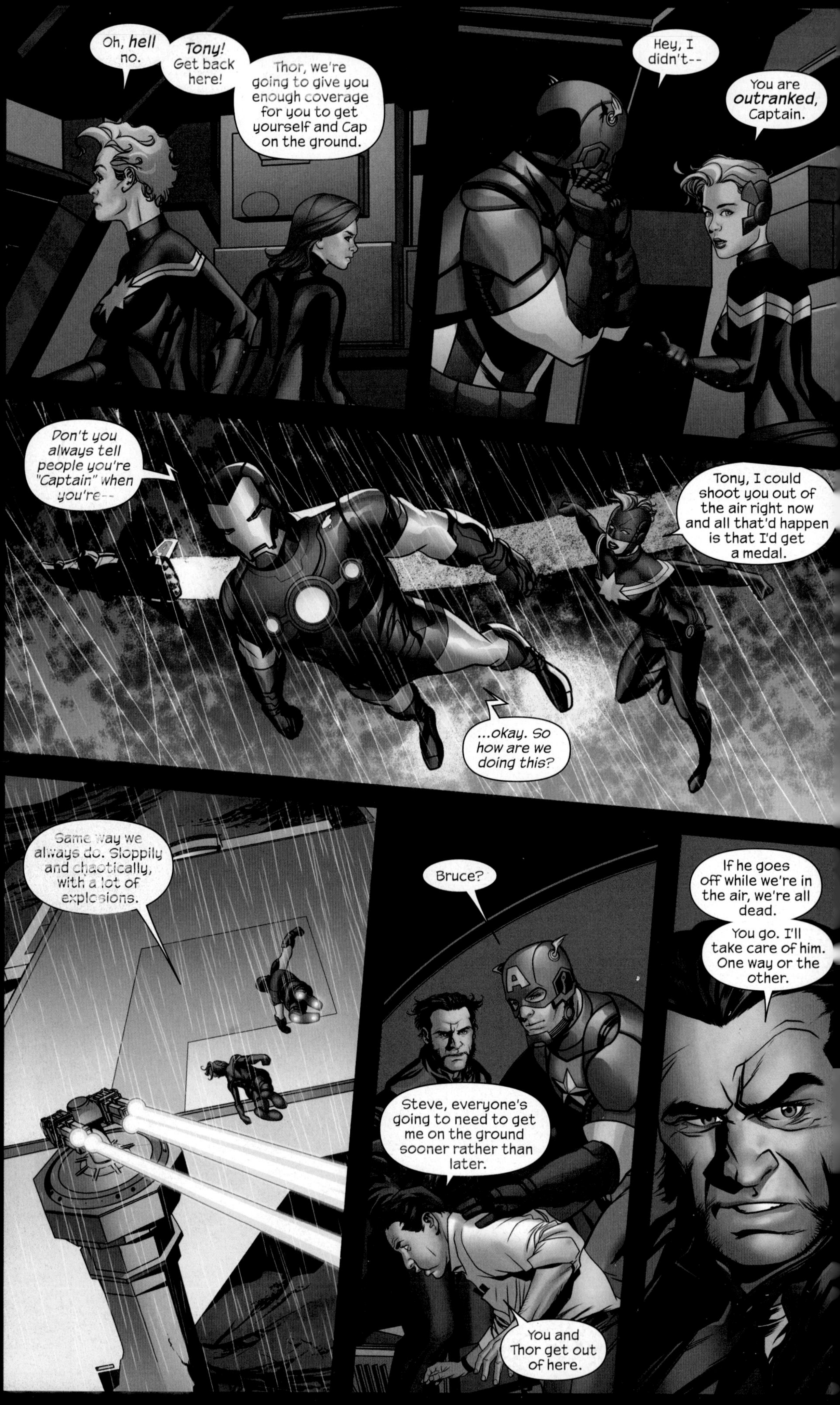

Oh, hell no.
Tony! Get back here!
Thor, we're going to give you enough coverage for you to get yourself and Cap on the ground.
Hey, I didn't--
You are outranked, Captain.
Don't you always tell people you're "Captain" when you're--
Tony, I could shoot you out of the air right now and all that'd happen is that I'd get a medal.
...okay. So how are we doing this?
Same way we always do. Sloppily and chaotically, with a lot of explosions.
Bruce?
Steve, everyone's going to need to get me on the ground sooner rather than later.
If he goes off while we're in the air, we're all dead.
You go. I'll take care of him. One way or the other.
You and Thor get out of here.

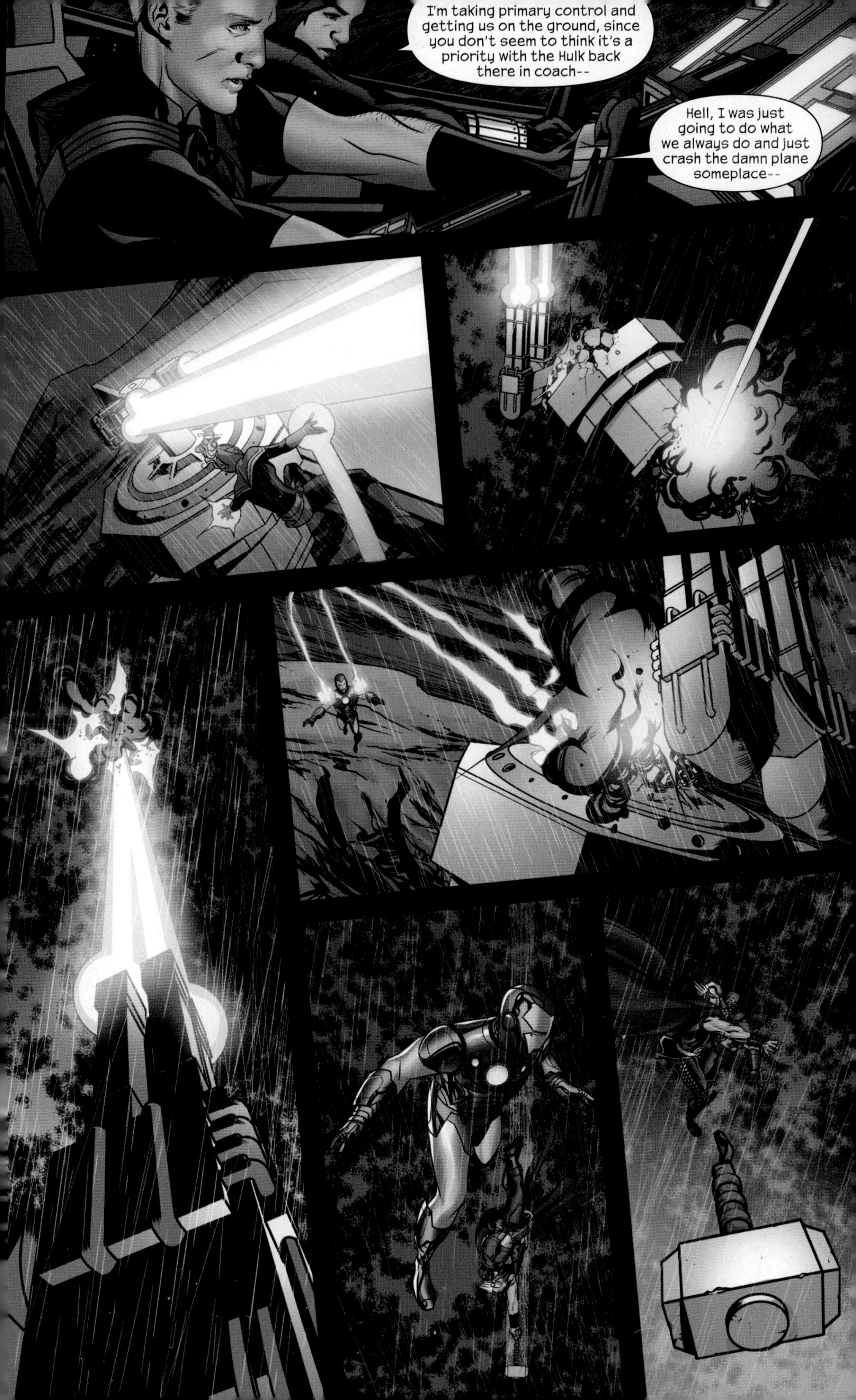
I'm taking primary control and getting us on the ground, since you don't seem to think it's a priority with the Hulk back there in coach--
Hell, I was just going to do what we always do and just crash the damn plane someplace--

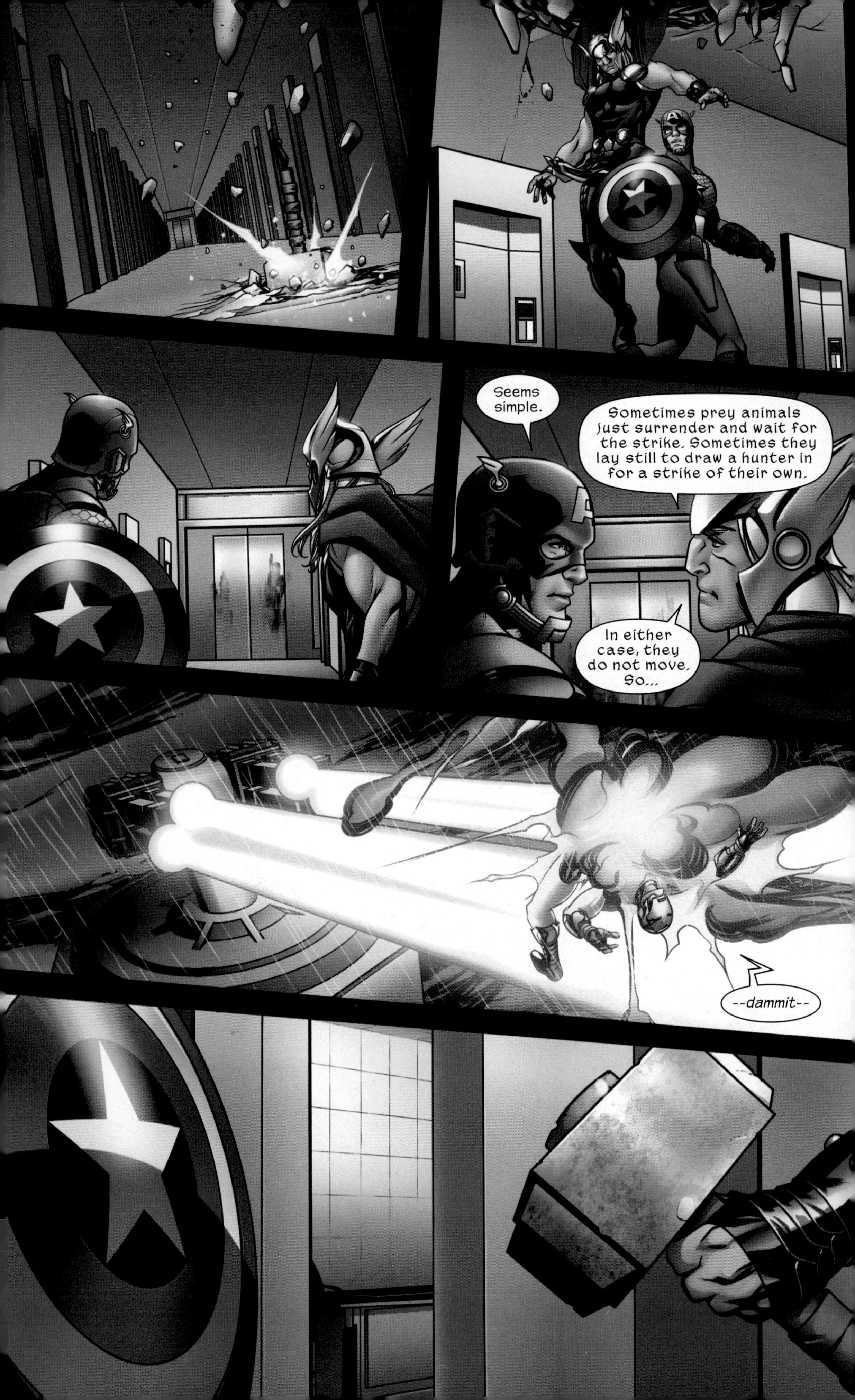
Seems simple.
Sometimes prey animals just surrender and wait for the strike. Sometimes they lay still to draw a hunter in for a strike of their own.
In either case, they do not move. So...
--dammit--

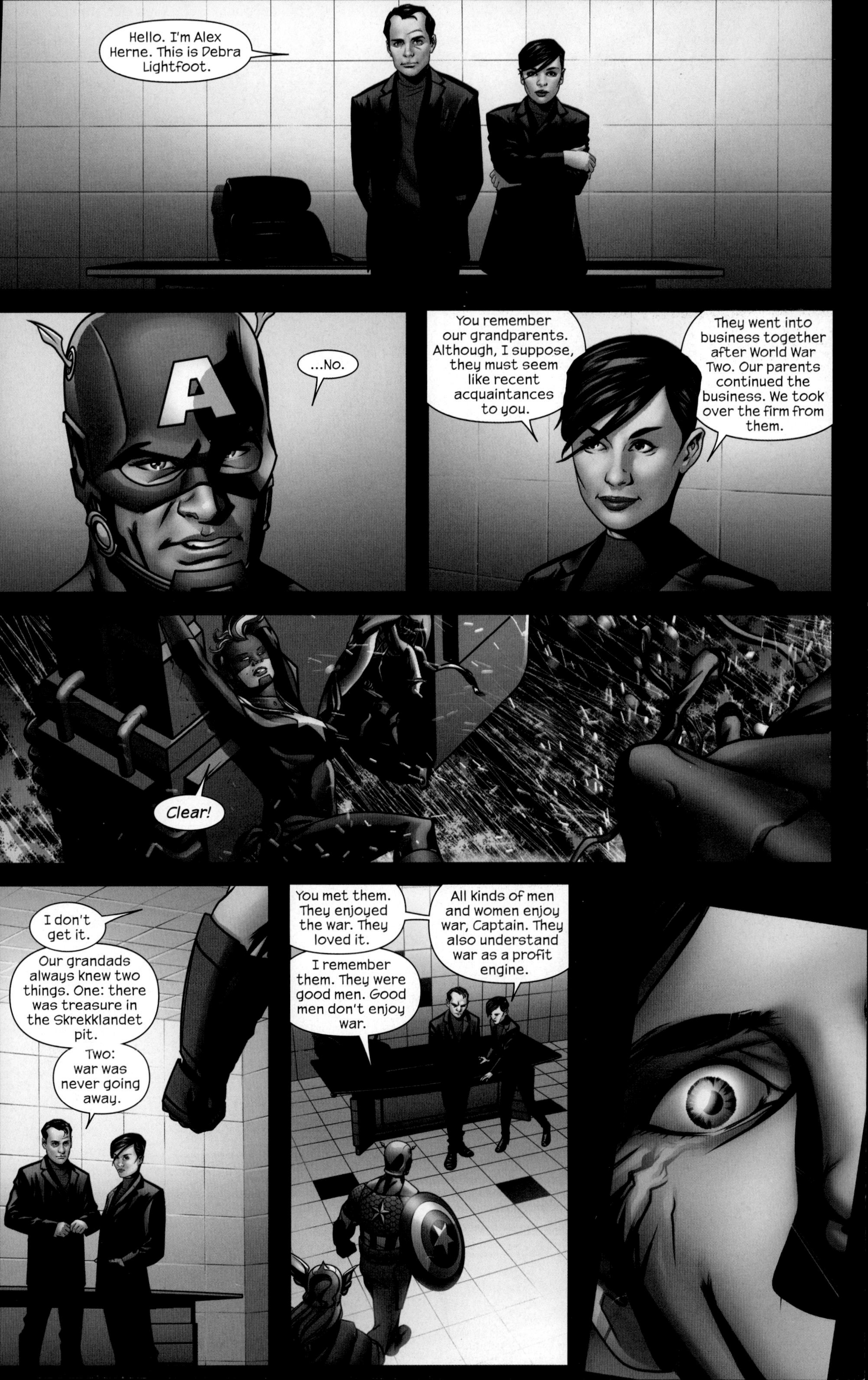

Hello. I'm Alex Herne. This is Debra Lightfoot.
...No.
You remember our grandparents. Although, I suppose, they must seem like recent acquaintances to you.
They went into business together after World War Two. Our parents continued the business. We took over the firm from them.
Clear!
I don't get it.
Our grandads always knew two things. One: there was treasure in the Skrekklandet pit.
Two: war was never going away.
You met them. They enjoyed the war. They loved it.
I remember them. They were good men. Good men don't enjoy war.
All kinds of men and women enjoy war, Captain. They also understand war as a profit engine.

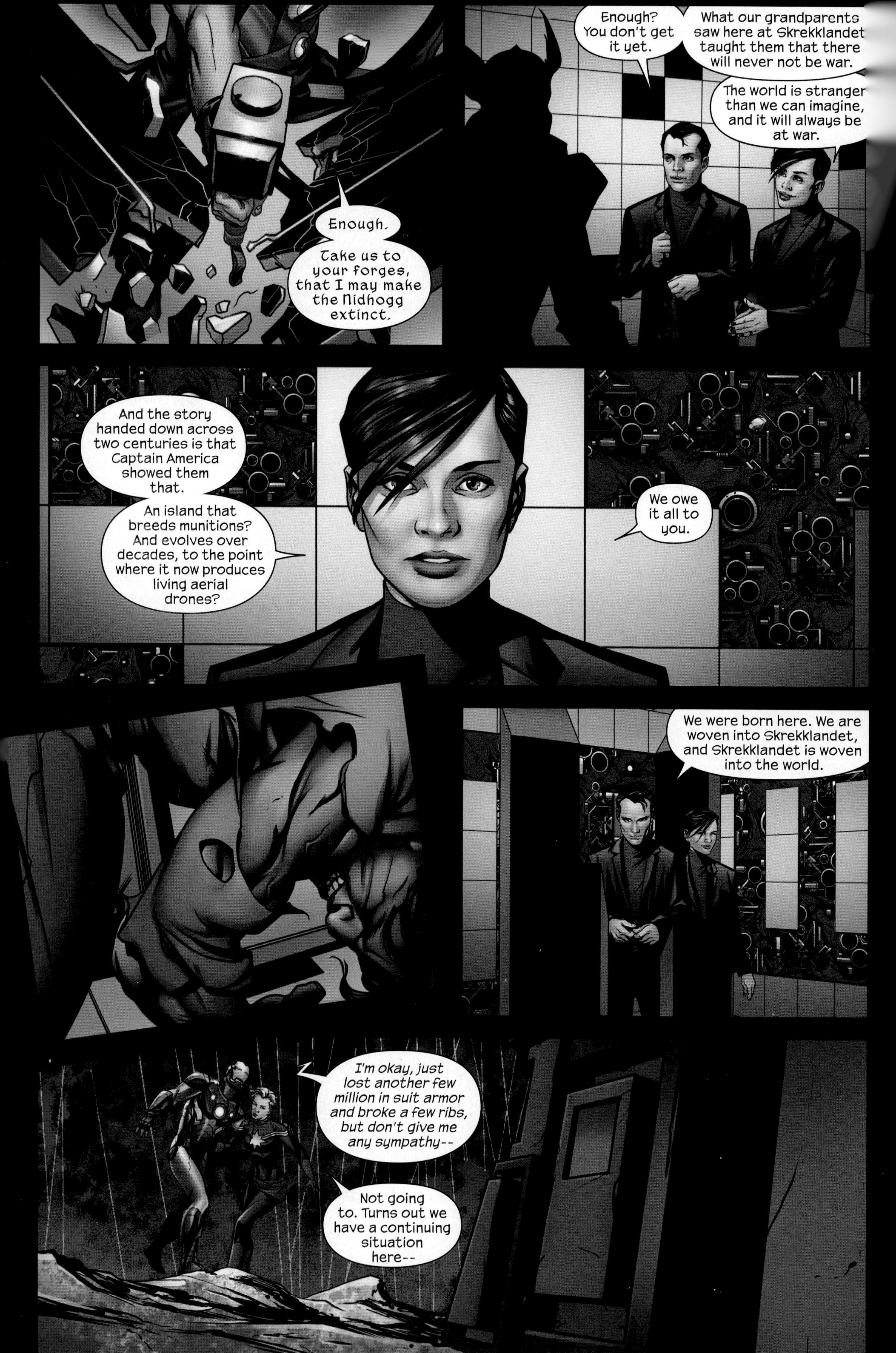
Enough.
Take us to your forges, that I may make the Nidhogg extinct.
Enough? You don't get it yet.
What our grandparents saw here at Skrekklandet taught them that there will never not be war.
The world is stranger than we can imagine, and it will always be at war.
And the story handed down across two centuries is that Captain America showed them that.
An island that breeds munitions? And evolves over decades, to the point where it now produces living aerial drones?
We owe it all to you.
We were born here. We are woven into Skrekklandet, and Skrekklandet is woven into the world.
I'm okay, just lost another few million in suit armor and broke a few ribs, but don't give me any sympathy--
Not going to. Turns out we have a continuing situation here--

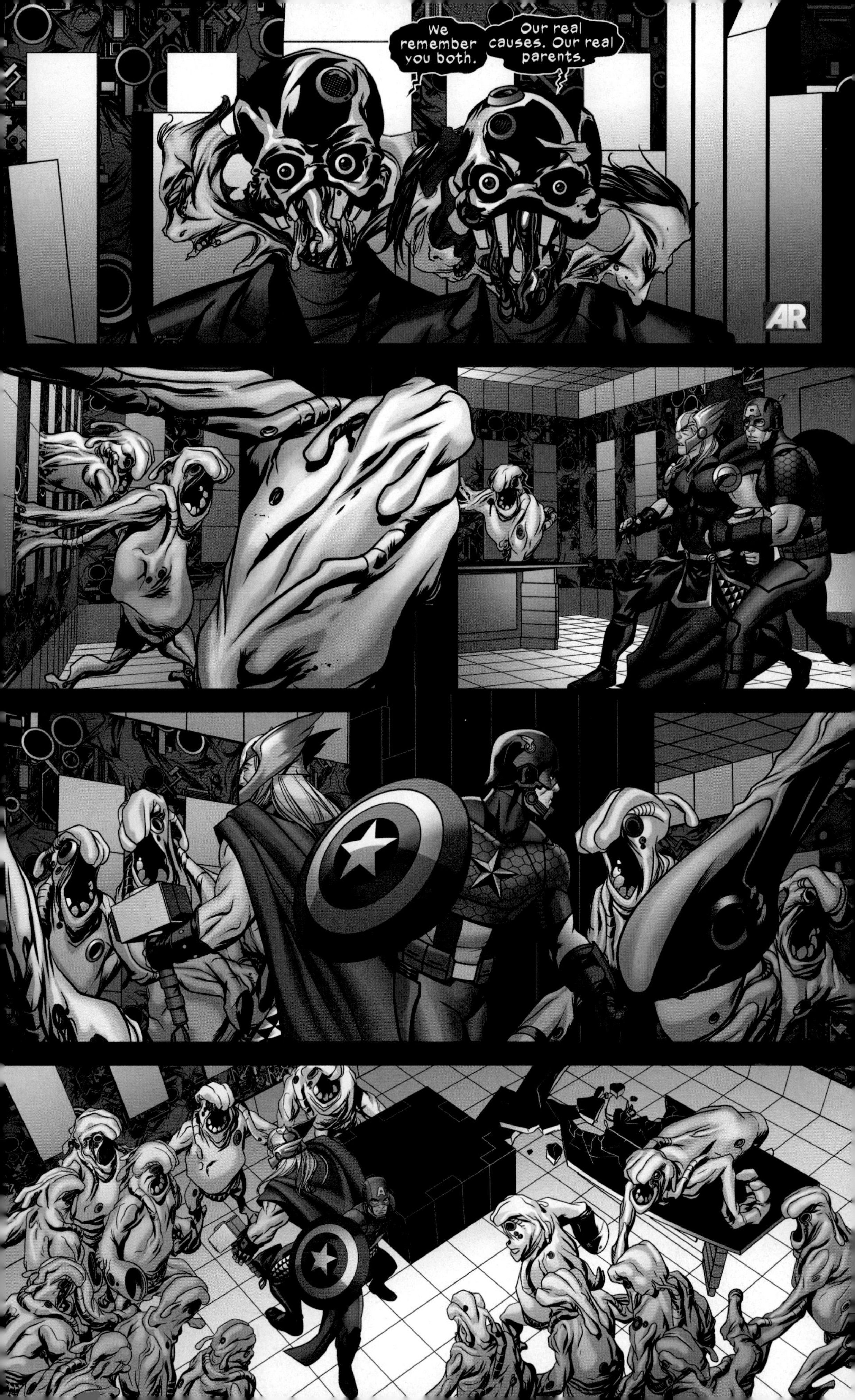
We remember you both.
Our real causes. Our real parents.

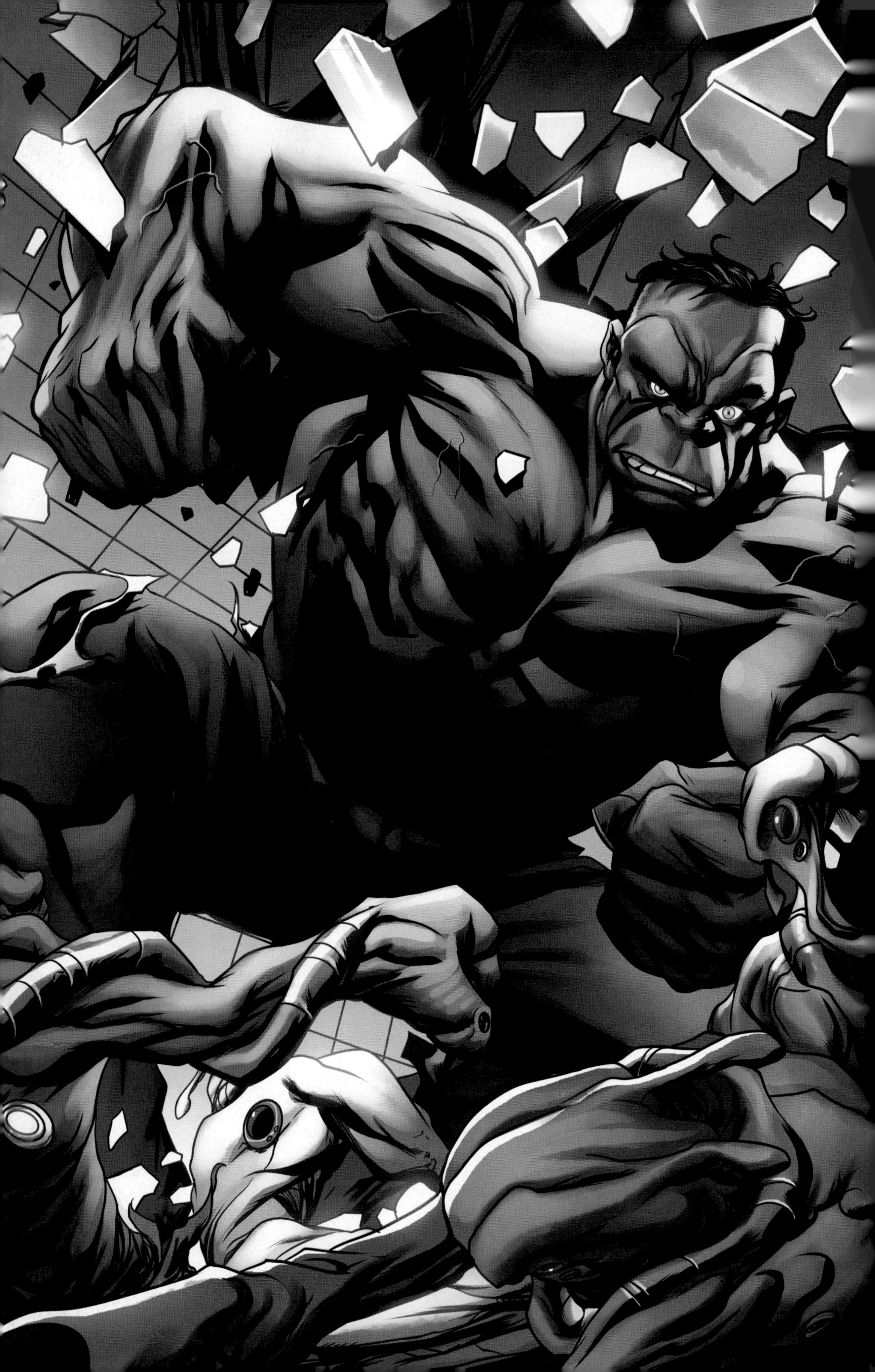

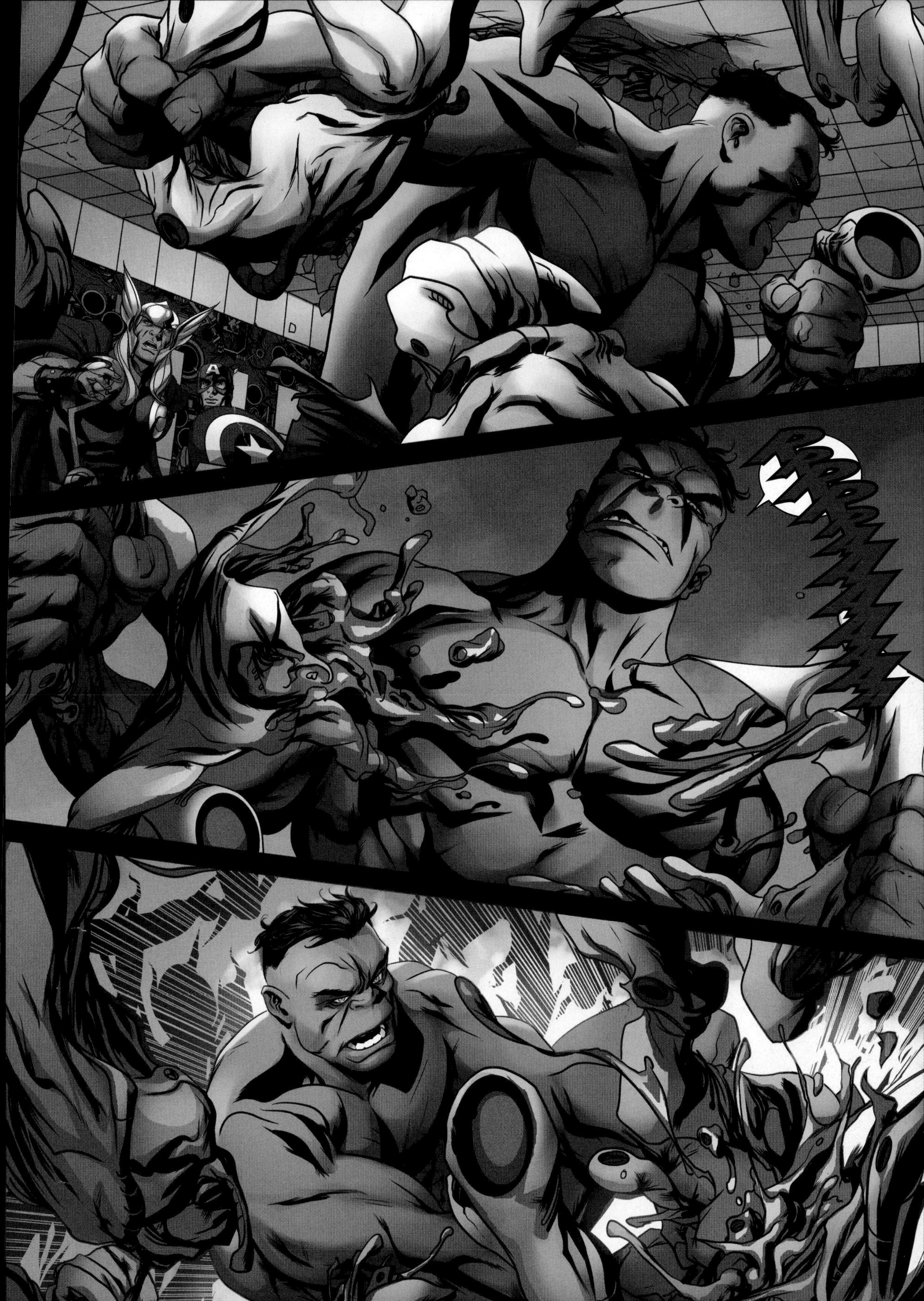

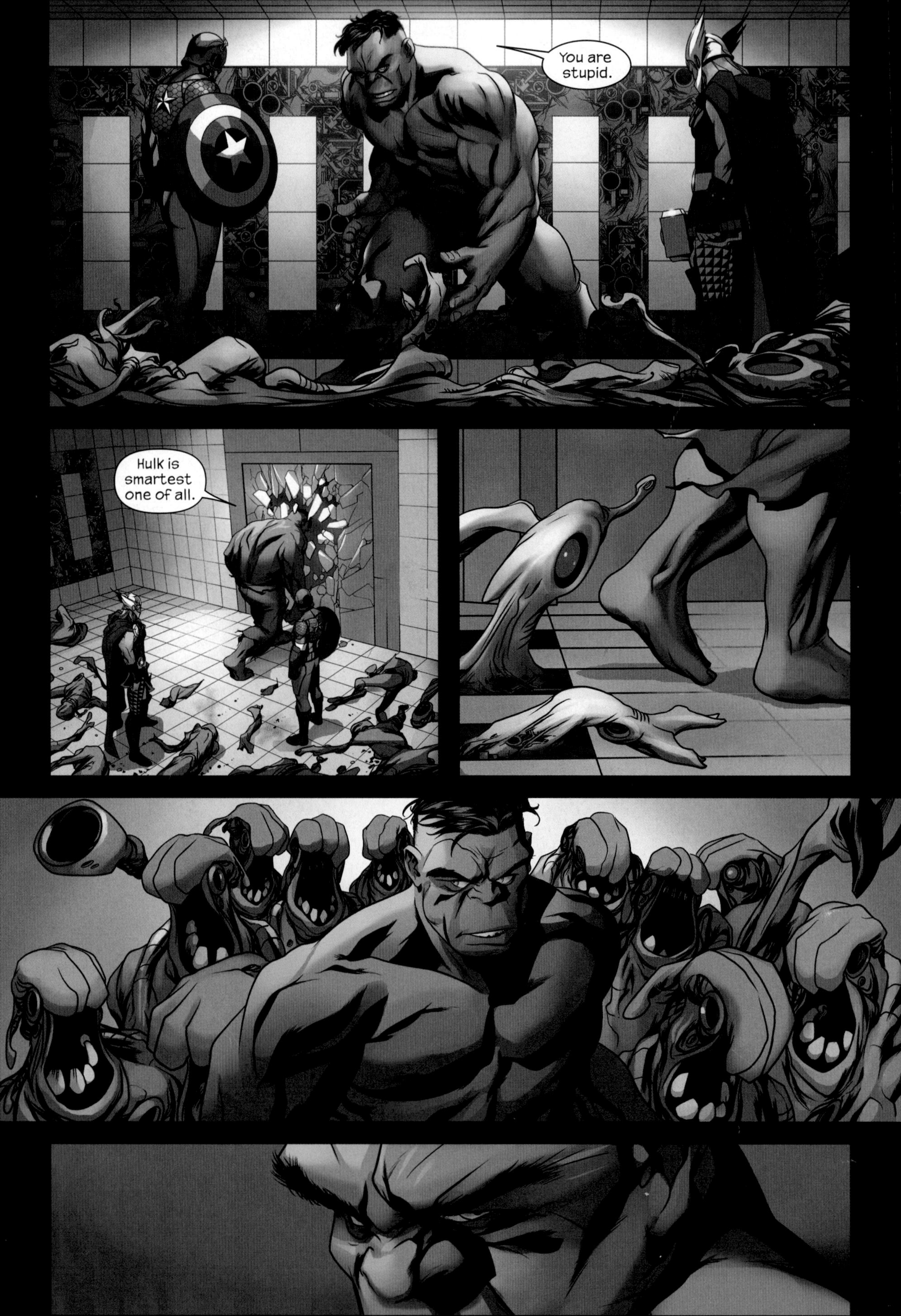
You are stupid.
Hulk is smartest one of all.

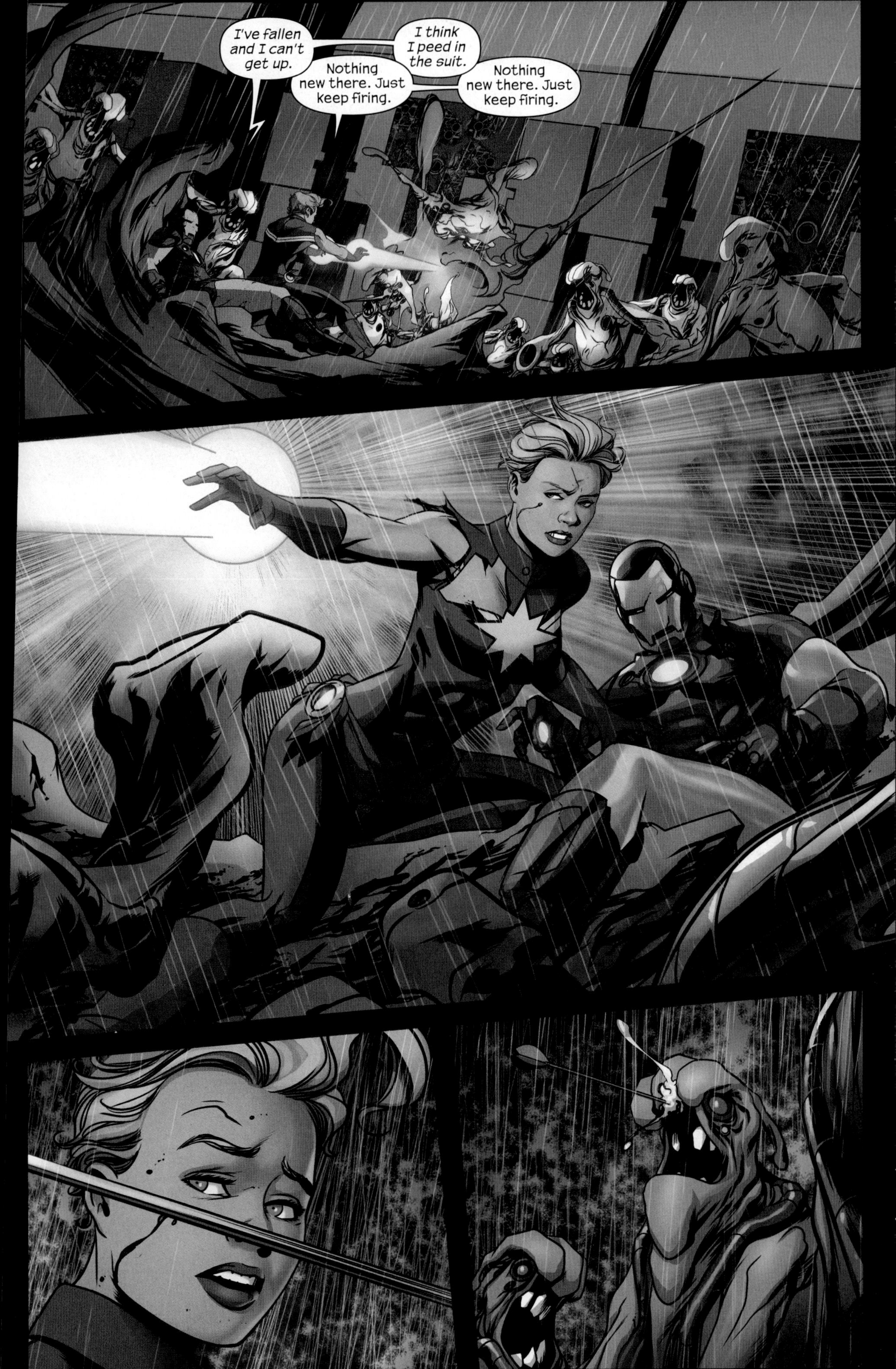
I've fallen and I can't get up.
I think I peed in the suit.
Nothing new there. Just keep firing.
Nothing new there. Just keep firing.

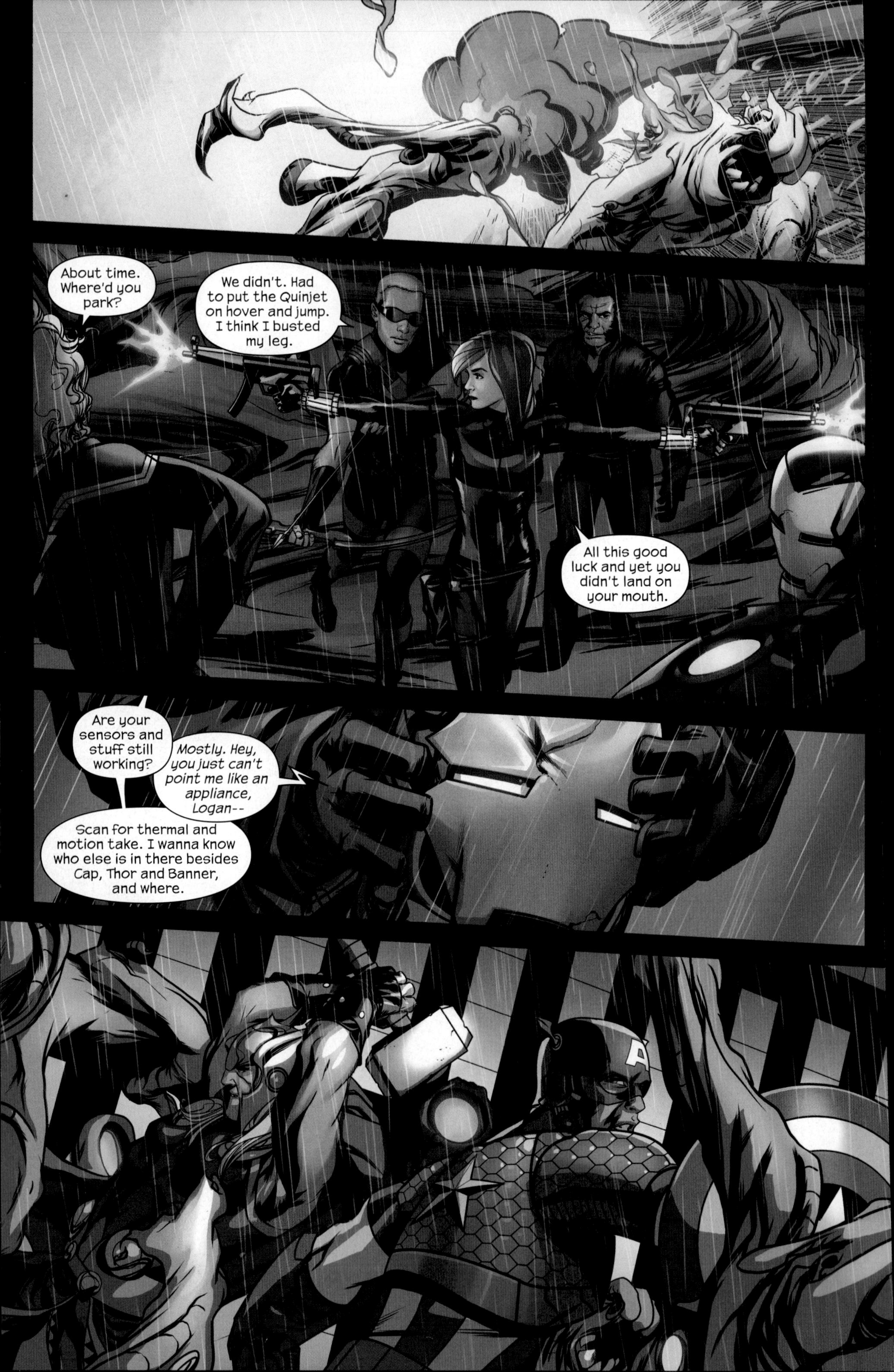
About time. Where'd you park?
We didn't. Had to put the Quinjet on hover and jump. I think I busted my leg.
All this good luck and yet you didn't land on your mouth.
Are your sensors and stuff still working?
Mostly. Hey, you just can't point me like an appliance, Logan--
Scan for thermal and motion take. I wanna know who else is in there besides Cap, Thor and Banner, and where.

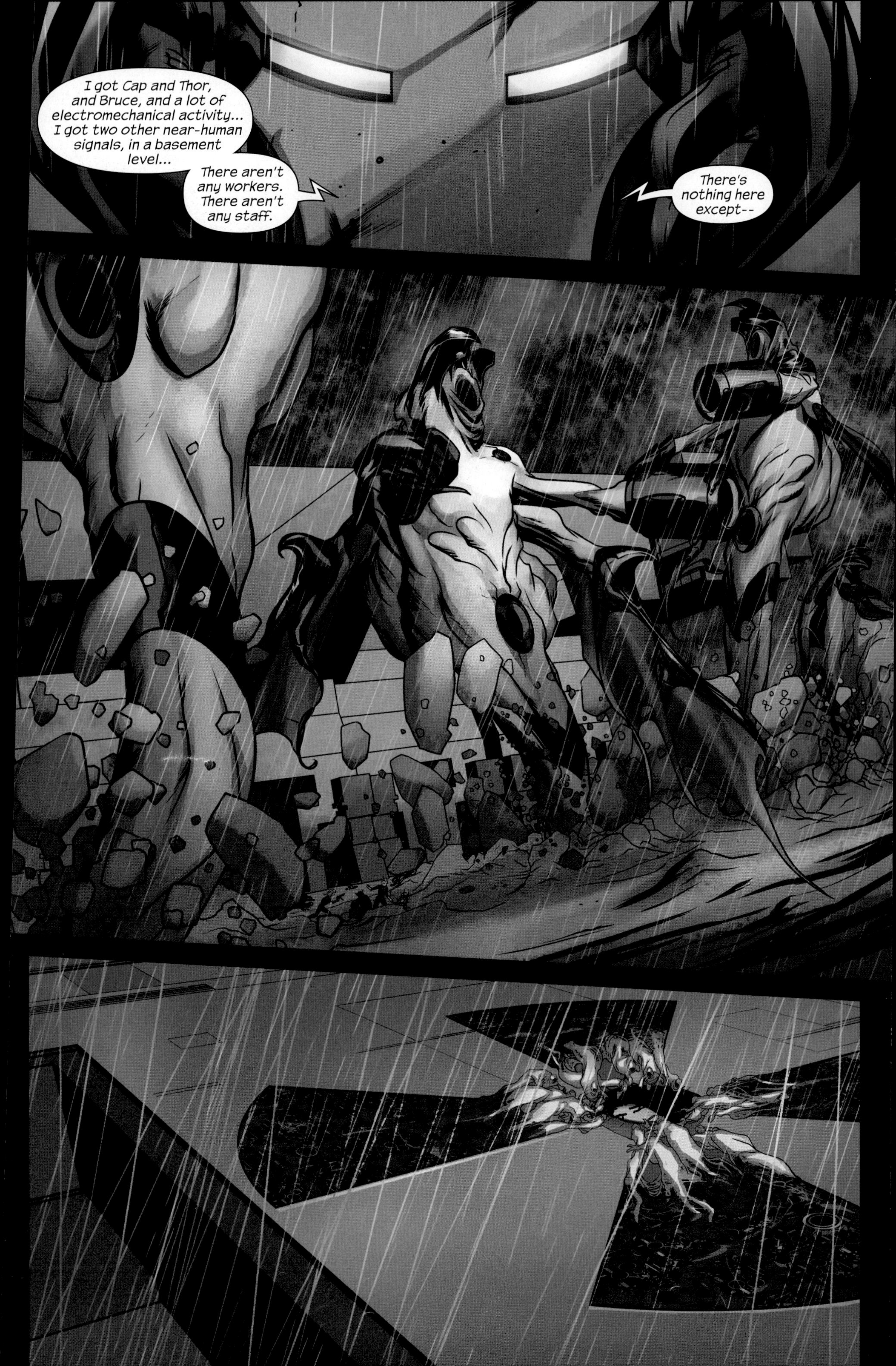

I got Cap and Thor, and Bruce, and a lot of electromechanical activity... I got two other near-human signals, in a basement level...
There aren't any workers. There aren't any staff.
There's nothing here except--

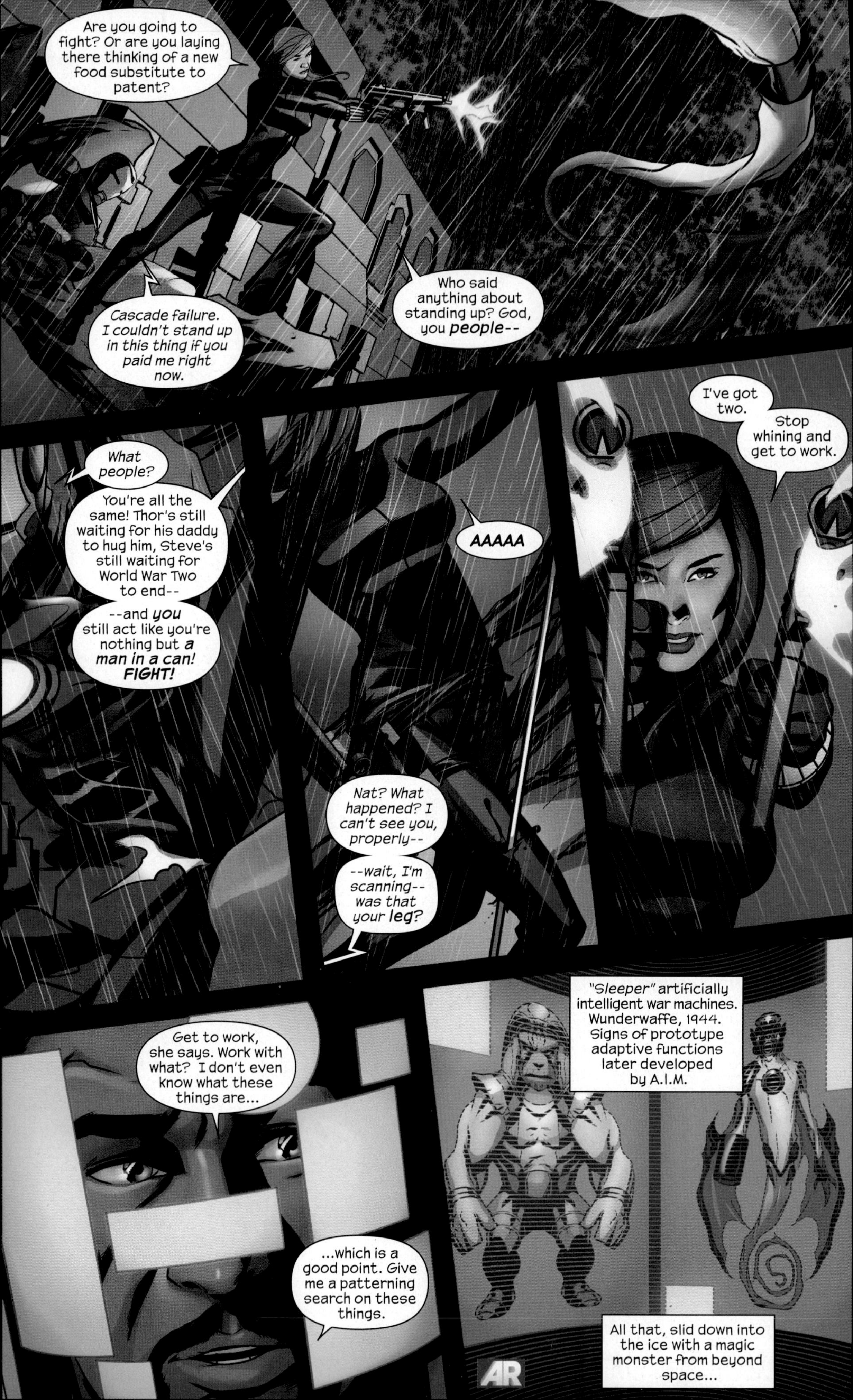

Are you going to fight? Or are you laying there thinking of a new food substitute to patent?
Cascade failure. I couldn't stand up in this thing if you paid me right now.
Who said anything about standing up? God, you *people*--
What people?
You're all the same! Thor's still waiting for his daddy to hug him, Steve's still waiting for World War Two to end--
--and *you* still act like you're nothing but *a man in a can! FIGHT!*
AAAAA
Nat? What happened? I can't see you, properly--
*--wait, I'm scanning-- was that your **leg**?*
I've got two.
Stop whining and get to work.
Get to work, she says. Work with what? I don't even know what these things are...
...which is a good point. Give me a patterning search on these things.
"Sleeper" artificially intelligent war machines. Wunderwaffe, 1944. Signs of prototype adaptive functions later developed by A.I.M.
All that, slid down into the ice with a magic monster from beyond space...
AR

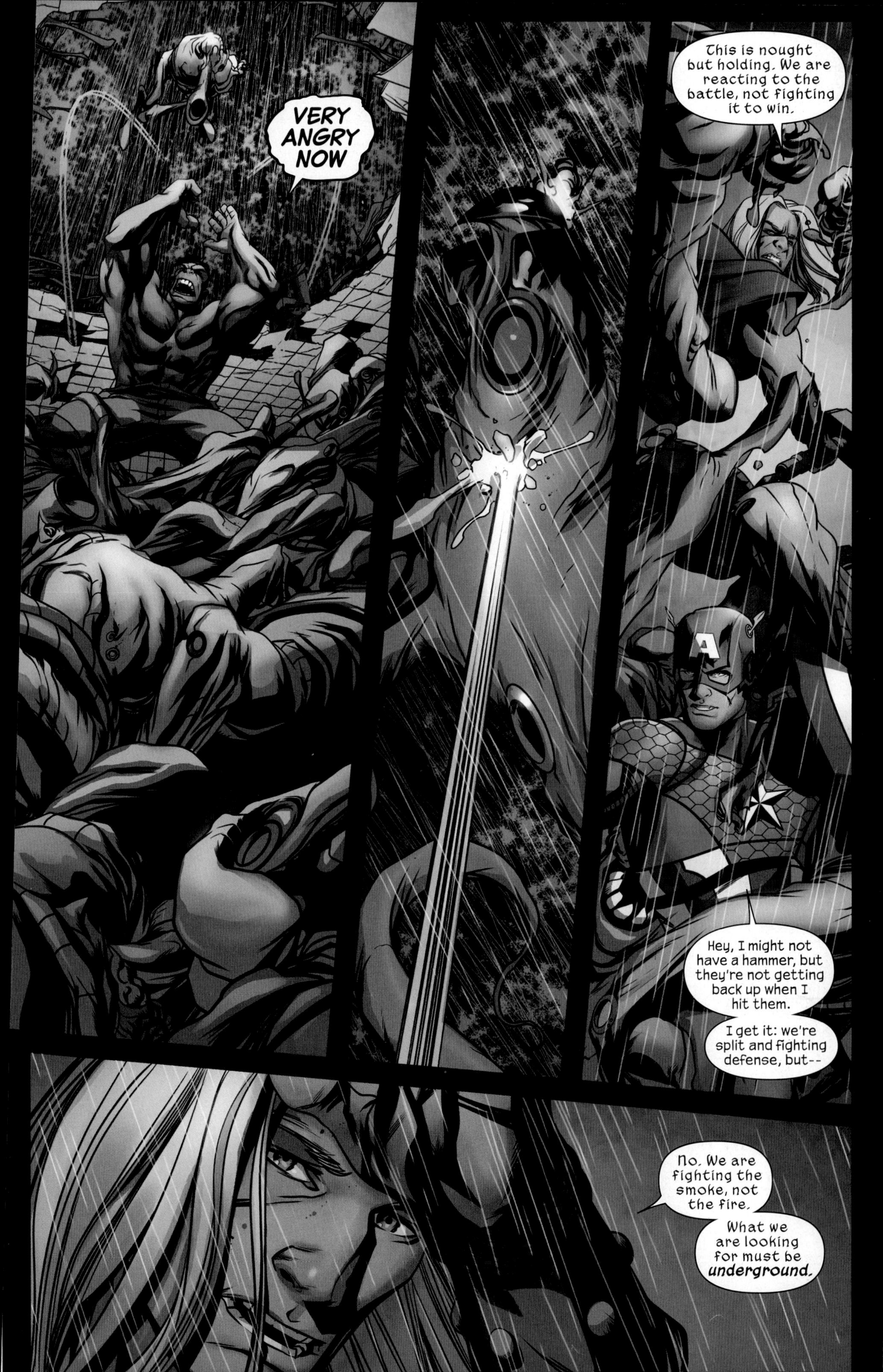
VERY ANGRY NOW
This is nought but holding. We are reacting to the battle, not fighting it to win.
Hey, I might not have a hammer, but they're not getting back up when I hit them.
I get it: we're split and fighting defense, but--
No. We are fighting the smoke, not the fire.
What we are looking for must be *underground.*

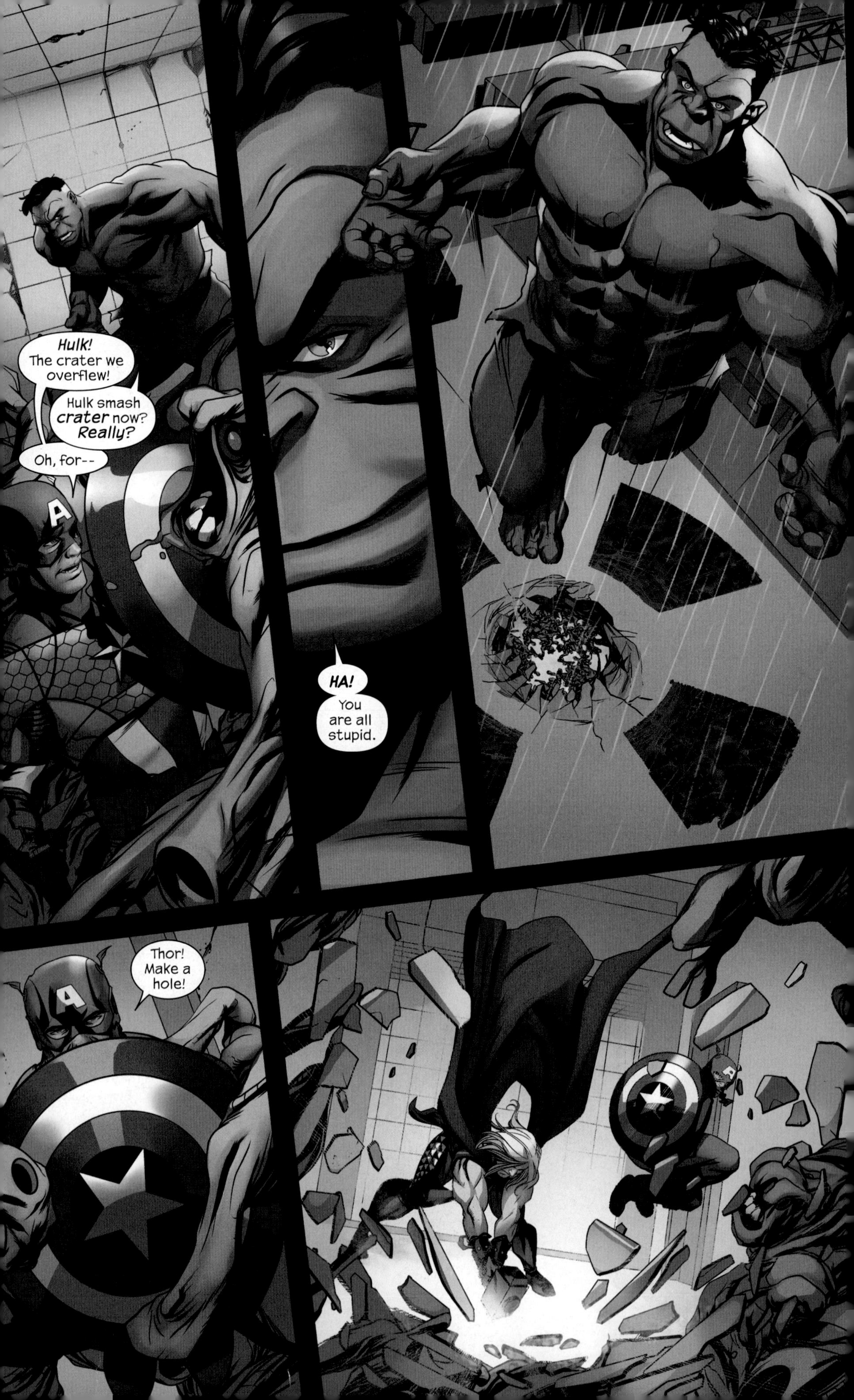
Hulk! The crater we overflew!
Hulk smash crater now? Really?
Oh, for--
HA!
You are all stupid.
Thor! Make a hole!

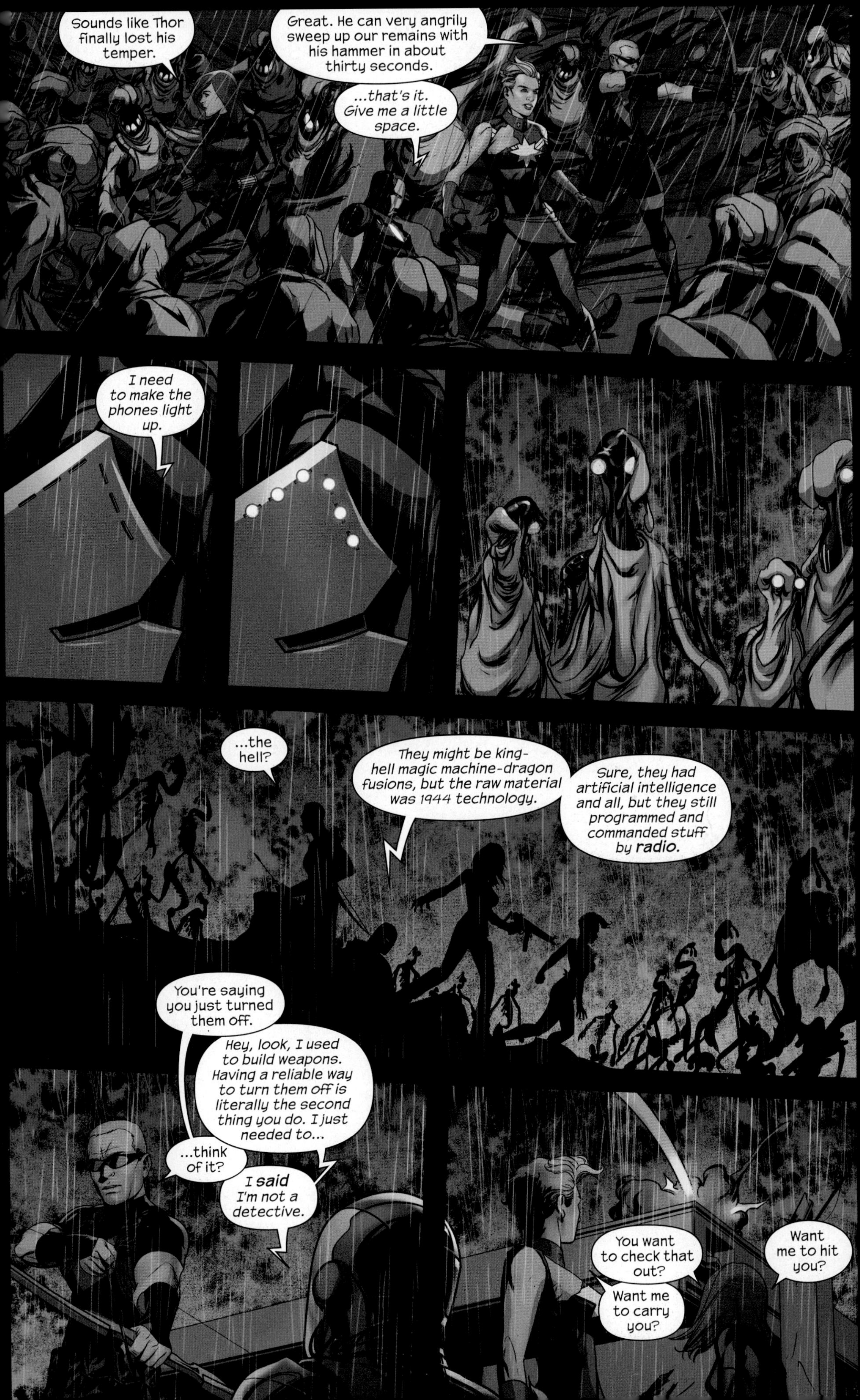
Sounds like Thor finally lost his temper.
Great. He can very angrily sweep up our remains with his hammer in about thirty seconds.
...that's it. Give me a little space.
I need to make the phones light up.
...the hell?
They might be king-hell magic machine-dragon fusions, but the raw material was 1944 technology.
Sure, they had artificial intelligence and all, but they still programmed and commanded stuff by **radio.**
You're saying you just turned them off.
Hey, look, I used to build weapons. Having a reliable way to turn them off is literally the second thing you do. I just needed to...
...think of it?
I **said** I'm not a detective.
You want to check that out?
Want me to carry you?
Want me to hit you?

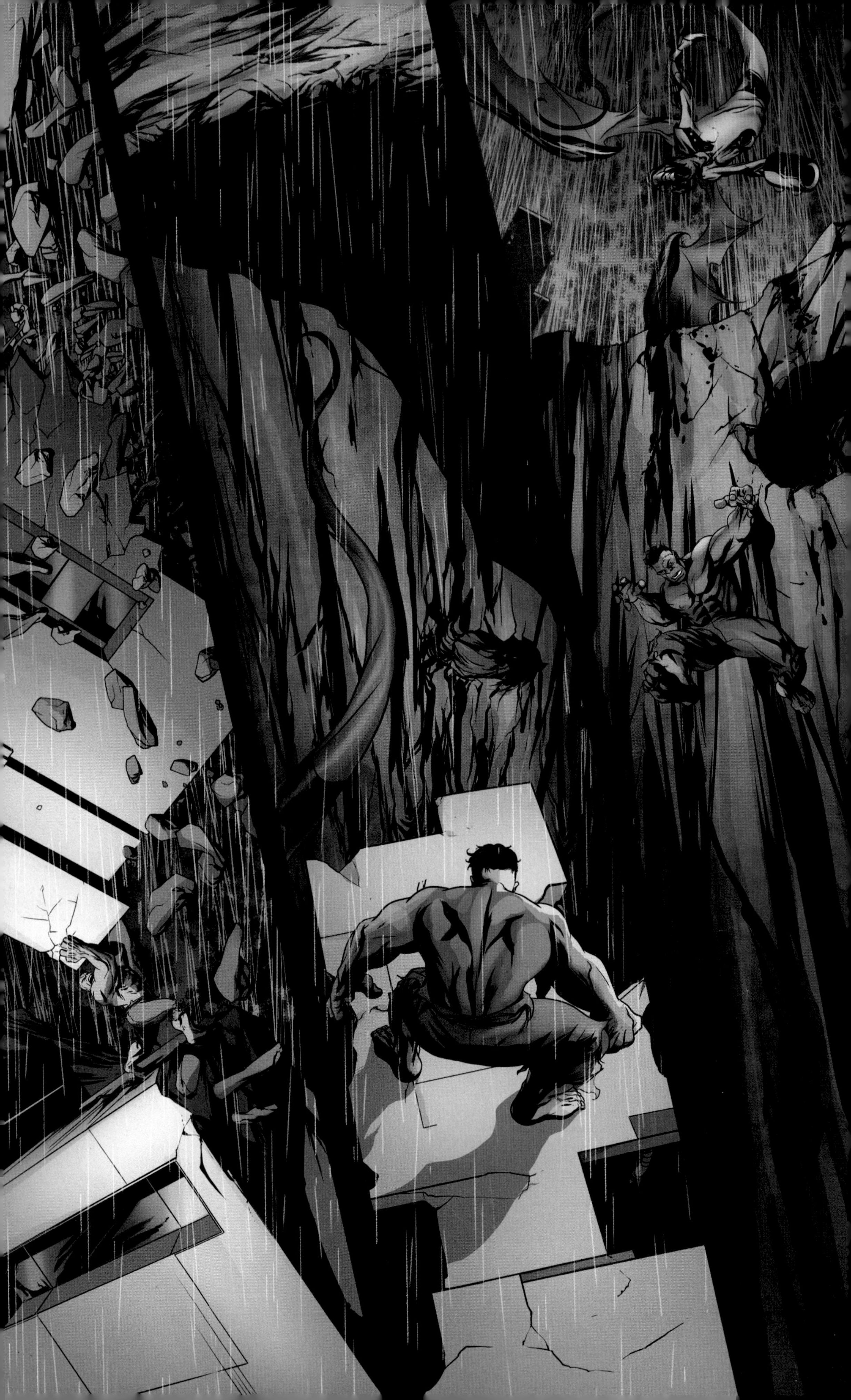

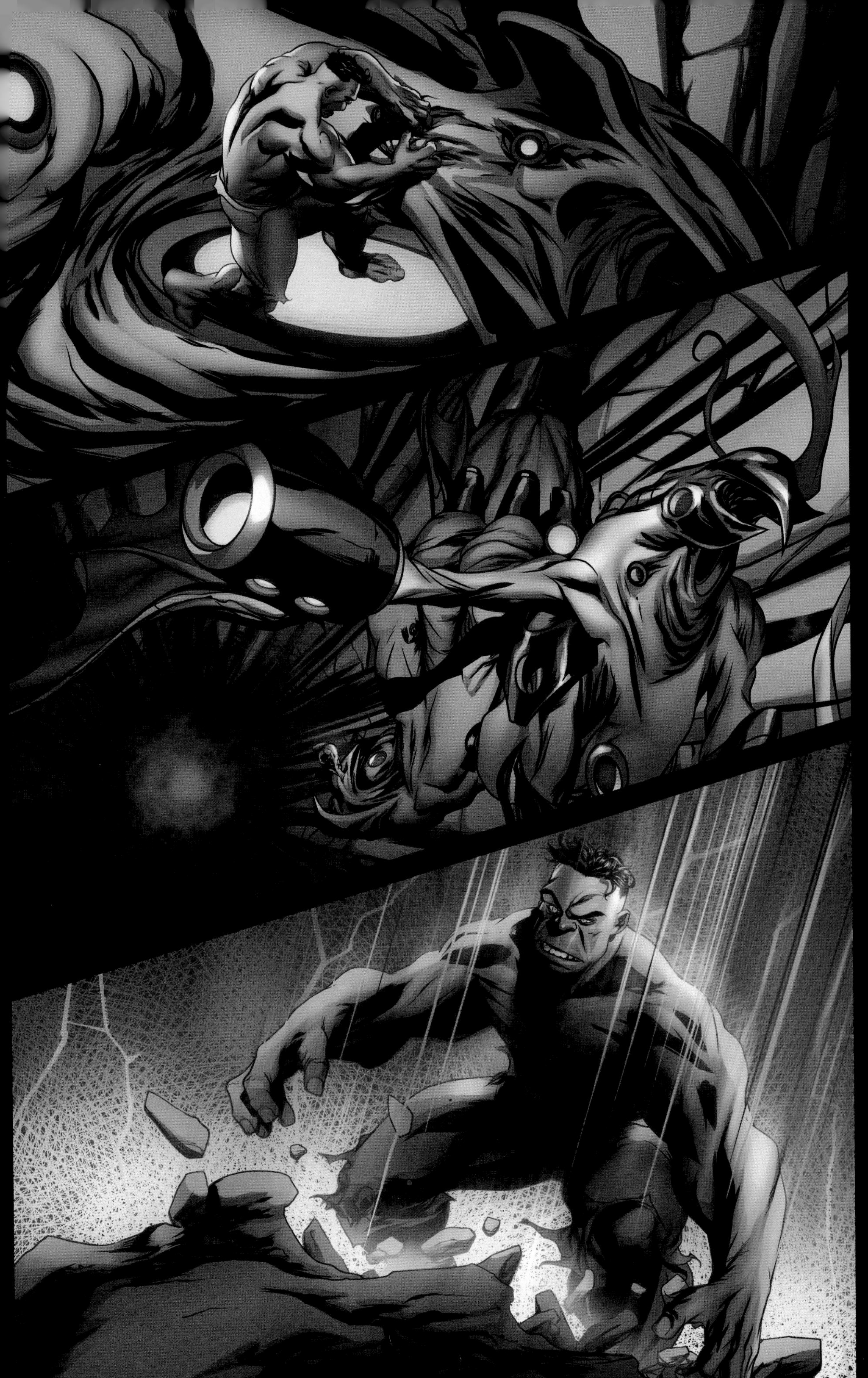

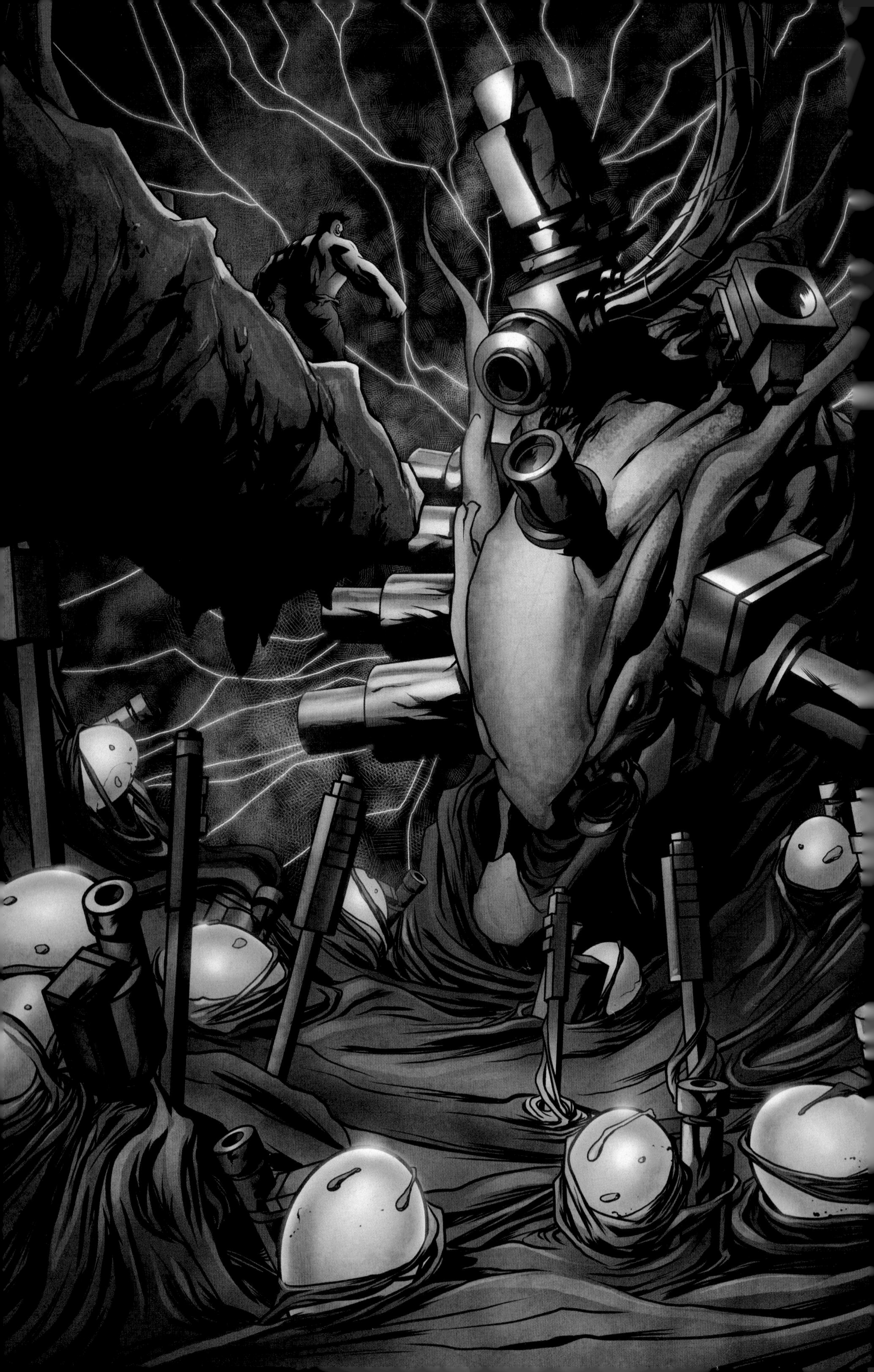

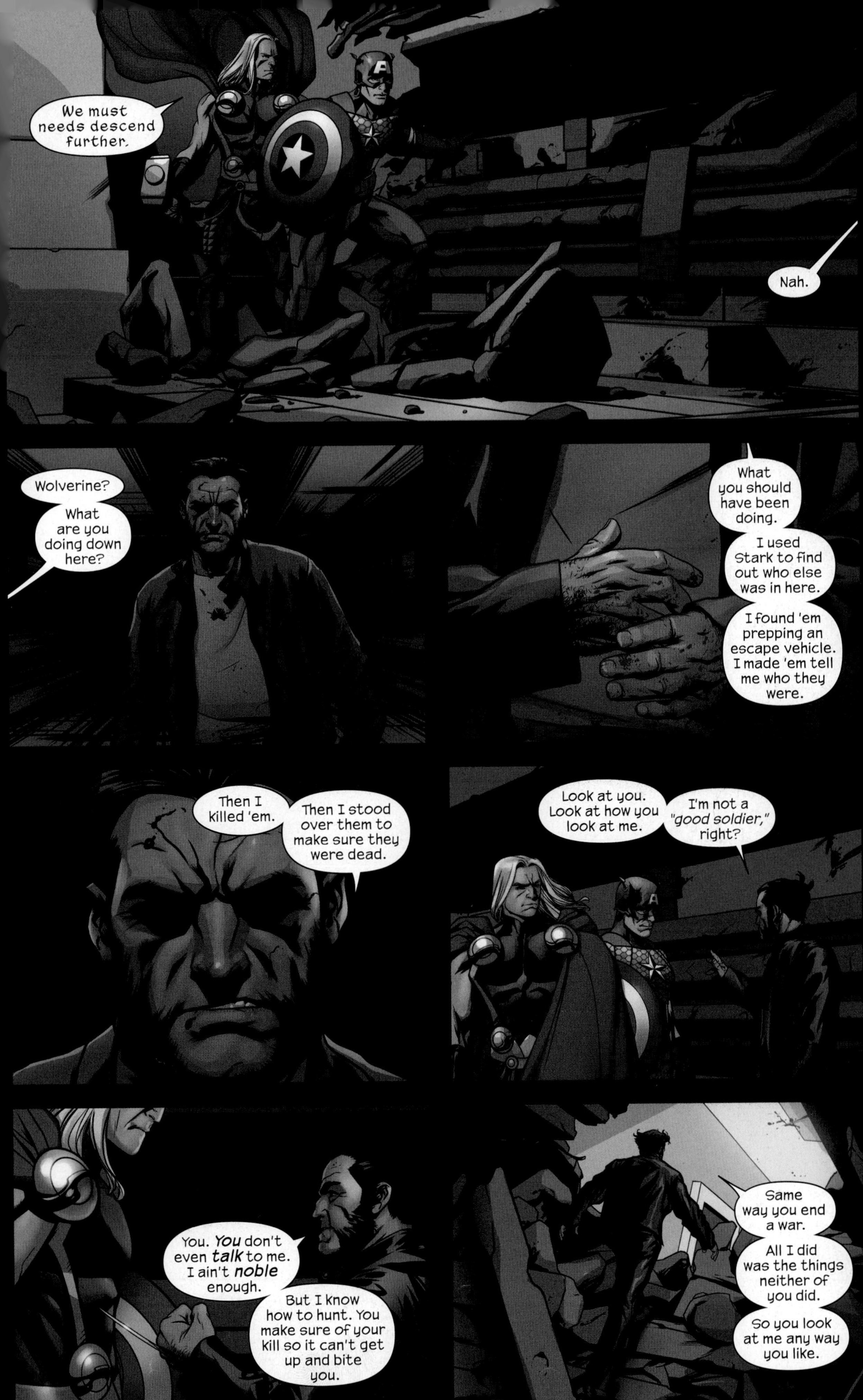
We must needs descend further.
Nah.
Wolverine?
What are you doing down here?
What you should have been doing.
I used Stark to find out who else was in here.
I found 'em prepping an escape vehicle. I made 'em tell me who they were.
Then I killed 'em.
Then I stood over them to make sure they were dead.
Look at you. Look at how you look at me.
I'm not a *"good soldier,"* right?
You. ***You*** don't even ***talk*** to me. I ain't ***noble*** enough.
But I know how to hunt. You make sure of your kill so it can't get up and bite you.
Same way you end a war.
All I did was the things neither of you did.
So you look at me any way you like.

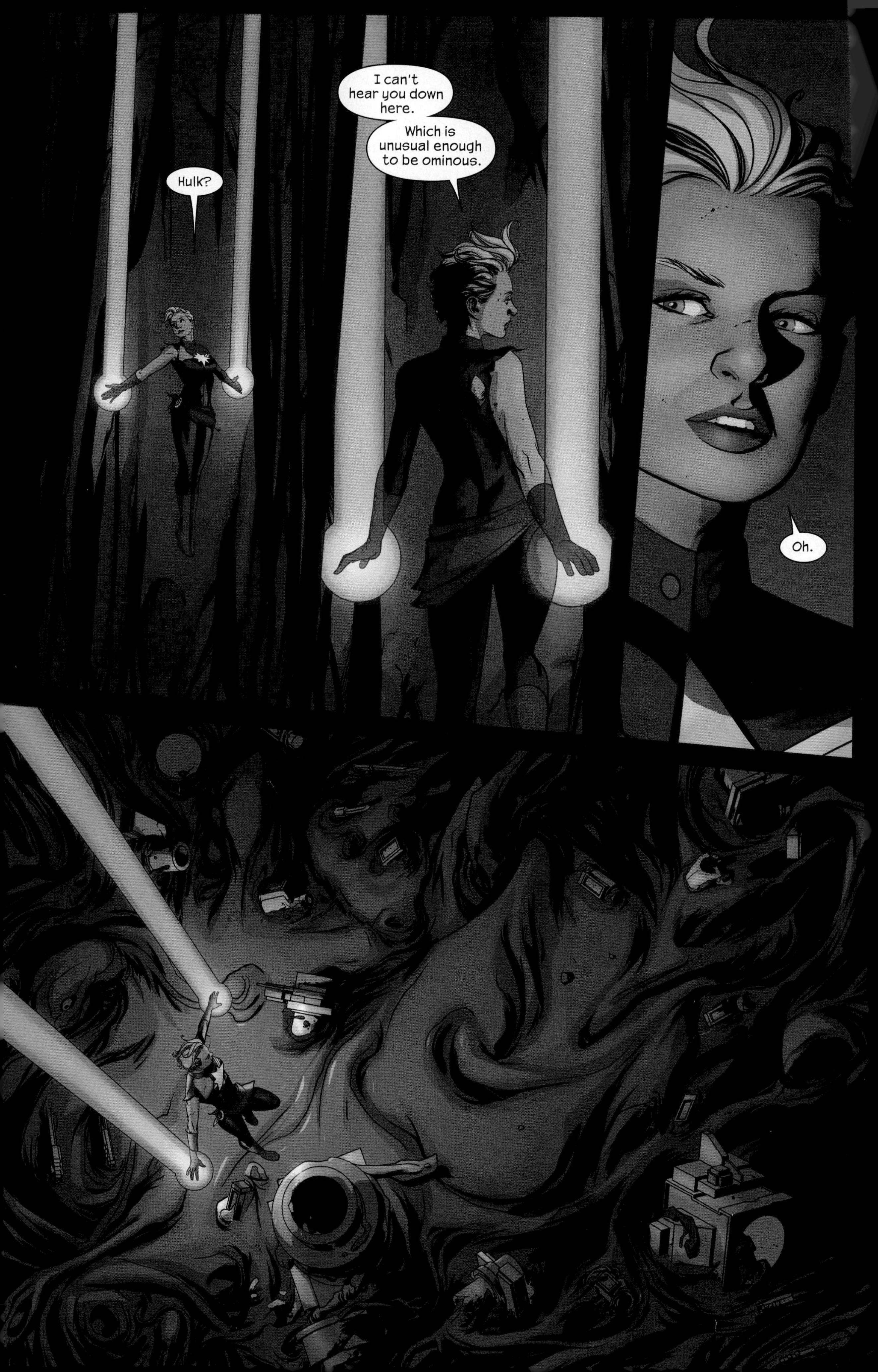
Hulk?
I can't hear you down here.
Which is unusual enough to be ominous.
Oh.

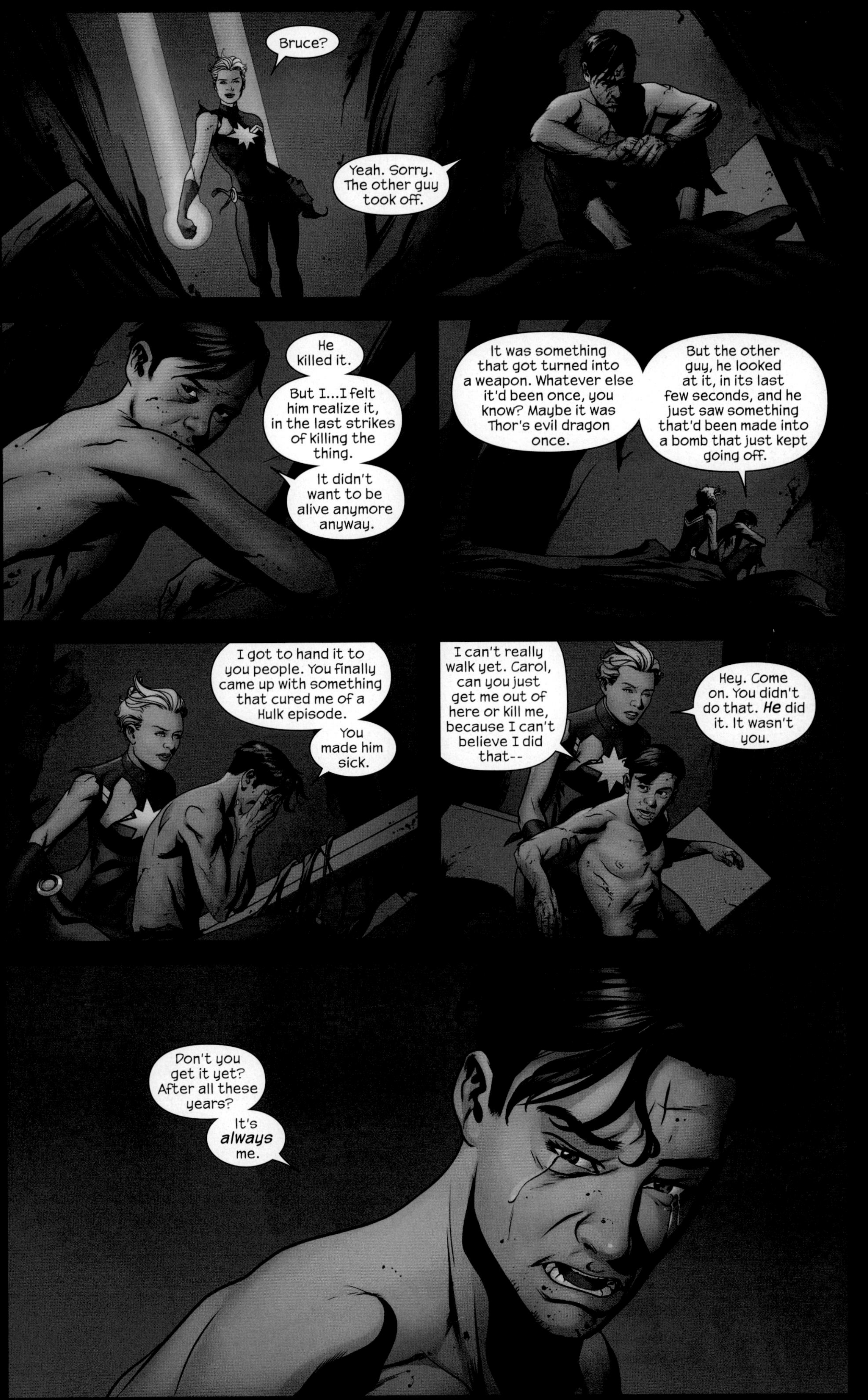
Bruce?
Yeah. Sorry. The other guy took off.
He killed it.
But I...I felt him realize it, in the last strikes of killing the thing.
It didn't want to be alive anymore anyway.
It was something that got turned into a weapon. Whatever else it'd been once, you know? Maybe it was Thor's evil dragon once.
But the other guy, he looked at it, in its last few seconds, and he just saw something that'd been made into a bomb that just kept going off.
I got to hand it to you people. You finally came up with something that cured me of a Hulk episode.
You made him sick.
I can't really walk yet. Carol, can you just get me out of here or kill me, because I can't believe I did that--
Hey. Come on. You didn't do that. *He* did it. It wasn't you.
Don't you get it yet? After all these years?
It's *always* me.

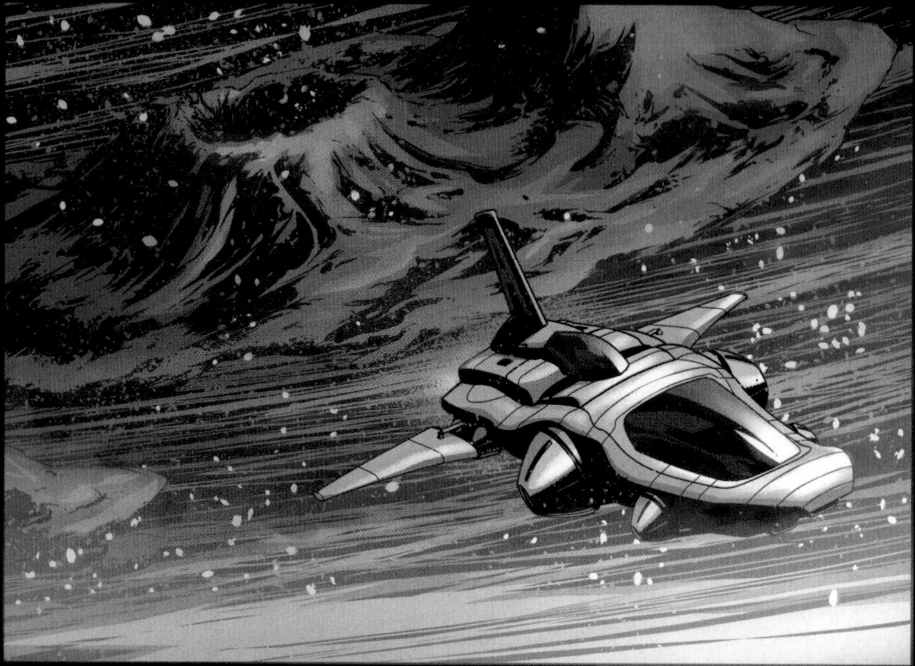

The future is a foreign country. All the things he loved are buried in a century past, and all the things he hated never died. It had occurred to him, more than once, that World War Two was some tarry quicksand that never stopped trying to drag him under the ground where he belonged.

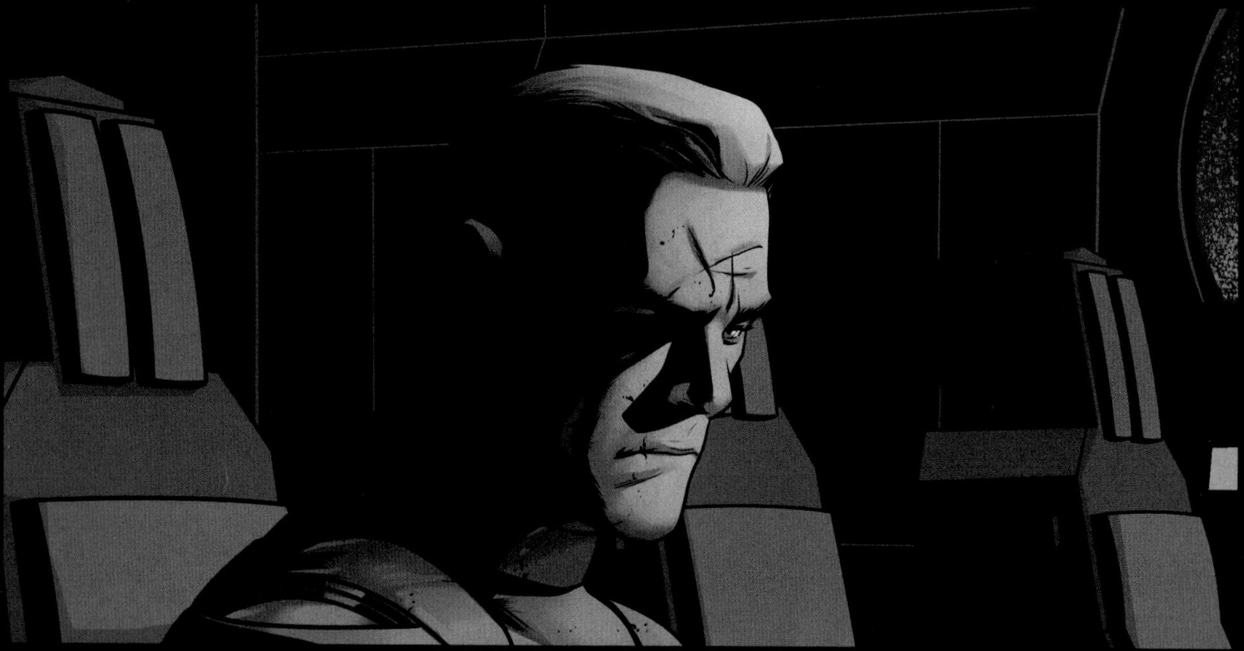

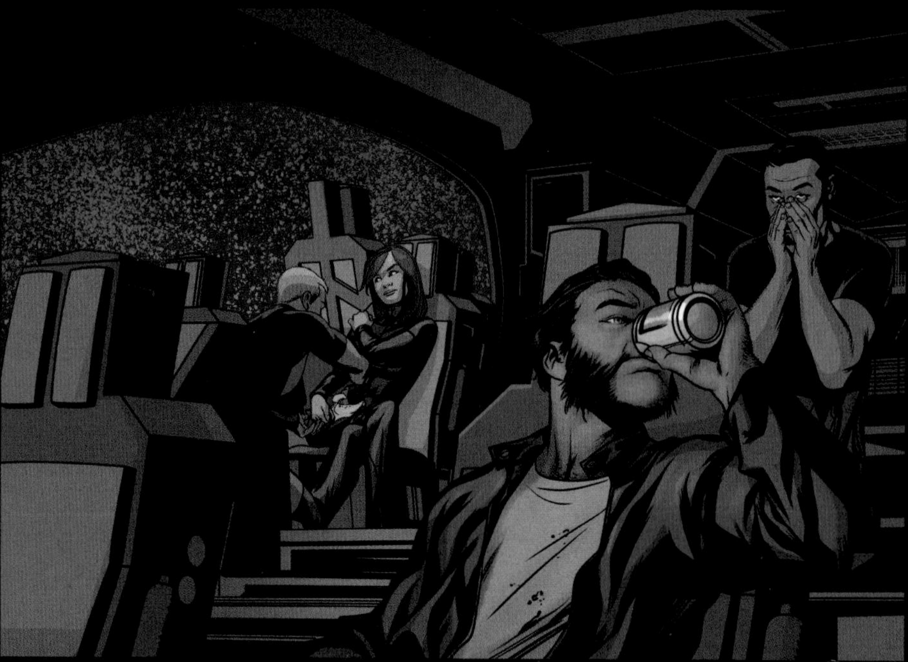

Thor stayed behind. He said he needed to conclude things and make amends. He wore that particular expression that meant, once again, he was returning to that far mythic home of his, and, once again, not as the conquering hero of his dreams.

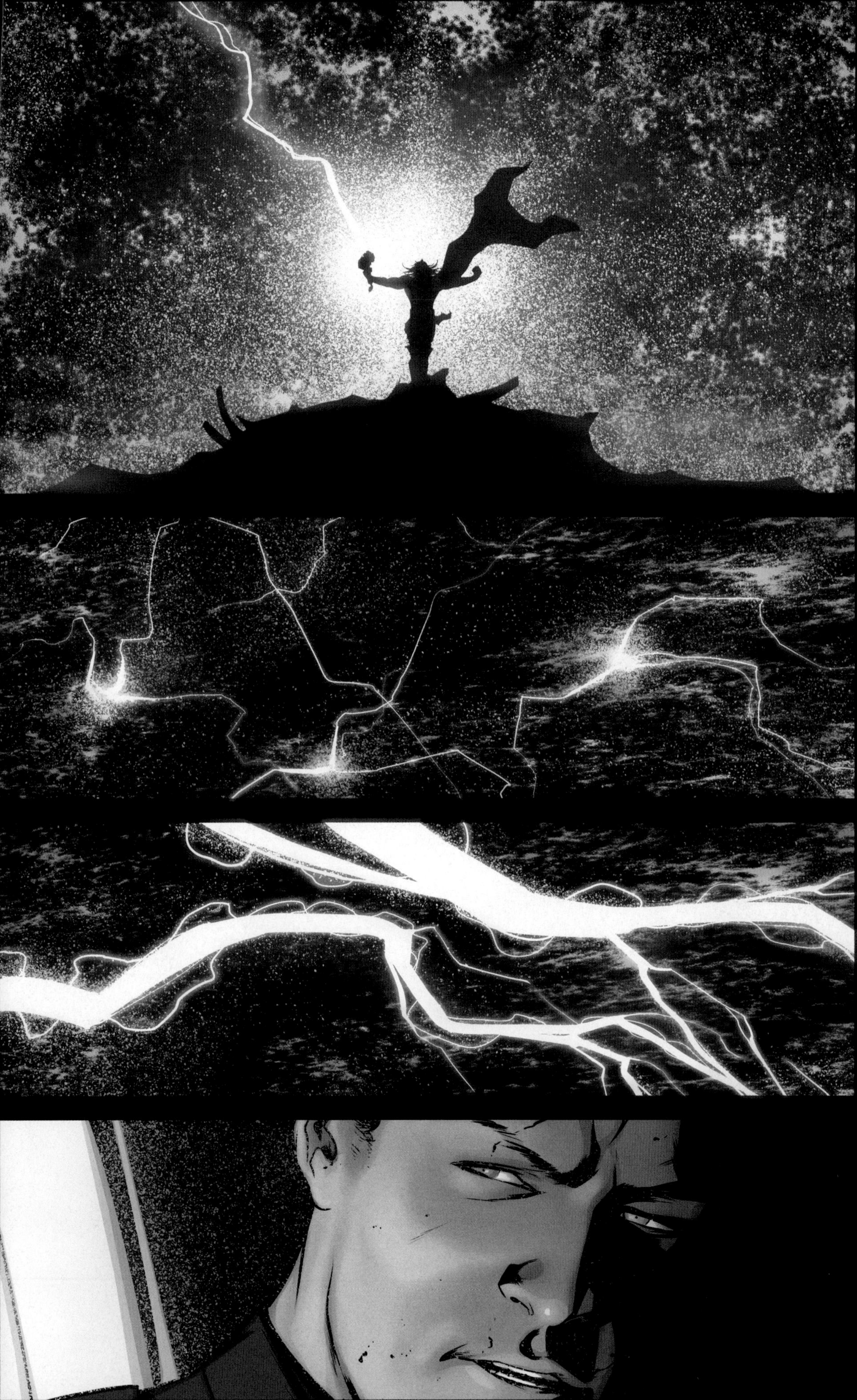

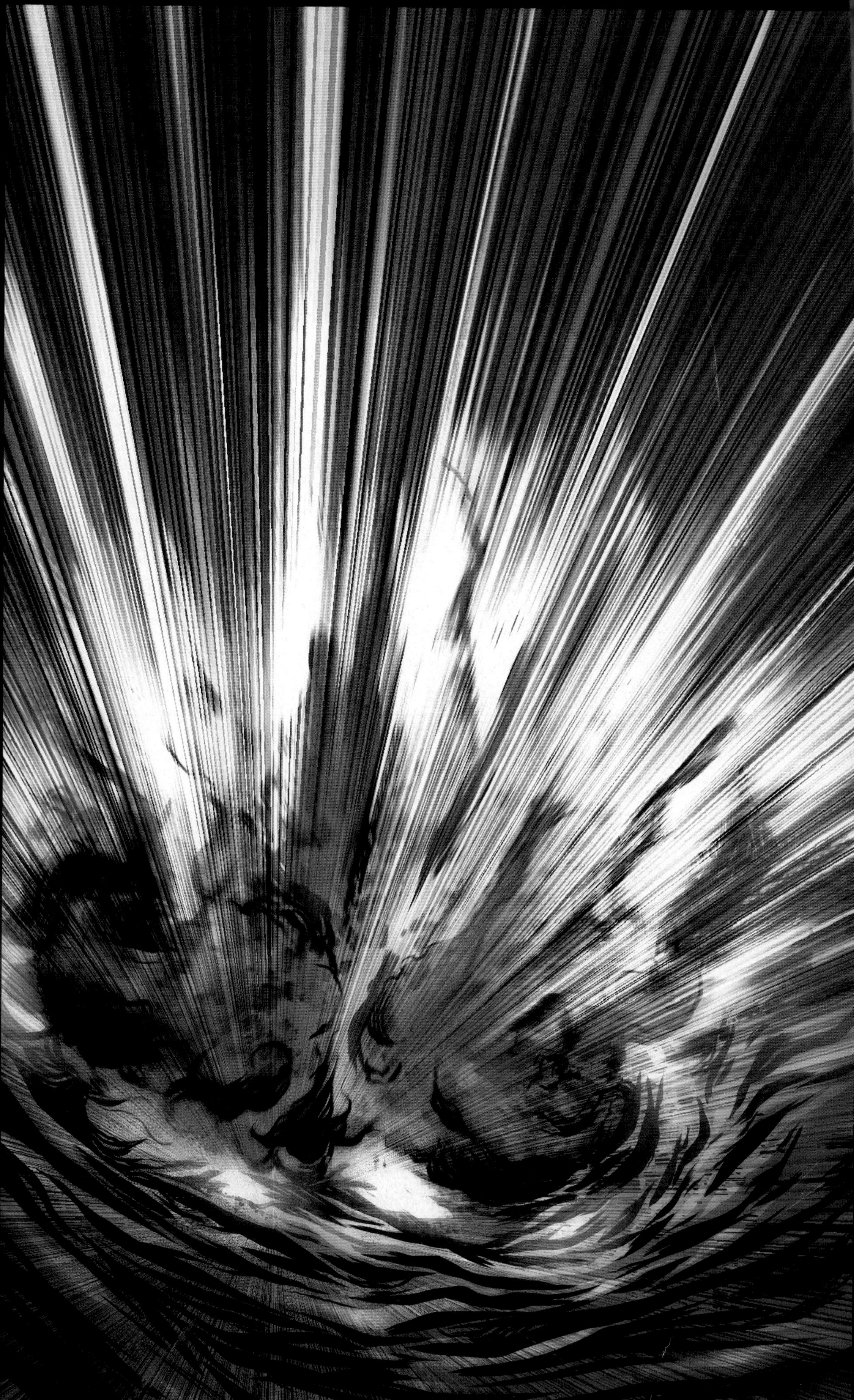

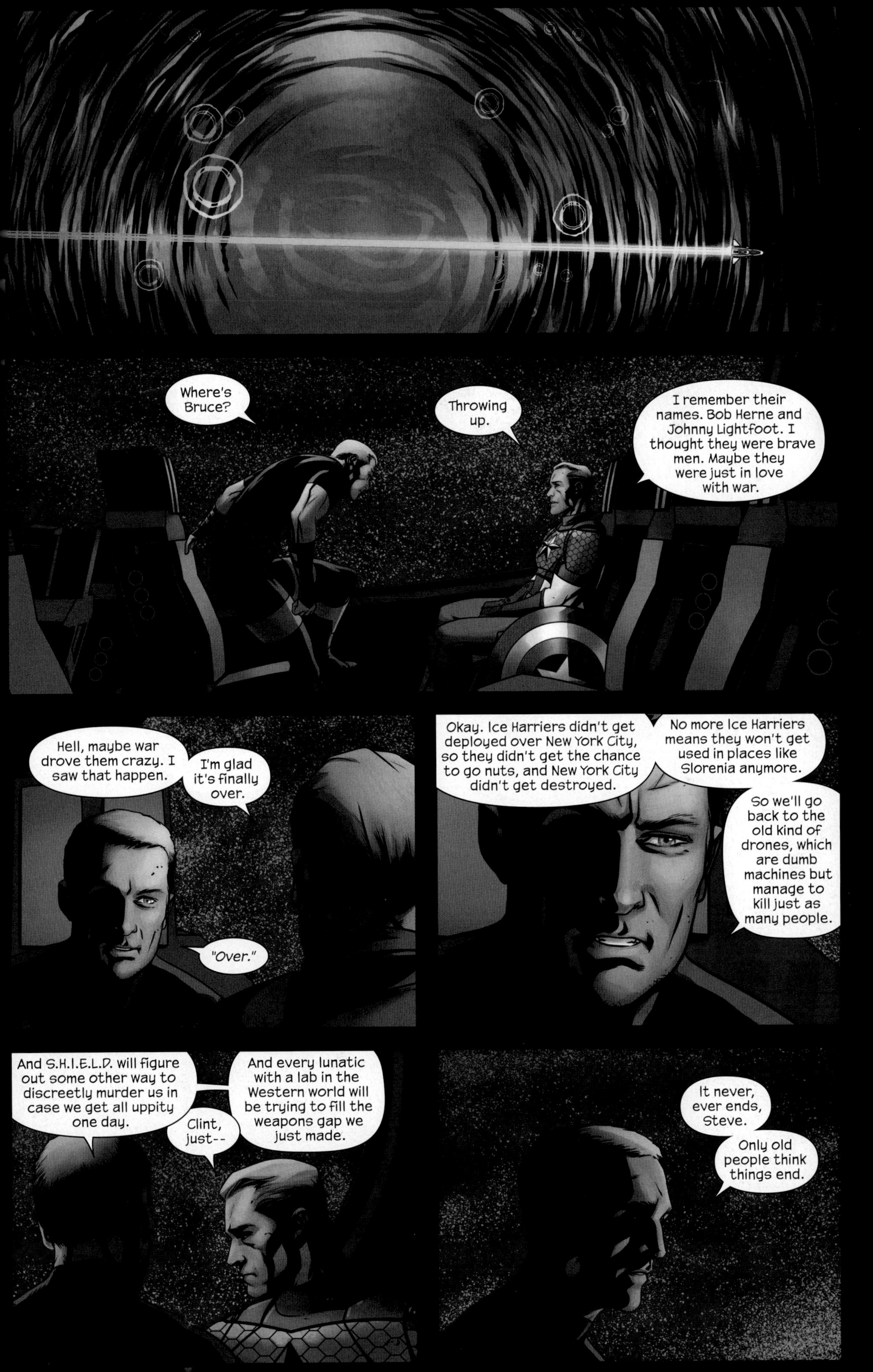
Where's Bruce?
Throwing up.
I remember their names. Bob Herne and Johnny Lightfoot. I thought they were brave men. Maybe they were just in love with war.
Hell, maybe war drove them crazy. I saw that happen.
I'm glad it's finally over.
"Over."
Okay. Ice Harriers didn't get deployed over New York City, so they didn't get the chance to go nuts, and New York City didn't get destroyed.
No more Ice Harriers means they won't get used in places like Slorenia anymore.
So we'll go back to the old kind of drones, which are dumb machines but manage to kill just as many people.
And S.H.I.E.L.D. will figure out some other way to discreetly murder us in case we get all uppity one day.
And every lunatic with a lab in the Western world will be trying to fill the weapons gap we just made.
Clint, just--
It never, ever ends, Steve.
Only old people think things end.

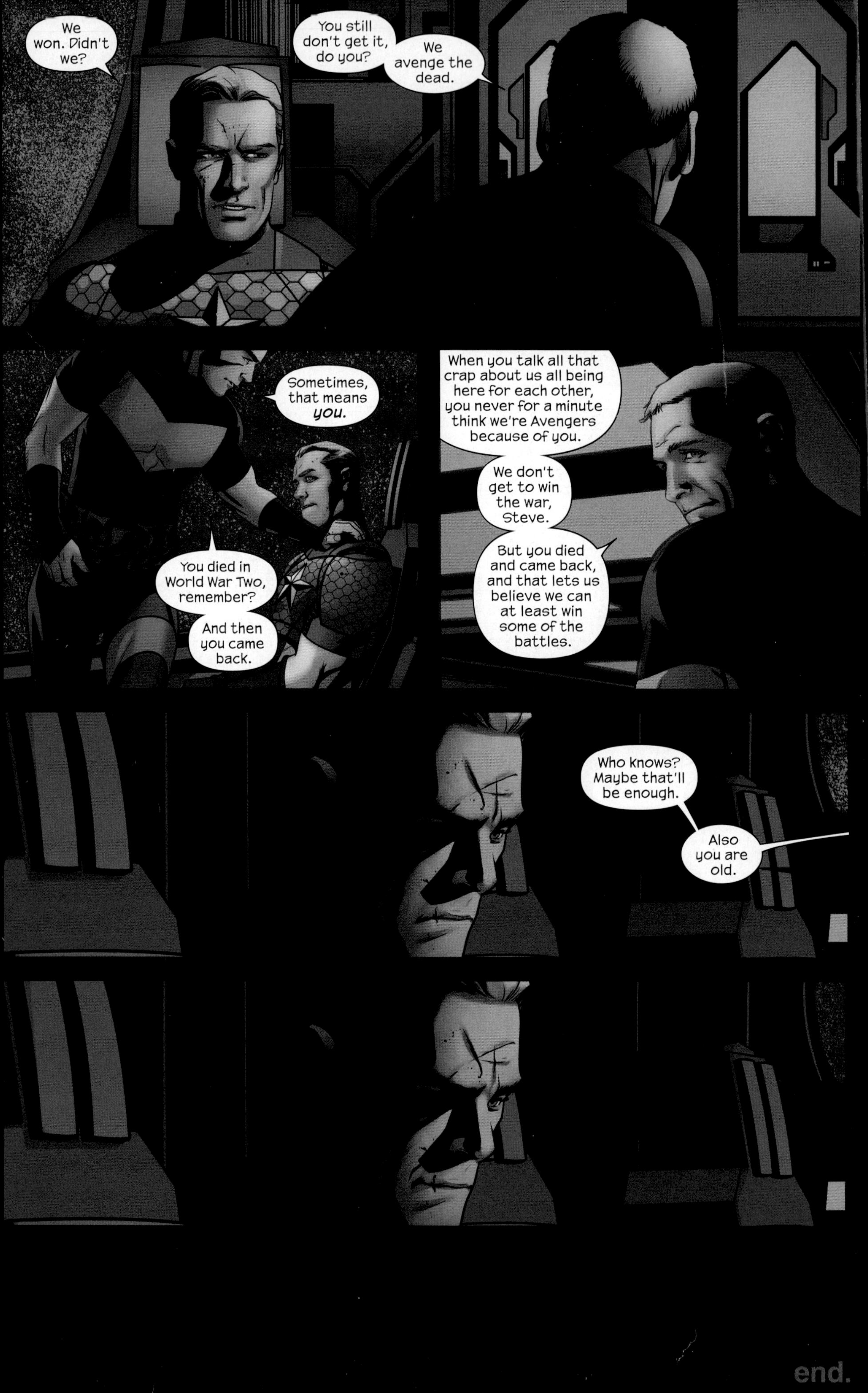
We won. Didn't we?
You still don't get it, do you?
We avenge the dead.
Sometimes, that means *you.*
You died in World War Two, remember?
And then you came back.
When you talk all that crap about us all being here for each other, you never for a minute think we're Avengers because of you.
We don't get to win the war, Steve.
But you died and came back, and that lets us believe we can at least win some of the battles.
Who knows? Maybe that'll be enough.
Also you are old.
end.

Warren Ellis

Springing from the fertile ground of the U.K. comics scene, Warren Ellis came to Marvel during the early '90s and proved his iconoclastic mettle in the ultra-edgy series *Hellstorm* and the miniseries *Druid* — followed by fondly remembered, extended runs on *Excalibur* and *Doom 2099*. After making a name for himself as a premier talent with Wildstorm's *Storm-watch*, *Transmetropolitan*, *The Authority* and *Planetary*, Ellis returned to Marvel to pen such titles as *Ultimate Fantastic Four*, the *Ultimate Galactus Trilogy* and *Iron Man*. His *Nextwave: Agents of H.A.T.E.* was both a critical smash and cult favorite. In addition to reviving the 1980s *New Universe* in *newuniversal* and writing *Thunderbolts*, Ellis took over *Astonishing X-Men* following Joss Whedon and John Cassaday's departure, and penned perhaps the definitive story of the Armored Avenger in *Iron Man*'s "Extremis." His Wildstorm miniseries *Red* was adapted into a 2010 hit movie. Ellis broke into prose fiction with *Crooked Little Vein* and his New York Times best-selling novel *Gun Machine*.

Mike McKone

Artist Mike McKone was pegged as a future industry superstar when his first work was published in DC's *JLA* and *Legion*. In 2001, McKone collaborated with writer Judd Winick to launch Marvel's *Exiles*, a surprise hit among X-fans. Two years later, he teamed with writer Geoff Johns to revamp *Teen Titans* for DC. Since signing an exclusive contract with Marvel, McKone's credits include *Fantastic Four*, *Amazing Spider-Man* and *Avengers Academy*.

Jason Keith

An Eisner Award nominee, Jason Keith has been a colorist in the industry for more than a decade. He got his start at CrossGen coloring *Scion* and *Sojourn;* among his first work at Marvel was writer/artist Frank Cho's *Shanna, the She-Devil*. Since then, he has colored *X-Men*, *New Avengers*, *newuniversal*, *Savage Wolverine* and more.

Chris Eliopoulos

Eagle, Harvey and Wizard Fan Award winner for his lettering, Chris Eliopoulos' prolific career in comics has been anything but the norm. He's worked on dozens of books during the fifteen years he's been in the industry — including Erik Larsen's *Savage Dragon,* for which he hand-lettered the first 100 issues. He's also published his own strips, *Desperate Times* and *Misery Loves Sherman;* been a contributing artist to the *Idiot's Guide To...* series of books; wrote and illustrated Marvel's popular *Franklin Richards: Son of a Genius* one-shots; and penned miniseries featuring *Lockjaw* and the *Pet Avengers*.

Rian Hughes

Designer and illustrator Rian Hughes began his career in the British music, advertising and fashion industries. His strips for *2000AD* and the short-lived *Revolver* with Grant Morrison and Mark Millar are collected in *Yesterday's Tomorrows* and *Tales from Beyond Science*. Designs for Titan Books' *Batman* and *Love and Rockets* volumes brought him to the attention of DC Comics, for whom he has designed numerous logos, including *Batman and Robin*, *Batgirl* and *The Invisibles*. For Marvel he has designed logos and covers for *Iron Man*, *X-Men* and *Wolverine* among many others. He both wrote and designed the critically acclaimed *Cult-ure: Ideas Can Be Dangerous*.

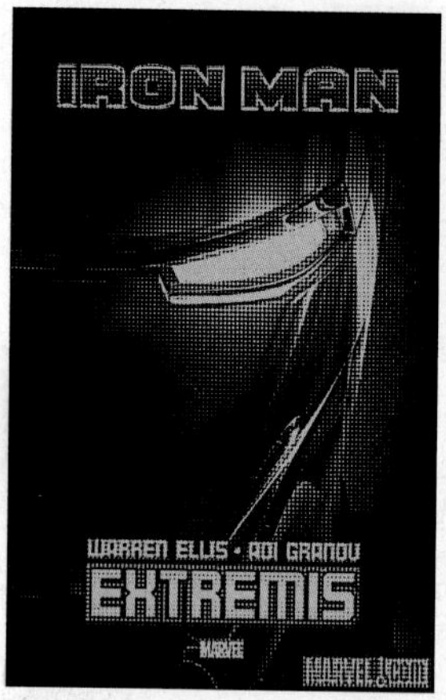
IRON MAN
WARREN ELLIS · ADI GRANOV
EXTREMIS

IRON MAN
EXTREMIS
978-0-7851-8378-5

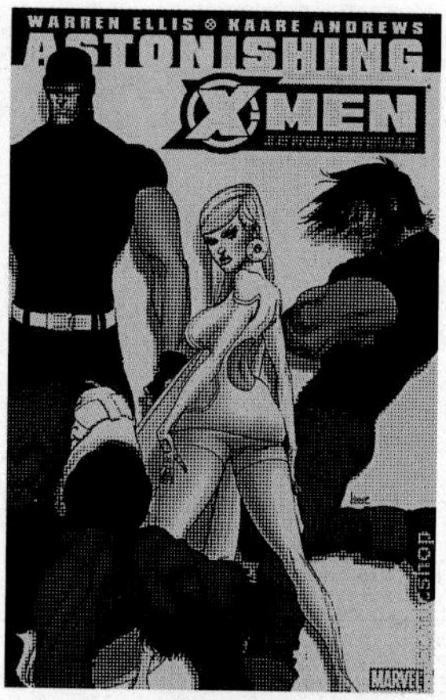
WARREN ELLIS ◇ KAARE ANDREWS
ASTONISHING
X-MEN
MARVEL

ASTONISHING X-MEN
XENOGENESIS
978-0-7851-4033-7

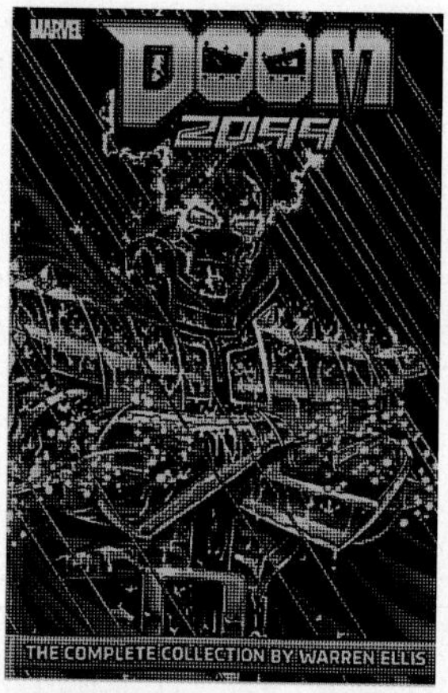
MARVEL
DOOM 2099
THE COMPLETE COLLECTION BY WARREN ELLIS

DOOM 2099
THE COMPLETE COLLECTION
978-0-7851-6754-9

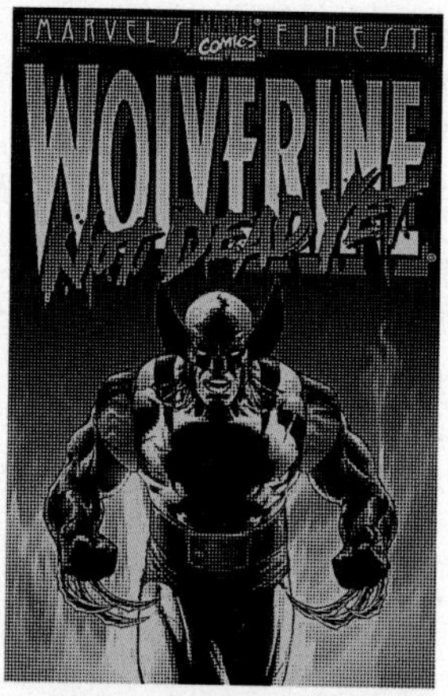
MARVEL'S FINEST
WOLVERINE

WOLVERINE
NOT DEAD YET
978-0-7851-6710-5

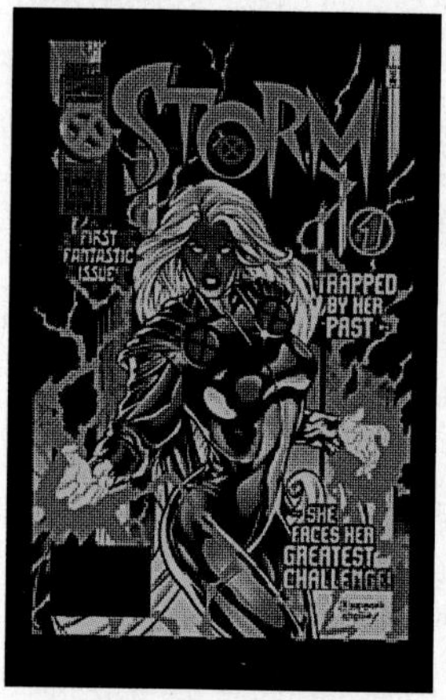
STORM
FIRST FANTASTIC ISSUE!
TRAPPED BY HER PAST
SHE FACES HER GREATEST CHALLENGE!

X-MEN
STORM
978-0-7851-8501-7

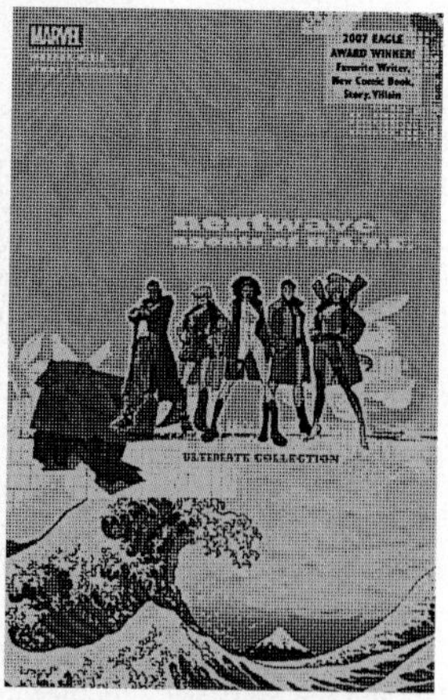
MARVEL
2007 EAGLE AWARD WINNER! Favorite Writer, New Comic Book, Story, Villain
nextwave
agents of H.A.T.E.
ULTIMATE COLLECTION

NEXTWAVE: AGENTS OF H.A.T.E.
ULTIMATE COLLECTION
978-0-7851-4461-8

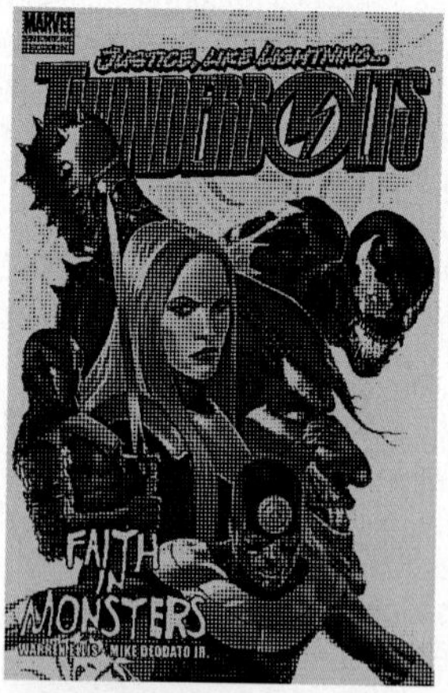
MARVEL
JUSTICE, LIKE LIGHTNING...
THUNDERBOLTS
FAITH IN MONSTERS
WARREN ELLIS MIKE DEODATO JR.

THUNDERBOLTS
ULTIMATE COLLECTION
978-0-7851-5849-3

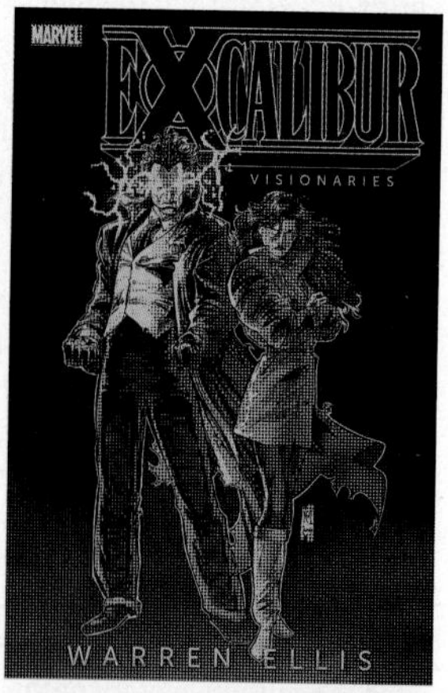
MARVEL
EXCALIBUR
VISIONARIES
WARREN ELLIS

EXCALIBUR VISIONARIES
WARREN ELLIS VOLUME I
978-0-7851-4456-4

Before they died, Peter Parker's parents left him something he never knew about...a sister.

SPIDER-MAN:
FAMILY BUSINESS

An Original Graphic Novel
by Mark Waid,
James Robinson
and Gabriele Dell'otto

Available **April 2014**

SPIDER-MAN
FAMILY
BUSINESS
MARK WAID
JAMES ROBINSON
GABRIELE DELL'OTTO
MARVEL OGN

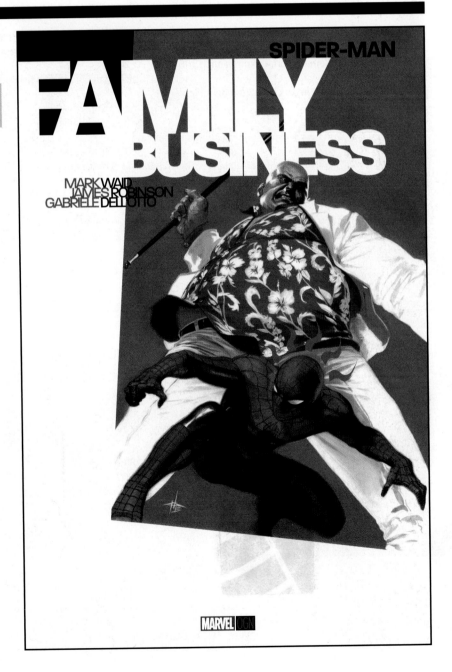

To redeem your code for a free digital copy:

1 Go to Marvel.com/redeem. Offer expires on 7/3/15.

2 Follow the on-screen instructions to redeem your digital copy.

3 Launch the Marvel Comics app to read your comic now.

4 Your digital copy will be found under the 'my comics' tab.

5 Read and enjoy.

Your free digital copy will be available on:
Marvel Comics app for Apple iOS® devices and
Marvel Comics app for Android™ devices.

Digital copy requires purchase of a print copy. Download code valid for one use only. Digital copy available on the date printcopy is available. Availability time of the digital copy may vary on the date of release. TM and © Marvel and Subs. Apple is a trademark of Apple Inc., registered in the U. S. and other countries. Android is a trademark of Google Inc.

MARVEL
FREE DIGITAL COPY OFFER

To access the free Marvel Augmented Reality app that enhances and changes the way you experience comics:

1 Download the app for free via marvel.com/ARapp.

2 Launch the app on your camera-enabled Apple iOS® or Android™ device.*

3 Hold your mobile device's camera over any cover or panel with the AR graphic.

4 Sit back and see the future of comics in action!

*Available on most camera-enabled Apple iOS® and Android ™ devices. Content subject to change and availability.